Juked

Juked

AUTHORED BY

NATHAN "NATE" HAYMER

EDITED BY

ZARA R. BROADENAX

GATHERING HOUSE PUBLISHING, LLC.

GATHERING HOUSE PUBLISHING

MADISON, ALABAMA

2023

Copyright © 2023 by Nathan "Nate" Haymer

All rights reserved. No part of this publication may be reproduced, distributed, or transmitted in any form or by any means, including photocopying, recording, or other electronic or mechanical methods, without the prior written permission of the publisher, except in the case of brief quotations embodied in critical reviews and certain other noncommercial uses permitted by copyright law. For permission requests, write to the publisher, addressed "Attention: Permissions Coordinator," at the address below.

Gathering House Publishing
P.O. Box 1044
Madison, Alabama 35758

Cover and Interior Design by: Gracena Gray, Gathering House Publishing, LLC

Editing by: Zara R. Broadenax, Gathering House Publishing, LLC

Printed in the United States of America
ISBN-13: 978-1-947351-21-9

First Edition
10 9 8 7 6 5 4 3 2

∞ This paper meets requirements of ANSI/NISO Z39.48-1992 (Permanence of Paper)

Dedication

This book is dedicated to all band directors (past, present, and future), all band heads (those who follow all the intricate details of band programs), and for all who just love marching bands and the excitement that they bring to sporting events.

Acknowledgement

I honor the many people who played an instrumental role in my life.

My mother, Patricia Bennett Rodgers. You raised three boys as a single mother from the time I was eight years old. You taught me the value of commitment and dedication.

My father, Norman Haymer, Jr. Your sense of humor, intelligence, and cut to the chase personality allowed me to grow and better understand how cold and cruel the world can sometimes be.

Niles B. Haymer, Sr., my twin brother who is older by six minutes. You and I shared a room for eighteen years. Throughout our many hard times, fights, and laughs, you have been the example of true brotherhood.

Norman Haymer, III, my older brother of four years. You have been a mentor and role model throughout my early childhood and adolescent years.

To the many teachers and band directors who played an influential role in my life. Mr. Blain Curry and Joe Evans (junior high school band directors), Glen Buckalew (high school band director), and Dr. Isaac Greggs (college band director). Thank you for pouring harmonies, melodies, and rhythms into my soul to create my background of music.

While all named above played a major role in shaping my morals, character, and knowledge, there are too many people to name who helped to mold and shape me through the years. Whether through positive interaction or through correction through discipline, I am thankful to all my teachers, mentors, church leaders, family, and friends that contributed to my drive to be successful.

Foreword

Building a reputation takes years of demonstrating good character, performing good deeds, and achieving success through merit, hard work, and determination. However, a single press of the "send" button by one-sided media or amateur detectives can attempt to destroy one's legacy within minutes. Despite the recent unfair treatment, people like Nathan Haymer deserve our admiration and respect for the mountains that he climbed to achieve the success that was far from effortless and never guaranteed. I know this, because I've been a witness for the last 45 years to a man who has constructed an insurmountable musical legacy that will one day be compared to great musicians in this nation. As Nathan's fraternal twin brother, I would like to shed some light on the dedication it takes to become *The Maestro*.

In the fall of 1985, I vividly remember being 7 years old and seated in the stands with Nathan at a very crowded Southern University football game in Baton Rouge, Louisiana. We were like two small flowers in a crowded forest of trees, trying to maneuver our line of sight just to see the field. People surrounded us with their flasks of whiskey, dressed from head to toe in Southern's "blue and gold" all while standing to their feet every thirty seconds with each throw of the ball. My mother was so into the game yelling at the "cheating referees" as I watched with intensity at every first down made. But I don't remember this day because of the football game, heck I don't even remember the other team. What stands out about this day, nearly 39 years ago, was Nathan staring in the opposite direction of the football field. His eyes were focused like laser beams on the producers of the soundtrack of Southern's football prowess…the Southern University Human Jukebox. With every swing of the Director's arms, clash of the cymbals, telescoping of the trombones and rhythmical sway of the Fabulous Dancing Dolls, Nathan was officially hypnotized. No, he didn't go into the *sunken place* at that moment, but instead he was elevated into a higher level of consciousness transcending his mind's normal preoccupation with child's play into a mind that became aware of the power of music.

In 1986, our parents divorced and my mother, who instantly became a single mother of three growing boys, moved us from Baton Rouge to her hometown of Gulfport, Mississippi. The move itself took an emotional toll on Nathan for years. Not only did our parents split up, but Nathan was now separated from his beloved Human Jukebox. YouTube wouldn't be invented for another 30 years and the only chance he had to grab a glimpse of the Jukebox was on the last Saturday in November on NBC's broadcast of the Bayou Classic. Even then, the short two-minute bit of the Human Jukebox was only the backdrop for Ahmad Rashad to blab on and on about other things not essential to the marching band right behind him.

During this time, Nathan didn't even have formal music training, he was just a master *beatboxer* mimicking drum machines with his mouth all day which always resulted in sibling fights at the dinner table. "Mama, he's spitting in my food!" I would shout. "You're just jealous you can't beatbox *My Prerogative* as good as me!" He would fire back. It wasn't until the age of 13 when Nathan received his first formal musical training at Central Junior High School in Gulfport, Ms. My mother admittedly struggled to make ends meet, barely being able to afford rent and keep food on the table. She would often say that her growing boys had the audacity to easily eat a loaf of bread and a pack of baloney a day. When it came to extra-curricular activities, if it didn't cost money, my mother didn't mind that we participated. But if there was a fee or any cost for said activities, then it became painfully apparent to us that my mother just couldn't afford it. So, while many of the kids in Nathan's junior high band had a parent to rent or buy them an instrument, he was left with left-over instruments that were broken, dented and out of tune. In 1991, his first instrument was a beat-up alto horn with a used mouthpiece. Nathan worked hours to repair the horn and once he started playing, he was immediately exiled to the backyard for the sake of our mental and eardrum health. Yes, the distressing sounds that flowed from that alto horn may not have been considered musical mastery then, but Nathan put in hours, days, weeks, and months of repetitive exercising on that raggedy horn. While all our friends were out playing basketball in the street, we could hear Nathan in the backyard blaring away ignoring the fluttering birds, the howling dogs, and the shouts of disapproval from the neighbors.

By high school, Nathan mastered many of the instruments in his marching band and became obsessed with marching formations. In our neighborhood, being in the band wasn't cool at all, friends would call him the *"Urkel of Musicians"* which Nathan oddly took as a compliment as he marched his way to becoming the first black drum major of the Gulfport High Marching Band his senior year in high school. In the late 90s, when he learned that I would be attending Southern University after high school, he balked at attending the same school because we were such archrivals after 18 years of being roommates. It wasn't until he met his idol, the legendary Dr. Isaac Greggs, Director of Bands at Southern, that within ten seconds of sitting down with him he became duty-bound to his first love, the Southern University Human Jukebox for life. His days as a student at Southern were spent mainly in the band room. While I was out being a student activist protesting everything from chemical plants to the food in the cafeteria, Nathan was becoming one of the most talented and respected members of the Human Jukebox. As I garnered all the attention as student body president, Nathan was garnering the attention and awe of those who mattered, Dr. Greggs and assistant band director, Lawrence Jackson.

Soon after graduating from Southern, Nathan wanted to fulfill his goal of becoming a band director. He wanted to focus on kids who grew up like him, whose parents didn't have much money or access to formal music training. He believed that playing in the band should be placed on a pedestal just like playing on the football field. Although the marching band is an art form and football are athletics, Nathan would often say that they both took years of training, dedication and a skill that could help pay your way through college. In 2001, Nathan became the band director at Washington-Marion Magnet High School in Lake Charles, Louisiana and I swear his band could put many college bands to shame.

In the summer of 2014, Mr. Lawrence Jackson suddenly retired leaving Southern University scrambling to figure out who would lead the world-famous Human Jukebox. The University was uncertain if the 36-year-old assistant director, Nathan Haymer, had the wherewithal to lead their prized possession. Being that there was no time to open a full search for a band director prior to the football season, Nathan was named the Interim Director of Bands of Southern University fulfilling a lifelong dream since that night in the stands in 1985. Although he was given the interim label, there remained doubters of his abilities to lead such a massive organization of well over 200 students with only three staff members. Then came his first halftime performance as Band Director of the Human Jukebox which launched his career into orbit!

Nathan had a way of reaching the millennials all while staying true to Southern's traditions. He continued the strong legacy of Dr. Greggs, all while bringing the Human Jukebox into the new millennium by creating the Human Jukebox into its own brand with a media marketing team, Human Jukebox logo with merchandise, Human Jukebox app, and even the Louisiana State Legislature approving of a Human Jukebox license plate. This band's halftime show was always a must see in person but, now a whole new generation of Human Jukebox lovers have been created through Nathan's social media platforms on Facebook, Instagram, and YouTube. The use of social media to reach out to alumni and the next generation of students is powerful because the young Nathan for years couldn't view his beloved Human Jukebox during his childhood.

Today Human Jukebox has millions of followers and viewership more than any other HBCU band in the nation. It was the Human Jukebox that was named the #2 band in the nation, only second to Ohio State University; and in 2018, Nathan was even named National Band Director of the Year. Today, there are hundreds of kids scrambling to Southern from New Jersey, Texas, Ohio, Michigan, and other states across this nation just to attend a high school summer band camp in June which started off years ago as a camp just for the locals. These kids will become future students, which makes the Human Jukebox the best recruitment tool for Southern University.

The "Nathan Haymer" I know is a man of faith who has never been the beneficiary of nepotism, cronyism, or luck to further his career. This is a blessed man who has worked hard for everything he's achieved in his young life despite the obstacles that were placed in his path to discourage him from climbing the mountain to success. Nathan Haymer's success story is what Southern University and other HBCUs should be about. You don't just wake up one morning and have others call you *The Maestro*. You have to earn it. And from the football field to the 2015 Fight of The Century in Las Vegas, Nathan has used the power of music to connect with the heart and souls of people across this nation earning the title, *The Maestro* and my brother.

Niles Haymer
Attorney-at-Law

Introduction

One year after being terminated as Director of Bands at Southern University and A&M College in Baton Rouge, Louisiana, I began to share my story and experiences with family, friends, and a trusted mentor, along with my desire to write a book highlighting my journey as a band director. I wanted to emphasize everything about my career other than a band director's formal or trained duties. In other words, band beyond the music or behind the scenes, which are the things that people do not know or see. Because I was still going through the legal battle of my life and arguably the biggest scandal that rocked the University, I decided it was best to wait until a resolution of the matter. Unfortunately, the legal battle ended with a sentence of thirteen months in federal prison. The unfortunate sentence to federal prison provided a golden opportunity to turn a negative situation into a positive one by investing much-needed time and attention to gathering my thoughts around the facts, successes, scandals, and fallouts that shaped my unique, high-energy, and wild career.

This book will stress the *Seven P's,* revealing the positive aspects of leadership: *Power, Prestige, and Position*, while placing heavy emphasis on the downsides of leadership: *Persecution, Problems, Pressure, and Politics*. I will leave no stones unturned as I share my truth with all of its successes and failures as a transformational leader, who re-energized the band culture for Historically Black Colleges and Universities (HBCUs), and the band culture nationally and internationally for the mainstream audiences. I have received many messages and videos from citizens of other countries imitating the Southern University Marching Band's success during my tenure as its famed maestro. The Southern University Band Program consistently ranked in the top 5 of all collegiate band programs in the nation during my tenure as their esteemed Director of Bands.

As you prepare for this journey in the world of Nathan B. Haymer, I ask that you do so with an open mind. Applying logic and formal problem-solving skills to my unique situation would make your head spin. There is nothing ordinary and traditional about my case, career, and the successes and failures that shaped them.

Nathan "Nate" Haymer
Author

"To thine own self be true; you can lie to me, but you cannot lie to YOU!"

-Nathan Haymer

Chapter 1

"Mr. Haymer, as a Southernite, you are an embarrassment to the University. Not only are you an embarrassment to the University, but you took advantage of the University as well! I HEREBY SENTENCE YOU TO 13 MONTHS IN FEDERAL PRISON ALONG WITH $78,800 IN RESTITUTION!"

March 30, 2021, will forever be the date embedded in my mind. Sitting in a courtroom at the federal courthouse in downtown Baton Rouge, I knew my life had changed forever. I heard the sentence and became overcome with emotions. I tuned the judge out and embraced my thoughts.

Just minutes before, I walked into the courtroom and saw my family and friends and although they were there, I still felt all alone in the cold and lifeless room as I watched the judge walk in wearing a solid black robe with a stern and solemn look on his face. I have always wanted to make my family proud, but overcome with emotions and feelings of failure, I knew this was not a proud moment.

Immediately, I thought of Niles and his unsuccessful run for judge. Visions of my move to Houston and leaving my family in Baton Rouge to navigate my mishaps and mess floated through my head. I blame myself for ruining the "Haymer" name but was it really all my fault?

The federal judge chosen to oversee my sentencing hearing was no other than Judge Brian A. Jackson, a 1985 graduate of Southern University Law Center. Even though Judge Jackson received his undergraduate degree from Xavier University of Louisiana, he was a native New Orleanian with ties and loyalty to Southern University and its leadership. He entered the courtroom, and the hearing began.

The legal proceeding started with Judge Jackson and the Assistant United States Attorney, Alan Stevens, speaking legal jargon. Mr. Stevens was submitting new evidence to tax an additional $45,000 of legal liability to me. "We don't have proof that Mr. Haymer misused this amount, but we have a theory that he did so," stated Mr. Stevens.

Immediately, my lawyers objected, and Judge Jackson overruled the objection. Today wasn't a trial, it was a hearing, and although a hearing is still a legal procedure, there was no jury. Nope, all I had was the opinion of Judge Jackson.

It was my lawyers' chance to speak on my behalf. My lawyers spoke passionately about my humanity. They talked about the lives that I touched and changed through my capacity as Director of Bands.

Since we were in the resurrection season and so close to the Easter holiday, one of my lawyers pleaded for the judge to have compassion.

The tears started rolling as I began to think, *who am I but a sinner? It is not up to me to determine my path as I believe my path, although painful, is destined by God, and through the pain will lie my purpose!*

It was my turn and as I approached the podium to speak, I could hear my mother crying. Her cry broke me and as I started to talk, I could not get my words out.

Gaining my composure, I stated, *"Your Honor, I led the Human Jukebox passionately and boldly as I had to be the example of strength and authority to many students that I led. It is with that same passion and boldness that I stand in front of you today to take full responsibility for my actions!"*

My fight was over. Even though I knew "life isn't fair," it was now time to accept my punishment. I am happy to see the light at the end of the tunnel and the completion of my three-year limbo journey. I finished my statement and instantly, Judge Jackson began his disapproving and chastising comments toward me.

Juked

Despite what the judge said, he's not the ultimate decider of my life's purpose and how I move on from this tragic situation. I was no different than any other band head when it comes to the love of music. My musical journey started as a young kid just like everyone else. However, my destination was to be the Director of Bands for Southern University and A&M College's Human Jukebox and now I'm a convicted felon. Here is my story...

CHAPTER 2

Ring! Ring!

One morning in late May 2014, I awakened to the sound of my phone ringing. I stretched and rolled over in bed to retrieve the phone. As my phone continued to ring, I looked and realized that I was familiar with the area code and the prefix of the number that was on the screen. It was a Lake Charles (Louisiana) phone number. I kept looking at the number trying to figure out who it could be. I have no idea who could be calling me this Monday morning. I realized that I was doing too much thinking and I just needed to answer the phone.

"Hello! Hello!" I said twice because I waited so long to answer, I was afraid that whoever was on the other end probably hung up.

"Yes! This is Reverend Tolbert, member of the SU System Board of Supervisors. I am calling to speak to Mr. Haymer!"

Immediately after college I lived in Lake Charles for five years, so I was familiar with The Reverend. I wasn't a member of his church, but I was invited to attend quite a few times due to band students, parents, and fellow band directors.

"Yes, this is he," I said using my business tone.

We were pleasant and passed through some small talk. Finally, Reverend Tolbert cut to the chase and let me know his reason for calling.

Juked

"Look! I am going to vote to make you the band director. You come highly recommended, and I seem to know some people in Lake Charles that are supporting you as well! You just have to promise me one thing. Promise me that you won't fight the young Vice-Chancellor of Student Affairs!"

"Sir, I have no intentions on fighting anyone!" I responded. "I just want to be the band director! It is my belief that…"

"Okay, good," stated Reverend Tolbert as he cut me off. "Because we are trying to make that young man the next chancellor of the Baton Rouge campus. I think that young man would re-energize SU and would be a positive change for the HBCU culture! There are people fighting us on this move, but I think we can get it passed at the board meeting this Friday."

This Friday's board meeting was at the forefront of my mind but not because of this conversation. No, the board meeting was ever-present due to the approval or denial of my Interim Director of Bands recommendation. Here this reverend is calling me about some administrator I don't know or even care about. I can't even get day-to-day business done.

As Reverend Tolbert continued his conversation on the support of the Vice-Chancellor and the importance of young leadership, I was becoming more frustrated. I have been trying to get things done like requesting the hiring of two assistant band directors, organizing the high school band and dance team summer camp, and understanding the logistics of the band's scholarship and travel budgets. Where's my phone call of support and discussion of my leadership?

As we ended the conversation, I struggled to awake and get moving. My head was throbbing and now I'm reliving this very strange phone call with the reverend. I forced myself out of bed to start my day, but I kept reflecting back to the conversation and the familiarization of the Vice-Chancellor's name, Dumas!

The name from the phone call was very familiar and got me thinking. A couple years earlier when I was the assistant band director, I was in the administration building on campus. I entered the elevator on the fourth floor headed down. On the elevator was an older lady who made me very uncomfortable. She and I were the only people on the elevator, and she just stared at me. She stared at me the entire ride down to the first floor. Being a true southern gentleman, when the doors opened, I gestured for her to exit first. Exiting the elevator, she stopped me.

"I'm sorry baby," she said with a voice of concern. "Are you a Haymer?"

"Yes ma'am," I responded with a mixture of confusion and being spooked.

"Baby, they set your daddy up!"

I looked at her wondering what she was talking about. Walking off she indirectly but directly said to me in passing the name Dumas.

The phone call from the reverend and the revisited memory of the lady in the elevator made me uncomfortable and curious. My father was a prominent attorney in Baton Rouge and well-known, but he had a past that I was very unfamiliar with. Slowly, it became extremely clear that I would need to know the details of his story since some of the people he associated with would now be in my circle.

Juked

Even though I knew I needed to call my father and have a heart to heart, I opted not to make that call. Calling my father would require me to rehash or reopen old wounds for him and I just didn't see the logic in that situation. Instead, I decided to call my mom. Although she knew a lot, she didn't want to go there!

"Nathan, you're going to have to talk to your father about that," was all my mother would tell me.

The conversation with my mother didn't last long, nor did it reveal anything. No better off before I called her, I decided to start to get ready for work. All the while, I relived the conversation with the reverend and revisited the memory of the older lady from the elevator.

My head pounding even more, it became clear that moving into the position of Director of Bands was walking into the land of POLITICS! It was an environment that I was not comfortable with or in. However, I was also getting an understanding that events between adults during my childhood were affecting my present and future whether I liked it or not. I just didn't understand the connection, influence and power related to my dad's former law partner, Walter C. Dumas.

Chapter 3

My week started off uncomfortable, confusing, and curious but I didn't fully comprehend the uncertainty I was stepping into at week's end. The long-awaited Southern University System Board of Supervisors meeting was about to occur. This was the meeting that would change my life. It was the meeting that prompted the conversation from Reverend Tolbert and jolted the remembrance of the lady in the elevator. Finally, it was the meeting that would fulfill my childhood dreams.

As a child, my parents signed me and my twin brother, Niles, up for soccer. On the campus of Southern University, my brother and I would run, kick, and block. However, one faithful day in 1985, my focus changed. On the soccer practice field near the parking lot where the band practiced, I heard the band very clearly. The music was my backdrop, my strength. It pumped the rhythm into my soul. The harmony matched my heartbeat and the melody reared as my spoken word.

One practice in particular, the band played Stevie Wonder's "Part-Time Lover" and my fate was sealed. I just about lost my mind and no longer was soccer the world in which I desired to reside. I had fallen in love with the SU Human Jukebox. Instantly, I found myself running towards the band mimicking marching with a high knee lift. Dare I say, I even attempted to imitate the signature *Jaguar-Rock,* the very ingredient that distinguishes the Human Jukebox's marching style from all the rest.

Immediately, the magical memory had me overcome with emotions. Today's events are the reason why I joined the band in junior high and high school. Today is why I endured all the "janking" from neighborhood kids since being in the band wasn't cool. This is the reason why I endured the hardships of being a crab in the SU Band along with graduating to become a band director. Finally, this is why I worked so hard and made personal sacrifices as a high school band director and college assistant band director. Everything pursued in my life since that magical day in 1985, has been encompassed in music to fulfill my seven-year-old version of success. Everything I have pursued from that childhood moment culminated on June 6, 2014, at that board meeting. I did it to be named the Director of the Southern University Department of Bands!

Besides the excitement and sense of accomplishment, I had a hint of disappointment. I was disappointed in the "interim" tag placed on the title. Arriving at the board meeting, I was disappointed with the agenda placed within the board packet and the fact that my name appeared towards the end. Finally, I was disappointed with the proposed salary of $61,500. No shade or anything, but that was only $20,000 more than my current salary as assistant band director at SU. I knew the salaries of the two Directors of Bands that preceded my appointment, and it came to me that Southern University has been lowering the pay with each new director and that realization started to frustrate me.

Members of my family came to the board meeting to support me. I'm so glad they did. They were able to help ground me. When I became frustrated, LaCara, my ex-wife, calmed me. My mother, Patricia Bennett Haymer Rodgers, continues to be my rock. Niles was my personal resource of information and his wife, my sister-in-law, Shermaine Haymer, was also a great source of support that helped to keep me calm.

To pass time and not be overcome or bored, I scanned the room and noticed the Vice Chancellor of Student Affairs. Instantly, I pointed him out to my family.

"That's him over there! The Vice Chancellor of Student Affairs. He will probably be my supervisor. I haven't officially met him yet, but I look forward to working with him."

Three hours into the meeting, my name is called. I could hear the rhythm of my heart beating. First it was at a normal lub-dub beat. But as soon as I heard my name, the beat accelerated. Unfamiliar with the procedure of the board, I didn't even know the vote had occurred.

Niles leaned over and said, "Nathan it's over and done. You're the band director now!"

Before I could react, a board member, Dr. Leroy Davis, summoned me to the podium to speak. I was unprepared. I had no speech and just started talking off the cuff. I was nervous and forgot to mention my family. However, Dr. Davis noticed them in the audience and reminded me to acknowledge them. I'm so glad he did.

"I would like to thank the Southern University System Board of Supervisors for your confidence in me to lead our great band, the beloved Human Jukebox! We will have a larger band with more excitement, this I can guarantee!"

One of the board members asked me about the Dancing Dolls. "We are all one unit! They will be more exciting too!"

Typically, a great speaker, that's all I recall saying. My nerves and emotions had gotten the best of me. I was just glad it was over and that I had gotten through it.

Even though we were towards the end of the board meeting, my portion was not the end. The last item on the agenda was the task

Juked

of deciding who would be the Chancellor for the Baton Rouge campus. I was interested in the decision since it would affect my ability to get things done for the students. However, the meeting took a turn for the worse and went into complete chaos. The board decided to go into an executive session and the meeting went long.

Ready to celebrate my new title and life's accomplishment, we left and went to dinner. While out, I attempted to watch the meeting on YouTube, but they were still in their private session, nothing was streaming live.

My phone was blowing up. Suddenly, I got a call and was told that the board was fighting internally. Some wanted the Vice Chancellor of Student Affairs. Others wanted the President of the Southern University System to become the President-Chancellor. Hours went by before the board negotiated a decision. The acting Chancellor would be Flandus McClintont who was previously the Vice Chancellor for Finance and Administration. The decision affected most of the departments that directly reported to the chancellor including the band and athletics. Later it was determined that the athletic director would report to Mr. McClinton and the band director would report to the Vice Chancellor of Student Affairs.

Personally, I didn't care or know if it was a good thing or not. I could work with anyone. I was excited either way. I was optimistic for the future of the band and the university in general. However, it was clear to me that this was the situation the reverend called me about.

Little did I know that the future would not be as bright as I hoped. The Vice Chancellor of Student Affairs is Brandon Dumas. He is the son of my father's former law partner, Walter, and now he's, my supervisor. Unbeknownst to me that when little kids don't get their way, they take their ball and run home! So, begins the battle!

Chapter 4

Although I have been serving in the position of Director of Bands for approximately two weeks, Monday, June 9, 2014, seemed and felt different. The official title gives the feeling of filling in or substitute teacher, even though the title started with "interim". I knew this would be temporary and soon I would move to being the actual Director of Bands, I just had to buy my time.

It was my first day officially in the seat and I faced more brick walls than ever. Set aside the fact, I received no formal transiting time or manual on how to operate. Instead, I got a list of important numbers on campus, a handshake, and lots of inherited problems. My predecessor, Lawrence Jackson or "Mr. J", was an accomplished band director and music arranger, and I admired his work. I loved how he infused so much power or sound into his arrangements. He also made me a lot of promises and only fulfilled one.

Mr. J told me that the numbers he was leaving were his allies on campus. "Nate, they'll be waiting on your call!"

The light bulb went off as if I was some crime detective solving the next big case like the TV show "Murder She Wrote" or "Scooby-Doo". This was my dream job, and I was very optimistic. No way Mr. J would set me up for failure. However, I had a lot against me when it came to the policies and procedures of the university. I had no experience in understanding the budgets or the process of spending money. I had no training in my fiduciary responsibilities or ethics as it related to my position. I was thrown the "hot potato" and was tagged "you're it" as it was my turn to figure all of this out.

July 5, 2006, I left my job in Lake Charles as the Washington-Marion Magnet High School Band Director to serve as the Assistant Director of Bands. Before resigning my high school position for SU, Mr. J promised I would be his successor and become the next Director of Bands. He promised when the days were coming close to his retirement, he would walk me around and show me the ropes while introducing me to the people who could help me become successful. Although he did keep his word on the timeline, the introductions never materialized. Instead, I got the list. I began to call everyone who was listed and to my surprise they were all nice and were waiting on me to call. I called every number except two: the chancellor's office and the Office of the President of the Southern University System.

Powerful people in departments are great for support with relationships and political connections on campus. However, I quickly realized the importance of treating people right. We often overlook custodians, receptionists, secretaries, etc., treating them as "small-time employees" while we trip over our own feet running to suck up to administrators. It is the "small-time employees" that run the University as they know the "ins and outs" of campus operations and procedures. If they love you, they can make your job and experience a pleasant one by making sure your paperwork, requests, etc. is at the top of the stack and signed by whatever boss who needs to review it. On the contrary, if they hate you, they will make your job a living hell! I told myself that I will never forget anyone on campus that helped me.

I had several issues to address. Hence, I had to devise a plan quickly. I needed to move the Human Jukebox from the dinosaur age to the technological age of social media. In addition, the band staff required pay raises. All band budgets must be increased and revamped. All band resources had to be renewed or updated. My biggest hurdle was the lack of support in my department. I had two positions that needed to be filled and I needed them filled quickly.

Juked

The morning of my first day found me jumping hurdle after hurdle and running into brick walls on brick walls. Unfortunately, I had never hired anyone before or received training from the University in doing so, so I went to the Office of the Chancellor for advice. None of them knew anything! Everyone I encountered kept their heads down not knowing what to expect in July when Mr. McClinton and Dr. Brandon Dumas was set to take the helm. I returned to my office frustrated.

As the day progressed to the evening, I stopped by the Louisiana Leadership Institute High School All-Star Band rehearsal just to be greeted with the same fakeness and confusion, but I didn't stay long to even worry about staff relations. I left the rehearsal to return to the office to finish making my band camp calls and emails to band directors, dance sponsors, and parents. First, I stopped by McDonalds right off the SU campus and grabbed something quick to eat. As I arrived at my office with my food, I noticed that the fax machine was flooded with papers and the red light on the machine was blinking, indicating that the machine was out of paper. I immediately put my food on the desk and reloaded the fax machine with paper. The fax machine went into overdrive for about 30 minutes shooting out sheet after sheet.

After eating, I began to count all the forms that were faxed in. I already had approximately 120 forms already in my possession that were filed. That night, I counted a little over 290 new registration forms. If what I was seeing was true, it would mean that the first event under my administration, The Southern University High School Summer Band and Dance Team Camp, would have record numbers as I had in my possession over 400 camp registration forms. Although I almost doubled the previous record, this was not a time for celebration. It was a time for panic. My mind went from panic to being angry with Mr. J for walking out and leaving me with a heavy load. This is the moment that I realized that I was stronger than I ever knew as my worry and panic turned into confidence and borderline arrogance! I made plans to storm the Office of the

President of the Southern University System the next day since I knew that he was the only one who could help me now.

That evening, I began to do my research. I called an old friend, Renardo R. Murray. Dr. Murray was the Director of Bands at Alcorn State University and worked previously with the president at Jackson State University during his short tenure as Interim Director of Bands at Jackson State University. The President of Jackson State University was now the President of the Southern University System. I knew Dr. Murray would be honest and helpful, which he was! He told me that the president was a straight shooter. He provided a wealth of advice.

The next day I went to the Office of the President of the Southern University System with a sense of urgency. I knew I just couldn't walk into any administrator's office and demand to see them without an appointment, but I didn't care!

"Good morning! I am Nathan Haymer, the new Director of Bands. I would like to speak to the president concerning an urgent matter. It is a matter of campus safety and a potential public relations nightmare for the University!" I told the receptionist as she looked at me with concern.

"He is not available at the moment; do you have an appointment?" the receptionist asked. She must have seen the look of frustration on my face as she told me to have a seat. She came from around the desk and began to speak to me softly.

"I am friends with Ms. Byrd, the administrative assistant for the SU Department of Bands. She and I have been friends for years. She told me what you're up against and I don't think that it's right! I am going to make sure that the president speaks with you, don't go anywhere!" As she walked off, I thanked her for the help and waited patiently.

Approximately 15 minutes passed and as my mind wandered on a band fan shirt that I would create as a token of my expression for all those who will help me to become successful on campus. "Mr. Haymer, the president will see you now!" The receptionist said. She winked her eyes and whispered, "Hold your ground and do not back down!" I nodded my head in approval and thanked her again.

As I entered the large and well-decorated office of the most powerful officer in the Southern University System, I didn't have time to even take it all in, but I did enjoy the view of the Mississippi River (The Bluff) that runs adjacent to the campus. "Thank you for meeting with me Mr. President! I have an urgent matter of campus safety and security that needs your immediate attention!" I said to the president as he paused to think of a response.

"Have a seat and let's talk about it!" he responded.

As I sat down, I continued to explain "I do not have a supervisor at the moment being that the chancellor is out on leave and the vice-chancellor not officially being my supervisor until July!"

The President interjected and began to explain the role of his office to me. "Well technically, I am not responsible for the day-to-day operations of the Baton Rouge campus or any other campus but tell me what's going on and I'll see what I can do to help!"

"We will have over 400 seventh through twelfth graders on this campus from all over the country! Right now, I only have one staff member and I am short two. Because I moved up to the director's position, I need someone in my old position as assistant director. I also need to replace a position that has been open since 2012!"

The president interrupted me as he was confused. "2012? Why hasn't it been filled in two years?"

I briefly explained about the issue between director, Mr. J, and longtime assistant director, Mr. Carnell Knighten. The president dismissed my attempt to explain and continued "I'll tell you what…I think that I can help you fill one position immediately, but the other position I am not going to touch! You will have to figure that one out with your supervisor when July comes."

The president began to yell a lady's name then she walked in the room. "This is my chief of staff." I briefly spoke to her as she looked at me in frustration. The President spoke, "Please assist our band director, he will tell you what he needs, and I want you to make it happen for him!"

"Ok, come with me!" said the chief of staff and as I followed her to the next office over.

"Thank you, Mr. President" I shouted and walked out of his office.

Dr. Murray was correct. President Ronald Mason, Jr. was a straight shooter and very helpful. However, his chief of staff seemed very frustrated. I proceeded to explain to her what I had just told Dr. Mason.

"Why in the hell did he just not take care of this before he stormed out of here mad about not being paid enough money!" Her comment was in reference to Mr. J, but I had no idea what she was talking about. Mr. J never shared with me anything about leaving because of his pay or being in the president's office.

"Ma'am, I don't know anything about that! I am just trying to get things together for my department."

"Are the funds available for the positions that you need to fill?" she asked.

"I don't know. I have no clue what funds being available mean or how to go about knowing how to find that information out. I don't know the procedures for hiring assistants. I don't know anything and that is why I am here."

"I can't believe this shit!" she said while shaking her head. "They are setting you up to fail, baby!"

I didn't know who "they" were that the chief of staff was referring to, but I did appreciate her tone and sense of urgency as she was talking with the same passion and emotion that I was feeling. The chief of staff picked up the phone. She had a five-minute conversation about my situation. "Do you have a person in mind that you want to immediately hire because that is what this situation calls for?" she asked.

"Yes, I do!"

"Good!" She responded. "Have them go online to fill out the application and go to the state police office to submit their fingerprints for the required background check!" As she continued to explain what I needed to have my new hire do to speed up the process, she began to make more phone calls giving orders to people on campus what to do to help me. She ended with "Go to Human Resources, they are waiting on you!"

"Thank you so much!" I shouted as I hurried and walked out of the door. As I passed the receptionist, I smiled and gave her a thumbs up!

I arrived in the Human Resources office with optimism. I had the president and the chief of staff in my corner, so I just knew that something was going to be accomplished today. My optimism was for a reason because as soon as I walked in the door, I was immediately assisted. "Sign here…Sign here…. Sign here!" As we flipped through the papers the Human Resources employee continued with "Mr. Haymer, I am here to help! My son is in your band!"

"Oh, really? Who is your son?" I asked.

She told me her son's name. He was a good kid and a music major aspiring to become a band director. "Oh wow…it's a small world! Your son is a good kid and great percussionist! I didn't say drummer, I said PERCUSSIONIST…there is a difference!" I told the employee with humor as we both laughed. She helped me tremendously as all I had to do was fill out the appropriate paperwork for the hiring process to begin.

When I walked into the band building, I immediately went to Ms. Byrd's office and thanked her for the tip that she gave the receptionist in the president's office.

"We are supposed to have each other's back, Nate! That is what I am here for," she said while laughing at my way of explaining to her what happened in the president's office and Human Resources office.

I was so excited and while I had so many questions, I was happy that I crossed at least one hurdle.

Chapter 5

The victory lap for the success of hiring an assistant was short lived. Immediately, I was faced with additional hurdles. Within the midst of celebrating, Ms. Byrd came into my office with folders in her hands and began explaining the band's travel budget and scholarship budget. More than just a secretary, Ms. Byrd is the true definition of an Administrative Assistant. She schooled me on both the travel budget and the scholarship budget.

"Everything that Mr. J did in terms of the band's travel budget and scholarship budget, I have right here! He already awarded some students for the upcoming fall semester before he left, so I also know how much money is left in the scholarship budget for the incoming freshmen. I know how much money is projected for this year's band travel budget as well! I just talked to the Executive Assistant to the Vice-Chancellor, and she confirmed everything that I am telling you."

When I looked at the scholarship budget for the first time, I was outraged. My blood pressure had to have risen because I was hot! "This is criminal! Only $90,000 for scholarships?" I asked.

"Nate, it's been like that for at least 25 years!"

"So, we have been getting a scholarship reduction over the years!" I told her as she looked at me with confusion.

"What do you mean?"

"I mean it's been $90,000 for 25 years, right?" She nodded indicating yes. "The price of tuition has more than tripled over that period of time so that means that the value of $90,000 in 1989, which was 25 years ago, was more than its value today in 2014!" As she agreed, I became even more outraged by her explaining more details.

"Oh, that's $90,000 for the entire year so that means the budget is split in half. You only have $45,000 for the fall semester and $45,000 for the spring semester. Mr. J used to bet on students not making the required grade point average (GPA) in the fall to keep their scholarships. That would give him extra money in the spring to give the students with the higher GPAs more money."

I couldn't take it! I had a severe headache! How did my predecessors do it? Ms. Byrd went on to show me that Mr. J already awarded $35,000 to students before he retired. This left me with only $10,000 to split among the freshman class.

It is my belief that all of the students in the band deserved a scholarship in some way, shape, or form. While everyone can't get a full scholarship, they deserve something as they dedicate and invest too much time and energy into rehearsals and performances. The students are the ones who make the crowd wave their pom-poms while saying "That's my band!" The students are the ones who must be student-musicians. This means that they are students first but still have to bear the load of a heavy practice schedule.

There wasn't a band member or Dancing Doll on the roster who received a full scholarship; no one did! As I looked at the list of students who were awarded scholarships, the highest of $1,500 were only going to a few students. A few more received $1000, but most of the list only received $500 per semester.

Juked

As I continued to become even more upset, I took a calculator out of my desk drawer and divided $45,000, the total amount of the scholarship budget for the semester, by 230, the total amount of students in the department. When I saw the answer, I threw the calculator to the floor! I could not believe the great Southern University Band operated like this!

To make matters worse, the resources of the band were in a state of despair. I knew that I would need outsourcing to bring the band to the next level. My solution was to create a marketing and brand management team. We were broke and my options were limited. I pursued two guys for this endeavor: Eric and Jabari. Both are Southern alumni with a strong connection to the band and school. Plus, they are former band members.

I knew each of them personally. I trusted and respected Eric more so than Jabari. Eric was the first person to introduce me to arranging music. He was two years ahead of me in the band. We played in the trombone section together which allowed me to observe the fact that he was very mean and thorough. Jabari and I played in the same band as well, but I didn't trust him.

I appreciated Eric's honesty about his partner being Jabari. I wasn't a big fan of Jabari's partnership with Eric nor was I a big fan of Jabari, as he appeared to be the band's biggest hater. I was hesitant to work with this duo, but Eric convinced me to speak with Jabari. We did a conference call that revealed a lot of things. We spoke about missed opportunities for the band and meetings with bad decisions. However, it still did not give me a great feeling about Jabari. The greatest thing to come from the conversation was a win-win proposition that made me more comfortable. "Hey man…we want to work for you! If you want to take a crap in the middle of the street, even though that will be a dumb thing to do, it's our job to market that piece of crap! It will cost the band nothing for our services. It will be our job as the marketing and brand management arm of the band to go and find the money through corporate sponsorships, partnerships, etc., the band will receive 80-percent of all our efforts, and we will receive 20-percent. It's a win-win situation for the University!"

I had to admit that Jabari had a point. I needed to give the proposal further thought and consideration. My trust for Eric was real and top of the list on why I should go into business with this duo. Even though I wasn't big on Jabari, I had a great history on building teams out of rivals. Jabari definitely wasn't a friend so I knew he would challenge my thoughts, decisions and not be a "yes man". I considered Jabari the band's biggest hater and wanted to offer him an opportunity to put up or shut up with sponsorships and times to make money. Jabari's 80-20 deal was no risk to the band or the university. Finally, doing nothing wasn't an option.

I had a vision. Unfortunately, my vision would require me putting my differences aside and working with a man I don't trust. Keep your friends close and your enemies closer. The proposal is what tipped me as I made the decision to go into business with Jabari.

"Have your attorney draw out the contract," I told them and further explained. "The decision isn't mine to make unilaterally. I would need the approval of the SU System Foundation's Board, the board's general counsel, and my supervisor."

While waiting on a decision, I mapped out a roadmap of goals for the department under my leadership. The goals were challenging, realistic, innovative, and bold because it was time to stop complaining about the problems and become the solution and change that the students needed and deserved! I began to put personal feelings aside and started depending on my unofficial Marketing and Brand Management Team, the MBM Team, with Eric and Jabari. I submitted my goals to them in hopes that they could begin the process of making professional slides, brochures, and digital material to submit to fans, alumni, and potential sponsors and partners.

    The MBM Team advised me on the upcoming Southern University Alumni Federation National Conference scheduled for July 2014 in Houston. We marked that as the date to have my new supervisor's support. Being the Vice Chancellor of Student Affairs, he was key to the political pull needed for success while holding the power to get the contract signed which was needed in making Eric and Jabari the official MBM Team of the Human Jukebox! Jabari put me in contact with a Houston based web designer who was responsible for creating the band's new Human Jukebox logo and new website. I had no time to wait and paid for the web designer's services out of pocket!

Chapter 6

Along with other campus directors, leaders, and department heads under the supervision of the new Vice Chancellor of Student Affairs, I received a formal email from him. The email was a basic hello, effective this date these departments fall under my division and looking forward to working with you. Surprisingly, my department was listed as "The Human Jukebox" and not the Department of Bands. True, my department had more ensembles than the marching band, but the marching band was the most visible and most popular, so I shrugged off the reference to the Human Jukebox only.

Since I received an email, it was the perfect time to set up a meeting with my new supervisor. At this point, I believed that developing a good relationship with my supervisor was key to being successful! I needed to make a good impression and change the negative perception he had of me. An ally of mine informed me that the Vice Chancellor thought I was arrogant, and he seemed to be jealous of my "popularity." His opinion seemed strange to me. During my years as assistant director, I never knew the Vice Chancellor. He started his job in 2012. During that time, I only reported to Mr. J, the Director of Bands.

Clueless to the reasoning on his thoughts of me, I quickly made moves to have him see the true me. I asked Ms. Byrd, my administrative assistant, to schedule a meeting with my new boss. Amazingly, she was able to get me a meeting the same day.

I walked into his office for my appointment and before I spoke, I saw all the TV monitors displaying pictures from many angles of the interior and exterior of the student union where his office was located.

"Thank you for meeting with me. I look forward to working with you!"

"Oh, no problem, Doc. Have a seat," responded the Vice Chancellor.

I looked at the Vice Chancellor before seating. Brandon Dumas was a young man, but he didn't dress the part. His style was from the 1960s or 1970s. He dressed the way my grandfather did. He wore dress slacks with a SU polo shirt tucked in and the slacks were pulled over his belly button. The legs of the slacks were wide, not like bell bottoms, just wide like what an older man would wear.

"I need your help."

"Ok, what's going on?"

Granted an opening to discuss the issues I faced; I took the opportunity to plant seeds. I explained the problem of the vacant second assistant band director position, provided details on my vision for the MBM Team, and accounted for the uphill battle I had been facing as the interim director.

Brandon attentively listened. Then he spoke, "Congratulations! I saw that you guys had a record-breaking attendance with band camp."

"Yes sir, we did! Thank you. Which reminds me of some things I need to run by you to ensure we can continue to host our camp with a high standard of excellence," I stated as I updated him on the registration process. I elaborated the story of the post office being behind with camp registration and payments and how my "fax now and pay later" system causes me to put stress on the director of residential life who oversees the campus dorms.

"There's so much that I need to cover with you, but I value your time. So, the most important item on my list is the assistant director's opening."

"You have to see Mac about the assistant position. I'll talk to him about it too. We have to make sure that the funds are available," Brandon responded.

Mac is the name they call Flandus McClinton, the Vice Chancellor for Finance and Administration and now Acting Chancellor. He would be able to notify us immediately if the funds were available for the position. I remember Mr. J not liking him and always characterized him as a "hard-nosed numbers guy!" He was a guy with no personality that stared at spreadsheets on computer screens all day and just said "No" to everyone and everything. He's been employed at SU for about forty years. He was old and set in his ways. Flandus McClinton was a guy that I didn't want to cross.

"I am going to do what I can to help you with this," Brandon said.

I was happy that he was cooperative, but I remembered the rumor about him thinking I was arrogant, so I continued the conversation by addressing the issue indirectly. "I don't know if we ever crossed paths in the past but as assistant director, I really walked with blinders on. I didn't say too much to administrators because one time I told Mr. J a directive from an administrator, and he didn't respond too kindly to it. I learned then just to walk from point A to point B with as little talking as possible!"

Laughing, he said, "Yes, I can understand that. Jack was a character. Why did he leave so unexpectedly? Was it because of the 2008 hazing case, because it's still not over yet?"

"I don't think so, but I was just as surprised as everyone else about his retirement. He didn't tell me either. I found out when I was called to the empty office on May 27, 2014. I worked hard to get here and all I want to do is serve our university!"

"I feel the same way man. Some people are saying the only reason I got this position is because of my father, but this is work. My father did get me here, but it's my work and achievements that are keeping me here!"

His father and my father were business partners at one time and there is history there. A history of his father as it relates to my father, and it was clear that he probably knew more than I did about their relationship as I was not as close to my father as he appeared to be to his. I changed the subject and looking back, it would have been safer to stay on this conversation than the one I started.

"What can I do to help you achieve your goals? If you need the band for anything, just let me know and we're there!"

He needed the band and wasted no time. "I'm happy to hear you say that. In addition to being over student affairs, I am also responsible for enrollment management."

I remember seeing his name on the board packet and was so consumed with my own pursuits that I really didn't pay attention. Gossip travels around SU faster than the speed of light. First, people were upset about him getting the vice chancellor position with no experience and "a fast-tracked Ph.D." from Jackson State University. Then, it was his quick salary increases starting at $85,000/year to $105,000/year and ending at $140,000/year. I didn't care. I had the position that I wanted but if Brandon had that type of power and influence, I wanted his help.

"I am starting a recruitment tour this fall! We have our own bus and I have a plan to increase the enrollment of the University and part of my plan includes using the band."

This was my first-time hearing about this tour, but I would be a fool to say no to my supervisor. I needed him for so many things that I wanted immediately and things that I would need in the future. I didn't necessarily want a pay raise for myself, I just wanted the same pay that Mr. J received. I also wanted Lorenzo Hart's, the percussion instructor/equipment manager, salary to increase immediately. Calculating all the things I need to get accomplished, I wanted to develop a partnership with Brandon. I needed to develop a good working relationship with him.

Brandon picked up the phone and called Mr. McClinton to ask about the assistant band director opening. Of course, he said "NO!"

"Don't worry Doc, I told you Mac is a very tough guy. I'll work on getting a 'YES' for you!"

I thanked him and changed the subject to talk about my final concern: MY INTERIM STATUS!

"I am glad you brought that up," Brandon said. "The Chair of the Southern University System Board of Supervisors isn't happy with you right now!"

I was shocked to hear this and Brandon had my full attention. I had no idea why she wouldn't be happy with me. "What do you mean?"

"Well, a number of band alumni reached out to her on your behalf. They stated that you should be the Director and not interim! You need to reach out to her because her support is necessary for you to become the permanent director. I can only recommend you, but the board has to approve it."

I appreciated the band alumni's support, but I had no idea that this was going on. I explained everything to Brandon. I knew he was right in stating that I needed the chair's support in order for me to get the approval.

Before I left the office, I wrote two numbers down. The first was the phone number for the board chair with instructions to call her after 6pm. The second belonged to Brandon. We exchanged phone numbers in hopes of having a better line of communication.

I left Brandon's office happy. I had a good feeling that we were going to work well together. The hour-long meeting resulted in me receiving an email stating that he was beginning the process of hiring the second assistant director. The only task for the day was to contact the board chair. I truly thought things were going well.

Juked

Chapter 7

I've become restless and didn't want anything to ruin my chances of becoming Director of Bands, so I waited until after 6pm to call the board chair just like Brandon advised me. I called at exactly 6:01pm and she answered on the first ring.

"Hello!"

"Hello. This is Nathan Haymer, Interim Director of Bands, I am calling to speak to the Board Chair."

"This is she!"

By the background noise, I could tell she was in her vehicle. "Did I call you at a bad time?"

"Oh, no. I am just driving home."

Bridget Dinvaut represented Louisiana's 1st Congressional District for Southern University's board. She is very well connected in Louisiana's politics. As she lives in New Orleans, she very well could be leaving Baton Rouge and be anywhere on Interstate 10.

"Okay, good. I would like to apologize for band alumni bombarding you on my behalf. While I appreciate their sentiment, I had nothing to do with them calling you. Furthermore, I will reach out to the Human Jukebox Alumni Association and ask them to stop!"

"Oh, no. There's no reason to do that," Bridget stated. "I am just happy to know that you didn't have anything to do with it. I also want you to know I was very close to Dr. Isaac Greggs and his family. Although I never played in the band, I know a lot about it. I am also friends with many alumni of the band who are much older than you. Mr. Haymer, I am a straight shooter and I have some concerns."

Ok. What are they," I asked very inquisitively.

"Well, some of the alumni I know don't think that you're the right fit for the position. Some are saying that you're too ghetto and others are saying that you can't write music!"

I paused. I knew now was the time to keep my cool. I gave thought to my response. I had too much to risk and lose. I wasn't going to blow my chances on hearsay and gossip. I have been a hothead at times. I may have gone off on people for good reasons but NEVER have I EVER been called "Ghetto!" Additionally, I wanted to ask her what the hell she had been doing the last 8 years or where she had been. I really wanted to know about the past four years. It is especially those years where I was the ONLY full-time music arranger for the Human Jukebox. That insult was personal. I've been through too much personally and arranged many top notched hits for the band to just be dismissed in such a manner.

"I don't know what the 'ghetto reference' is so I am not going to entertain that, but when it comes to writing music, the job of the Director of Bands is similar to a head football coach. The head coach doesn't run the offense or defense. The head coach is the manager. It is his job to keep the coaches on task and develop a winning strategy. My job as Director of Bands is similar in that I will have assistant directors who will be charged with writing music while I write the drills for halftime and oversee the entire program as an administrator."

"Ooh, I love that answer and sports analogy," Bridget stated in a snooty tone as if she was Queen Elizabeth II. "So, you're saying that you'll be able to lead a team of talented music writers?"

"Oh! Most certainly," I replied while maintaining my professionalism. I didn't want my "ghetto antics" to show up by correcting the term writers to arrangers.

"Well, I want to use a band analogy for you, Mr. Haymer! What do you call the leaders? Umm ummm?"

"Section leaders."

"Yes, that's it! Section leaders. And don't they sit first chair?"

"Yes, they do!"

"Ooh, see. I do know something about band," she replied as she gave a snooty laugh. "Ok, so you are the section leader and you're first chair. It's up to you to defend your chair or lose it."

Wow! Her analogy stung! I knew exactly what it meant! She must have known of someone who was interested in the job and was warning me that if I couldn't produce that I would be replaced before the season was over!

Without sounding bothered by her threat, I responded "I totally understand, and I don't have a problem defending my chair!"

"Good! Now there's **one** more thing. I heard that you were inquiring about your salary being too low?"

"Yes, that is true. I am doing the work of the Director, so I feel that I should receive the same salary as my predecessor, Mr. J!"

"I set your salary at $61,500, which is $20,000 more than you made previously! What incentive do you have to work harder to become the permanent director if we gave you everything upfront? Your salary will stay at $61,500 until you earn the directorship!"

"Well, I received my check at the end of June and my salary is still $41,500. I just hired an assistant director who's making the same salary as me and will be hiring another assistant who will make more than me because his salary will be $45,000!"

"Just be patient, Mr. Haymer!" she said with that same snooty-unconcerned-condescending voice. "I am sure that your supervisor is making sure that your paperwork is processed!"

Chapter 8

I met with Eric and Jabari and told them that my supervisor was on board with approving the contract that they submitted to me. I gave a copy of the contract to Brandon and to Preston Castille, General Counsel of the Southern University System Foundation Board. Now, we were just waiting on Attorney Castille to approve the contract or notify me of any concerns. Even though I was hoping the process would be quick, in reality I expected a small delay since Attorney Castille was also busy running for president of the SU Alumni Federation. To help the process along, I had an appointment to meet with Attorney Castille later that week at the law office where he practiced privately located in downtown Baton Rouge.

The week passed and it was now time for my meeting with Attorney Castille. At this meeting he advised me not to go with my choice for the Marketing and Brand Management team because he had some serious concerns.

I arrived downtown to Attorney Castille's office that overlooked the city of Baton Rouge. I was astonished by the nice view! Baton Rouge doesn't have much of a skyline, but this building is the tallest in the city except for the Louisiana State Capitol building. I must have waited about ten minutes for Attorney Castille to see me, but I didn't mind at all. I was enjoying the view of the city.

The receptionist said, "Mr. Haymer! He's ready to see you. Follow me, please."

I followed her to a conference room with glass walls. I thought it was rather formal to meet in a conference room at a huge table with 16 chairs just for a meeting between us!

"Good morning, Mr. Haymer," Attorney Castille said as he shook my hand. "Have a seat!"

We engaged in small talk for a couple of minutes. He then placed a folder on the table and slid it in front of me. He asked me to open the folder and I did. In the folder were results of a background check on Jabari. The report was damning with a lot of details about Jabari. The information was quite troubling and the most troubling was the legal problem. Apparently, Jabari partnered with someone to promote a concert and failed to deliver on what he was contracted to do. The report also revealed many personal things including the foreclosure of his home.

As I read, Attorney Castille sat silently until I looked up at him.

"Now, do you understand my concerns?" He asked. "Look Nathan, I played the trumpet in the Opelousas High School band in the 1980s. Although I never played in the band as a student at SU, I always admired the band and Isaac Greggs. I want you to be just as successful as he was and part of that is being fully aware of who you're dealing with! I will submit these findings to the foundation's board, but I didn't want you to be blindsided by the discovery. You can take that copy with you and let me know what your final decision is. I'll submit it to the board if your recommendation is still a yes!"

I thanked Attorney Castille for the insight and for taking the time to meet with me. "Good luck in your mission to be alumni president!" I knew it was very close to election time and as the Director of Bands I stayed neutral because I knew whoever would become President of the SU Alumni Federation I had to work with in some way, shape, or form.

After leaving the building and getting into my vehicle, I called Jabari. I wanted to tell him the disturbing news and he was furious. Instantly, he started to explain the legal problems and other damning details, but I cut him off.

"Look man! I've made my decision, and this report doesn't change my mind! I will scan this information and send it to your email! I just want you to know that the board will see the report as well, but my decision is final!"

We continued our conversation and Jabari mentioned his ability to call a few people. I was glad that he was going to contact people on the Southern University System Foundation (SUSF) board on his and the band's behalf. The board's vote was the final say so. Upon approval, Eric and Jabari would be working for them on behalf of the band.

Eric and Jabari called me more than a dozen times a day. Every day we talked about the "same ole same ole". I was pushing hard to get the contract signed so that they can "put up or shut up"! I needed the MBM team to produce half of what they promised. If they could do that, then the annoying phone calls and getting into the business of things that are beyond the scope of their duty would be worth it!

While working to get the contract signed, I received a call from Brandon. The call gave good news and bad news.

"Hey man! Mac approved the position for a second assistant director! Does Brian Simmons have a master's degree?"

"No, he doesn't. I am encouraging him to get his master's. When I was first hired in 2006, I was in the process of completing my master's degree, but I was still hired!" Everyone knew that I hired Brian Simmons fresh from completing his bachelor's degree.

"Oh no! Brian is good. It's just that Mac told me that your next hire must have a master's degree and some experience. Between us, Mr. J called a board member concerned that you were making the wrong staffing decisions!"

I thought Brandon's comment was odd for two reasons. First, Mr. J and I talked about Brian Simmons months before his retirement. He knew that I was going to hire Brian whenever my day came to be the director. Last, if Mr. J was so concerned about my decisions, then why did he let the second assistant position freeze after the death of Carnell Knighten, former longtime assistant/associate director? He also transferred the position from band to the music department. More importantly, why wouldn't Mr. J just call me instead of a board member? I couldn't believe that he would do that to me! As much as he and his family complained about Isaac Greggs being "extra" after his retirement. Well, if what I was hearing from Brandon was true, then Mr. J was being "extra-extra," but I didn't want to believe this. Still, I continued to listen to Brandon.

"It's your staff. You can hire who you want. They just must have a master's degree!"

I listened to Brandon and okayed his comments. He instructed me to write the requirements for the position and submit the appropriate paperwork to Human Resources so the position could be advertised appropriately.

I was heartbroken. I had a person in mind that could develop a good working chemistry with Brian Simmons to build a dominant force that will take over the band world. The person I wanted was also my crab brother who also worked with me as a high school band director. Eddie Rideau is the name of my first choice, and he would have been a great fit. It was upsetting for Brian Simmons as well. My relationship with Eddie was different after this. He never treated me differently, but it was hard for me to face him. I let him down! I fought for many things that were less important and I should've fought harder for him. I don't think Brandon Dumas had anything to do with this but in my mind, Mr. J and Jabari were my prime suspects!

It was clear that the powers that be felt they could influence decisions that affect my leadership and my business. It was also clear that certain powers wanted a particular person to have the second assistant director of bands job. The person everyone was bidding to have the job is Kedric Taylor.

Juked

I have worked with Mr. Taylor before; therefore, I knew his strengths and weaknesses. As far as his experience, I already knew what he was capable of. Working with Mr. Taylor wasn't a question of his experience and what he can bring to the table, rather a question of his character and how it can destroy the table!

Mr. Taylor came to visit me at the office. During his visit he referenced us working together and expressed his interest in the job. I heard him out and told him to apply. We shook hands and I walked him out of the office. He was definitely my "Plan B". He was the only applicant for the job. I had others who sent their resume or expressed interest in the job, but none officially applied.

We conducted the interview a week later. Mr. Taylor was nervous under pressure. I noticed how he was stumbling over his words. The Executive Assistant to the Vice-Chancellor for Student Affairs (VCSA) and the Director of Student Life both asked excellent questions concerning student academic success, the role of assistant band director, and other non-musical questions. They left all the band and music topics to me. I didn't ask Mr. Taylor anything because he was already having a tough time fumbling through the questions that were asked by the other two interviewers.

"Thank you for your interest in the position, I'll be in touch with you!"

I told Mr. Taylor as we concluded the interview. He thanked everyone present and walked out of the conference room. We were in the Office of Student Affairs on the second floor in the student union. I wanted to shake Mr. Taylor up and interview him in a place that was unfamiliar. I thought the band hall would have made him too comfortable, but if I knew that he would fumble the interview like he did, I wouldn't have made it as formal. The executive assistant to the VCSA said, "I don't know about him! He seemed to be too nervous." We all laughed as I assured them that although he fumbled the interview badly, he could do the job.

On the next day, I called Mr. Taylor, and I could tell immediately that he was in a rehearsal with his high school band.

"Hey man! You need to get out of that band room and get some rest. You have a lot of work to do," I said jokingly.

"Hey what's going on?" he said quietly. I can tell that he didn't want his students to know what was taking place because he was talking in a "sneaky tone."

"I am not going to hold you long, I know that your students are around, but you're going to have to break their hearts! I am calling you to let you know that you've been selected to be the Assistant Director of Bands!"

"Oh, for real?" Mr. Taylor responded with no excitement. In fact, the whole moment was quite uneventful.

"Yes! I am going to get with my supervisor to find out when you need to report to campus and fill out the appropriate paperwork. You will need to turn in your letter of resignation to your principal and school district as soon as possible because we have work to do!"

"Alright! Thank you, man. I'll do that," Mr. Taylor responded very dully. I didn't think much of his lack of excitement because I could hear the students playing on their instruments in the background and I thought maybe he wanted to break the news slowly to them. Losing a band director can be a traumatic experience for a student as I experienced the same thing when I told my high school students that I was leaving them for SU back in 2006. They were not happy at all!

As a day or so passed, Mr. Taylor did exactly what I asked him to do. He turned in his letter of resignation. I was prepared to make the announcement of the addition of Mr. Taylor on the band's social media platforms, but the VCSA asked me to hold off as they were still doing all of the processing in Human Resources. Something didn't sound right about that because the process for Mr. Simmons moved quickly. Then I remembered that the

Juked

president's office classified Mr. Simmons as an emergency hire. Again, I had to learn how to remain patient.

Within a week, I received a text message from the VCSA… "You can move forward in the process of hiring your assistant director, but the funds are unavailable!" I was confused. In order to start the application and interviewing process, funds had to be approved by Human Resources and an administrator or I wouldn't have been allowed to move forward to conduct an interview.

I was very upset by the text message. I began to think…*I am already depressed by calling my crab brother, Eddie Rideau, to tell him that I couldn't hire him after I promised him the job. Now I must call Kedric Taylor after he submitted his letter of resignation to let him know we don't have the funds to hire him? I cannot do this again!* After going through a ten-minute panic attack, the VCSA texted again, "Use the funds from your band camp to pay Mr. Taylor's salary.

"How do I do that?" I responded. My supervisor's use of text messaging, in serious situations, caused even more confusion, but it was his preferred method of communication. He continued with… "Go to the comptroller's office. I've already instructed one of the account managers on what to do and they will set it up for you!"

Not thinking of the consequences that it may lead to, I did exactly that and was able to announce Mr. Kedric Taylor as the Assistant Director of Bands and the final addition to the SU Department of Bands' talented team. I was happy to get over another major hurdle as we were fully staffed and ready for the fall. I wanted the staff to have all the advantages that I didn't from being disconnected with Isaac Greggs during my first four years as assistant, to being overworked and underpaid as the band's only arranger during my last four years as assistant! As happy as I was to finally have my complete team in place, the consequences of this day would haunt me for the remainder of my tenure as Director of Bands for several reasons to come!

After close to two months of going back and forth, the MBM team is official! The contract was approved and signed by all required University officials, including myself and my direct supervisor, Brandon Dumas! Jabari signed the contract with a fancy celebratory pen and as usual, he was doing the most! I was happy that we crossed over another hurdle. I was happy for the MBM team as Jabari stated, "Business as usual is no longer!"

The MBM team's first plan of action was to go after individuals who sold band merchandise such as T-shirts, decorative license plates, etc. The MBM team had a point, the band wasn't receiving any profits from those sales. They also went after "Jukes (former members of the SU Band)" who recreated or rebranded the band's signature "S" shirts. I supported them with this move as well. Their motto *Business as usual is no longer!* meant that we had to start doing things the right way. Anyone selling band merchandise would require permission from the University's Collegiate Licensing Company (CLC) director as it would give them a license to sell and give the band a percentage of the profit. Because the CLC director was also the CEO of the SUS Foundation, I had no problems with the MBM team's plan of action due to their contract being under the supervision of the SUSF as well.

News of the MBM team and their new role would cause conflict between them and the Human Jukebox Alumni Association. It was something that I wanted to stay out of, but the politics and Jabari's disrespect to the Human Jukebox Alumni Association would bring me into yet another battle that I didn't foresee but should have seen due to his troubling history as the founder of the original band alumni association that failed! I haven't even put a band on the field to perform yet and I was already tired in my new role! It was now time to focus on the product, the Human Jukebox, and stop lending my energy to the side show, but the MBM team would continue to act as the troubled child that reminds you to pay attention to them every day!

Chapter 9

Up to this point, I have dealt with politics, staffing, marketing and brand management, Dancing Doll tryouts, and developing a good relationship with my supervisor. I'm ready to work with what I truly care about and the reason why I'm back at my alma mater.... The Southern University Band! However, before I could focus on the good stuff, I have to deal with the MBM team's distraction prior to band camp.

Before band camp began, I met with a local activist and entrepreneur that expressed interest in helping the band raise funds. His magazine company was an online black urban media platform that highlighted many stories and events around the Baton Rouge area that didn't necessarily make it to the front page of the newspaper or local TV news. He mainly covered unreported or underreported news for the black community.

After our initial meeting in my office, Gary Chambers and I hit it off good. I was excited to hear his ideas and enthusiasm for the SU Band. We agreed that he would produce a documentary covering the band's historic past and present. He would start filming the documentary on the first day of camp with the freshman class and conclude the documentary with the band's debut performance at the first football game of the season. After getting the necessary clearance from the VCSA and the Acting Chancellor, we had the greenlight to start the filming project. This project was approved before the MBM team's contract was signed and bringing them on board was a nightmare since Jabari didn't want any parts of it.

"Hey man! Remember you said that if I took a crap in the middle of the road and as stupid as it would be to do so, it's your job to market it?" I told Jabari. "I am the director, and I don't report to the MBM team, it's the other way around! With that being said, I am doing the project!"

"Well, you said you didn't want a 'Yes Man' and I ain't one. So, I am telling you that it is stupid!"

"Thank you for your sentiments, but we are doing the project!" I stated boldly as I hung up the phone in his face.

As a student of history, I was more interested in the project not because of what it could potentially raise in revenue for the band, rather, for its historical significance. As much history as the SU Band has, it has never done a good job documenting its history. This project would help with that. Gary Chambers will interview former band members as far back as the 1950s and 1960s to present date.

I began the university band camp with the "crab class of 2014." Before I could really get into my groove, I got an annoying text from Brandon about referring to the freshmen as crabs. I was in the middle of my welcome speech, which was being recorded by the band's media team and Gary Chambers' media team. One of the newly appointed assistant directors, Brian Simmons, approached me and whispered, "Check your phone!"

I paused to check my phone. I saw a text from Brandon about something that I posted on social media welcoming the "Crab Class of 2014." I guess that he had a point as he referenced the 2008 hazing lawsuit! I used the word "crab" and freshmen interchangeably in my social media posts. I was able to multitask by asking Mr. Simmons and Mr. Taylor to come up, introduce themselves, and give the "Freshman Class" their expectations while I edited my post and returned a text to Brandon to let the "micromanaging pest" know that it was corrected.

We managed to make it through our first week with no major problems. A few students quit, but that was a normal thing every year. At the end of the week, I had a solid class of approximately 90 freshmen. I was happy it was Friday and after 4:00pm, I surprised

Juked

the freshman class by giving them the rest of the day and weekend off! I was tired! After getting a good night's rest on Friday night, I woke up Saturday morning around 9:00am. I received some calls from the band staff and MBM team, but the most unusual call was around 11:00am from a former student. This student used to do most of the video work for the band when I was the assistant director. I didn't know what he wanted. He never really called me so; I was sure it was something important.

"Hello Mr. Haymer! Sorry to call you on a Saturday, but I still have the contact number for Sonja Norwood. She gave me her number about two years ago for Director Jackson to use, but he never wanted me to reach out to her. Do you want her number?"

"Yes, please give me her number!" I said excitedly. The number had a Los Angeles area code. I continued, "I'll tell you what. Call her for me and see if she wants to talk to me first and if she does, then I'll call her."

"Okay!"

Sonja Norwood is a graduate of Southern University who was instrumental in guiding the success of her children, Brandy and Ray J., and many other artists in the music industry. Being an Artist Manager is a very intense and tough job, but to do it a black woman is something that I won't even attempt to "MANsplain." What I will explain is the unfair judgment that women get for being firm, tough, or a "boss," when men do it all the time and are called a mogul! Sonja's reputation exceeds her, and I was hoping that she would want to talk to me. I was nervously thinking of what to say to her to get her support with the Human Jukebox. In less than five minutes the former student sent me a text, "She's waiting on your call!"

"Thank you!" I responded as I dialed her number slowly. Because of my respect and admiration for her, I will not share the details of the initial call with Sonja; but what I will say is because of my call followed by numerous calls within a week's time span, I gained a powerful ally that would prove to be invaluable to my tenure as Director of Bands. I initially introduced her to "Nate," the shy and humble person who I naturally am. In a matter of weeks, she had to deal with "Haymer-Time," the person who I am when it's "lights, camera, and action!" She was responsible for many of the ventures and projects that the MBM team would eventually attempt to take the credit for as I will reveal throughout the crazy journey in the world of Haymer-Time!

Chapter 10

I faced many obstacles that first football season as the "Interim" Director of Bands. Even though my conversation with Sonja Norwood was great, it quickly went left after that. First, I wrecked my car. There, I'm finally admitting it. I wrecked my car!

The entire band was present for camp, and I was working them according to my favorite motto, *"All night is All right!"* As the band worked throughout the week, I kept the same schedule of not getting out of rehearsal until after 1:00am! We would rehearse marches first from 8:00am to 11:30am, then pop tunes from 1:00pm to 4:00pm, then break for dinner. From 6:00pm to 8:30pm we would continue rehearsal on pop tunes and after 8:30pm, we would go to the practice field for marching fundamentals. Depending on the day, we would finish outside rehearsal at 11:30pm or 12:00 midnight then go back to the band hall and play through a few more tunes! I wouldn't dismiss the band until I was tired!

On August 13, 2014, I was more tired than I ever admitted. After giving a directive to Mr. Simmons and Mr. Taylor about splitting the 6:00pm-8:30pm rehearsal time equally so that both can rehearse the band, I drove home around 7:00pm. My goal was to be back for marching rehearsal outside on the practice field at 8:30pm. But this day I was living the saying of "Man plans, and God laughs." If the saying was true, then God was having a personal comedy show at my expense.

I lived approximately 14 miles away from campus. I was less than 5 miles away from home and I WRECKED MY CAR! All those long practices affected me, and I truly had no clue. Apparently, my body shut down and I fell asleep while driving. I ran into the median of the highway. The crash tore my front bumper and the grill off, and it bent the hood. All I remember was the sound "BOOM" and getting out of the car in a panic! I was so scared from the impact that I needed a moment to take it all in and collect myself.

The strangest thing about the entire situation was the fact that no one stopped on the busy highway to even check on me. Everyone kept it moving and the moment became metaphorical to me! I told myself the following: *Haymer, the things we stress over aren't that important. One day you're here, the next day you're gone, and the world will keep turning as if you never existed. You're going to kill yourself trying to prove something that you don't have to prove! If SU doesn't make you the permanent director, then quit! Life is too precious to be doing this to yourself!*

In this moment, I finally let go of the harsh words of the SU System Board of Supervisors' Chair, Bridget Dinvaut. Her words about not losing my first chair faded as if itis it was no longer important to me.

Suddenly, I was a firecracker of powered emotions. I felt powerless at that in that moment, and I also felt powerful. Thanks to the crash, I had a reality check with myself. However, I was still stubborn. I ripped the hanging front bumper off my car and tossed it in the back seat along with the grill. I got back into my car and drove home. Thank God that I wasn't hurt! My car was wrecked up and jacked up, but still drivable. I made it home and called my insurance company to file a claim. I refused to get a rental car replacement until the next morning. I texted my staff letting them know to take the band to the field and that I would be late.

I drove to the band's practice field on campus around 9:00pm. With my megaphone in hand, I jumped out of the car yelling the instructions for the students to get in their assigned spots on the field to start drill. I could hear the students' comments as my staff came over to me with a dazed and confused look. I kept a straight face and lied through my teeth.

"Everything Alright Fellas! I just had a tire to blow out."

I was too embarrassed to reveal the truth and there was no way I was going to admit the truth that night. I carried on with practice and my story. My poor 2009 Nissan Maxima never drove the same!

My accident was just the beginning of God's comedy tour. Two weeks later, not only I, but the entire band would face embarrassment at the hands of the University of Louisiana at Lafayette's campus police.

It was the first football game of the season and time for the first performance of the new era of the Human Jukebox. I had no doubt in our first performance as I designed it to be something different than what the Human Jukebox fans were accustomed to while keeping all the traditions and customs. There's a fine line or "tightrope" one must walk when planning performances for the SU Band. Our fans grew tired of the same old same, but if we tried to do anything that was too far out there or too much of a change, then we would often hear the phrase "That ain't Southern!" This simply meant that the fans want the same old SU with a new twist. Change is good, but too much change too soon wouldn't be accepted. This performance would test my "tightrope" theory.

Ready to put everything on the field, we arrived on campus ready to give all the fans a show when we were greeted by the campus police, police dogs, and other high-tech police equipment.

"Get back on the bus now," yelled the campus police. Students hurried back on the bus, surprised to see dogs in the vicinity of the bus door areas of all five band buses. While on the phone with the Chief of the Southern University Police Department, I exited the bus in full regalia which consisted of my director's suit and hat.

"Chief, what are they doing?"

"Mr. Haymer, this is crazy! Apparently, they received a Homeland Security grant from the federal government. Their chief explained to me that the grant mandated that they use the equipment for every home game. Since this is the first game of the season, we are their test run!"

One of the best decisions that I made was to have the SUPD escort us on all away game trips. In doing so, the police could get us through any city quickly bypassing traffic lights and other traffic situations by coordinating with law enforcement in the areas that we were traveling to or through. Also, the chief was an instrumental ally as she would often prevent me from getting into trouble! Chief always kept me calm by explaining to me what's going on before something happens or making sure that she or an assigned officer were always close to me to prevent anything from happening.

"Apparently these white people don't understand the historic context or the optics of having dogs, police, and police equipment surrounding buses full of black people!" I stated.

Suddenly, I felt like we were starring in a deleted scene from the movie "Mississippi Burning." The campus police were making a scene, and you could hear fans make comments about how "the band must have drugs on the buses." Of course, while all of this was happening, Brandon Dumas and Mr. McClinton walked up. They observed the situation and inquired on what was happening. I informed them of what our chief of police told me.

"Let's just stay calm! We will handle this situation with their administration on Monday morning, but right now let them do whatever they have to do!" Brandon told me as he and McClinton walked away in a concerned manner.

We had completed our personal visit to the civil rights movement of the 1950s and were ready to unload the buses. It had rained earlier in the day and now it was wet, and the humidity was thick enough to cut it with a knife. As we marched towards Cajun Field, I turned around to look at my band. They looked like Roman Soldiers with steam all around them coming up from the ground as the sun was evaporating the water from the wet pavement. It was a beautiful scene. As we entered the stadium to cheering fans and set up in the stands, there were two ULL Officials close by with headsets.

Juked

"Hi! I am Amy with ULL Athletics, we are here to assist you." She said as she handed me the game day itinerary and headset. "We need you or your designee to wear this headset at all times because there are many times that we have to run promotions and neither band can play!" Predominately White Institutions (PWI) lacked interest in the bands playing during timeouts, after scoring touchdowns, and other breaks in the game. I knew that this would be a disaster, but I complied with Amy.

When a HBCU plays a PWI in football, the fans know the HBCU will more than likely not win. Our fans know that if nothing goes our way during the game that night that they had one thing that they could take pride in, their beloved Human Jukebox being unmatched and incomparable to our PWI counterparts. Due to this simple reason, I knew that I would eventually piss Amy off! It was a true clash of the cultures as I ignored the headsets and gave the orders for the band to play while Amy went to go get backup to enforce the rules! Finally, I explained to Amy, as she was literally red as a crawfish from her anger, and I could see tears forming in her eye.

"Look around you! There's a sea of Gold and Blue in this area among an ocean of Red and White everywhere else. I have to see the gold and blue colors every Saturday and they were growing frustrated with me because the band wasn't playing anything. Amy, I understand your job and the trouble that I am causing for you, but I have a job too and a decision to make. I'd rather make you mad, than to make them mad! We will probably never see each other again after tonight, but I have to see them every week!" I stated as I pointed to the sea of Blue and Gold. Amy walked off and I was right because I never saw her again after that!

With seven minutes remaining before halftime, I initiated the tradition in which the director tells the students to prepare their minds for a good halftime performance. I was confident that the "lightly seasoned" show that I planned for them would go over well. The time came and we performed. Our halftime show was the statement heard around the HBCU band world. There is a new era of the Human Jukebox. I received a lot of praise for the attempt to do something new while holding on to our traditions, I also received criticism. Overall, I was satisfied because either way, the competition was looking without knowing what to expect. I was also satisfied because I took a chance by doing something out of the box and was pleased by the results. Besides, I would rather do something new and fail than to do the same old boring and stale predictable things that our fans grew tired of.

There were some things that I knew our first performance would yield, and there are some other things that I couldn't have predicted using my wildest imagination. I'll start with the predictable. The talents and abilities of Brian Simmons, Assistant Director of Bands, were unmatched even before he realized it. I knew that some people didn't understand why I would hire someone with no experience as this was a rare move by any SU Band Director, but they didn't know the history like I did. Two of the most legendary arrangers in the history of the SU Band were hired fresh out of school with no experience. The hiring of Brian Simmons in 2014 was no exception as history was simply repeating itself!

What I didn't foresee was not ordinary but has become the norm of today. I was caught off guard by the celebrity tweets of the band's performance. Pharrell re-tweeted the band performing his 2014 hit "Happy" as we made a smiley face on the field, and this was major! I often criticized the MBM team for operating beyond the scope of their duties, but their ability to get Pharrell to retweet our performance was within their job description as it is literally the essence of marketing and brand management! I was so happy for our new social media attention. Between the re-tweet by Pharrell and Brian Simmons' viral arrangement of the British Rock Band, Queen, "Bohemian Rhapsody," the Human Jukebox took social media by storm and revolutionized the role of marching bands in the social media age! The implementation of our subliminal new logo with the right placement in the videos along with the editing and use of multiple cameras for different angles sent the message that we were in the forefront of a new aged revolution. Soon, other

Juked

bands would follow to duplicate our professional look and I had no problems with this. I knew if they were following us, then they were right where they needed to be, which was standing behind and following the leader, the Human Jukebox!

Chapter II

I've always said that social media and technology was man's biggest blessing and man's biggest curse depending on how you use it. The Human Jukebox's use of social media promoting our brand definitely elevated us to another level as the band's Facebook page grew from 14,000 followers to over 100,000 followers during my tenure. Even with our success on social media, we had to prove another point. The band had become so popular during our first two performances against PWIs that we were criticized yet again for being whitewashed or a celebrity band. It was finally time to face our first HBCU opponent to prove that the Human Jukebox could still blow the stadium down! Power is necessary as it is another trademark of the Human Jukebox and became a trademark of many bands in the Southwestern Athletic Conference (SWAC) as well.

The first victims of the Human Jukebox were the Alcorn State University Sounds of Dyn-O-mite Marching Band. It would be the first time that the HBCU band world could make a true assessment of the Human Jukebox's high quality powerful sound! We battled so many rounds with Alcorn in the 5th quarter exposing their shallow book and lack-luster arrangements. Their best song of the night was "Slave to the Rhythm" by Michael Jackson and it went downhill after that. The standout song for us on that night was "We are One" arranged by Kedric Taylor, Assistant Director of Bands. That would be his first hit with the Human Jukebox. Because of his experience, people expected him to succeed, and I was happy that he had a hit as well. The Alcorn game established the dominance of the Human Jukebox for the Haymer-Time era by putting the band world on notice that we are not just a social media band, we've been doing this for years!

Perhaps the biggest and most anticipated matchup of the season was the Boom-Box Classic! This was no surprise as it was the most

Juked

anticipated battle every year among band heads, but 2014 would prove to be different. We made a contractual agreement with the Jackson State University "Sonic Boom of the South" Marching Band to perform in a battle of the bands the Friday night before the SU/JSU Saturday football game. The battle was scheduled to take place in the Athletic and Assembly Center on the campus of Jackson State University. This was huge! Two of the top HBCU bands could finally battle without the interruptions and distractions that the football game often brings, and this was truly a band head's dream.

Both schools' band directors and administrators agreed to a performance that would give JSU and SU a fifty-percent profit split. JSU agreed to provide the SU Band with a meal after the battle and lodging for Friday night. We were set and ready to go, but what looked good on paper was a disaster in execution! Here is when I know that I must be the only show on God's comedy special!

We arrived in Clinton, Mississippi (the outskirts of Jackson) to our motel and discovered that the travel agent that the JSU Band Staff used had us in six different motels. The motels were in poor condition! They literally looked like the type of motels that you rent by the hour. There was no way that I could fathom that the Director of Bands at JSU and his staff would think that these accommodations were acceptable.

I called the JSU band director frustrated, and he was immediately concerned. He asked me to call his assistant director who was also a graduate of SU and former Director of Bands at Norfolk State University in Norfolk, Virginia. I was familiar with the assistant director. He was the one who spearheaded the communication between both schools to make the event possible. I didn't think he would find our lodging arrangements acceptable, either. After a short phone conversation with the JSU director and assistant director, the travel agent called me.

"How could you put my students in such terrible living conditions?" I asked.

"Look, I don't know what you were expecting! The hotels aren't five-star. It was the best that I could find." he responded.

"Sir, I didn't expect a five-star facility, but I didn't expect a negative five-star facility as well. Come on man! Have you seen this place? All the motels are a dump except for two. I need you to come over here to view the facilities with me or we won't be able to perform due to a breach of contract! The contract stated for us to be provided a lodging facility, not 6 facilities."

The travel agent became very frustrated with me as I kept demanding him to come over and see the dump. He finally agreed as we waited on our buses. It took him approximately 45 minutes to arrive. The assistant director from JSU wanted us to come to campus and perform while they worked on resolving the issue, but I no longer trusted him. I also didn't trust the travel agent. I started to consider the JSU's assistant's comment about coming to the battle as the issue gets resolved. Then, I thought *What incentive do they have to take care of us after the battle is over and they made their money?*

The travel agent finally arrived. I looked at him and I was angry. At this time the SU Chief of Police came to stand close by me. While in a "heated" discussion with the travel agent, I received a phone call from someone at JSU.

"Hello!"

"Yes, this is the Dean of the College of Liberal Arts at Jackson State University, I am calling to speak with Director Haymer."

"Speaking!"

"I understand that you are in Clinton. Why are y'all way out there?"

Although I never met the dean, I was shocked that she asked me that question and not the band staff at JSU being that she was their supervisor. After explaining to her what transpired, the dean told

Juked

me that she would call me back. At this time, the travel agent came back to let me know that he can put one third of the band in the Red Roof-Inn, another third in the Best Western and the remaining third in the Holiday-Inn. I did a walk-through of the facilities and finally agreed to the terms even though I was still upset that it took so much energy to get a resolution. Within 20 minutes of agreeing to the new terms with the Travel Agent, The Dean from JSU called me back.

"Mr. Haymer, I have some good news! I managed to book you 80 rooms at the Marriott in downtown Jackson!" The dean said excitedly.

I was puzzled because that's all that we needed in the first place. Since I already accepted the accommodations from the beeper carrying travel agent, I declined the dean's offer especially since the students were already putting their luggage in their rooms.

"Thank you for your help! I wish we would've had that option earlier!"

"Well, when you get a dean to handle your traveling you get first class treatment. I don't know why you dealt with the assistant band director!"

I don't know what she meant by that, and I didn't want to know. I was just happy to get the nightmare over. As we ended the call it was obvious that the Human Jukebox, the Band Staff, and the SUPD were all angry and the Sonic Boom was going to pay for it.

I did not care what the MC of the battle was talking about. This was not a come to Jesus moment! This was war and we brought it to the Sonic Boom that night!

Game day was HELL!! We had to leave our respective lodging by noon. Therefore, I had to carefully plan the day because we had nothing to do from noon to game time at 6:00pm. After eating at a local restaurant, we stopped by a high school to use their practice field to run through our halftime show. Unfortunately, we didn't stay long. The practice field's grass was high and not leveled off. We ended practice before I initially scheduled which caused us to make it to the stadium earlier than expected. We waited on the buses until about 4:15 PM and began to unload to march in for the game.

I told my staff to just keep their eyes straight ahead and keep it moving! As we made it to the gate to enter the stadium, a JSUPD officer told us that we could not enter, and Mr. Taylor asked her why.

"Because this is OUR HOUSE and we tell you when we want you to come in," the JSUPD officer responded!

At this time, I was already in the stadium passing her as she jumped in front of the Dancing Doll Captain to prevent them from entering. The captain had a confused look on her face, and I couldn't hear what the JSUPD officer was telling her.

"Let's Go!" I yelled at the Dancing Doll Captain. She strutted around the JSU officer with the rest of the Dolls, the drum major, and band behind her! I yelled "BLADE HEAD!" as an indication for the percussion to start the cadence. We marched in the stadium and took our places in the stands. By the time we were set up in the stands, another officer came up to the band.

"COME HERE RIGHT NOW," he screamed. I looked around to see who he was talking to like that. He continued, "I AM TALKING TO YOU!"

"I am not going to leave my students. You can come up here and talk to me!" As he walked up the stairs in my direction, the SUPD came around me just in case he tried something. I told my staff, "Anything that he attempts to say or do to me, he's going to have to do it in front of everyone!"

The officer finally made it to me. "What is your problem? I should arrest you!"

Juked

"Arrest me for what? I understand that y'all didn't want us to come into the stadium before your band, but please tell me what law that I broke by entering an open stadium on game day, which is my job description. I understand the rivalry between the schools but are you an officer of the law or are you an officer of your feelings?"

The officer didn't even respond to me, he just walked off. It was a good thing that I had the SUPD with me not only because the JSU officer at the gate lied and told my supervisor that I cursed her out, the SUPD Chief fixed the situation for me, but because I probably would have been arrested for cursing out the JSUPD had the SUPD not been present.

I knew that the JSU Band Staff was angry that we played over the Sonic Boom as they were marching in! That's the nature of the beast in the SWAC! Besides, JSU was notorious for doing the same thing to all their visiting bands. It was time that they got a dose of their own medicine!

October 17, 2014, the week before the Boom-Box Classic at Jackson State University, I had a huge victory regarding my paycheck. By the end of August, the paperwork for my salary increase went through. I finally received the interim salary and the back-pay for the difference of what I was supposed to make in the months of June and July. Although my salary was significantly low, especially in comparison to my counterparts at other HBCUs, I finally felt respected! However, in October, things changed!

Unbeknownst to me, I had a "guardian angel" fighting on my behalf through the inner workings of the University. My "guardian angel" was a member of the SUS Board of Supervisors and became another invaluable ally in my attempt to reinvest and re-energize the Human Jukebox. Because of her efforts and many others, the SUS Board of Supervisors voted to confirm me as Director of Bands, changing the interim status to permanent.

My supervisor informed me that a search would not take place for my position like the SUS Board Chair initially wanted. They would still advertise the position for the required number of days and whoever applied that qualified for the job would be interviewed. Also, I had to apply for the job that I was already doing.

A week after submitting my application, I became impatient. "Are there any applicants for my position?" I asked a source who worked in a position on campus who knew all of the inner workings.

"No! Also, if no one applies then the process can be extended if your supervisor and/or board chair wants to do so."

This was all I needed to know because I had a plan. I was tired of the games that SU was playing so I decided to speed up the process. I called my friend and classmate Miguel Bonds, who was the Director of Bands at Talladega College in Talladega, Alabama

"Hey! I need you to go online and apply for the Director of Bands position here at SU!"

I knew that he must've thought that I was clearly out of my mind, but I wanted to speed up the process. By asking Mr. Bonds to apply, I knew that my supervisor and his "puppet masters" on the board would by-pass the interview process and recommend me for the position immediately AND it worked. A few days later, I received a notice from my "on campus source" that someone applied for the position. After five months of doing the tough work in the director's seat, I finally achieved my ultimate goal in life by officially becoming the Director of Bands at Southern University with a salary of $76,500! Just like The Notorious B.I.G. said, "Mo Money, Mo Problems!"

Chapter 12

The beginning of the end for me was around the corner and I didn't even know it. After the Boom-Box Classic with Jackson State, my career was a double agent. In the 14th year of my career and at the young age of 36, I achieved my lifelong career goal by being promoted to The Director of Bands at Southern University and A&M College. I was so young with so much of my career and time still ahead of me that retirement wasn't a thought. It felt a lifetime away! Due to my youth, I had a lot of "fight" and "bite", and this would be attributing factors to my downfall. Being only 36 years old, I didn't care about the consequences. I determined that whatever day would be my last, the band program I left for my successor would be in much better shape fiscally, have updated and better performing equipment, and newer uniforms than the band I inherited.

As a black male in America, I know I have a bullseye on my back. However, the Bayou Classic in the year of 2014 was the year the bullseye on my front started to appear. When I stepped into the job, I wanted to turn the Human Jukebox into America's Band. For this to happen, I comprised a plan with achievable, measurable, and obtainable benchmarks. One benchmark was to seize on opportunities that had the potential to go viral.

In August of 2014, I was very passionate about planning halftime performances that were different from what SU was accustomed to. During this same timeframe, a young man came into my office stating that he wanted to propose to his girlfriend and asked me if it was possible to do it during the band's Bayou Classic Halftime Show. I told him to come back in a week so I could give the idea further thought.

I really liked the idea because I've never seen it done before. Plus, he had a diamond company that was based out of New York City backing him in his efforts to be creative with a marriage proposal. Over the course of the week, I'd seen many unusual marriage proposals from a simple YouTube search, but none were done during a band's halftime performance. I contacted the management company that runs the Bayou Classic to discuss what I wanted to do for halftime, and they told me that it was my choice. This was just the opportunity I knew we needed. I met with the young man the following week and told him that we would do it!

Bayou Classic was here, and we seized the opportunity. The "Bayou Classic Marriage Proposal Performance" went viral. It was just the positive exposure for the band and the University that I wanted. Social media, national publications such as ESPN and SB Nation, and international publications like the Daily Mail were constantly playing our show.

The show was a complete hit and beautiful. It consisted of a big wooden box on wheels decorated as a big gift. A little girl, the girlfriend's daughter, pops out of the box with the ring to give the man to propose to his girlfriend. Simultaneously, the band began playing Patti LaBelle's "If Only You Knew," while spelling out MARRY ME on the field. To ensure that everyone knew what was going on, Darrin Bedell, who has been the band's announcer since 1996, started narrating what was taking place. The crowd went crazy!

Monday morning the nightmare began. I was summoned to Flandus McClinton's office to discuss the halftime performance with him and Brandon Dumas.

"We initially thought it was you proposing to your girlfriend, but when we found out that it was for someone else, we became confused." McClinton said. "It's been said that the New York Diamond Company, who advertised their company during the halftime performance, paid you to do it!"

Juked

I was very confused and offended that McClinton would accuse me of getting a "kick back!" As I went to explain my purpose for the performance, I was told, "Perhaps you should submit your halftime plans to Dumas and me to view and approve from now on!"

I was offended but kept my cool. By this time, I've had enough of the job. I just wanted to hurry and end the season. Someone was not happy with me. I was going to find out who it was because I was tired of the micromanagement!

If the "Bayou Classic Marriage Proposal Performance" was the bullseye's target to slay me, then "A Message from Nathan Haymer" posted on YouTube was the nail in my coffin and I didn't even know I was dead. The video wasn't created to end my career. Nor was it meant to be the ammunition used for my demise. No, the video was created on a day I was frustrated and wanted to reveal the "truth" about the band's detrimental state.

I asked Garrett Edgerson, the director of Human Jukebox media, to come to the band hall to record me. I placed band instruments on the floor. I went to the uniform room and randomly selected a band uniform. I told Garrett to start recording and I began to talk about the problems that we were facing. I did not rehearse, nor did I do multiple takes. I just talked candidly as I picked up the instruments, uniform, and walked through the building to show the leaky roof and ceiling tiles. It was easy for me to talk about the problems because I lived with them for eight years at that point.

After recording the video, I sent it to Brandon. I knew that I could not post the video without the knowledge and consent of him or McClinton. As much as I wanted to, I didn't tell everything. I knew if I spilled all the beans, I would have been fired on the spot!

For instance, I didn't speak about the Bayou Classic Battle of the Bands profits. On the Friday night after Thanksgiving, the Bayou Classic hosts a Greek Show and a Battle of the Bands which fills the

New Orleans Superdome to half capacity or an approximate 30,000 to 35,000 people. The profits are split evenly between The Southern University System and Grambling State University. I'm not sure what GSU does with their half of the profits, but I can tell you that a whopping 0-percent of Southern's profits went to the band. To keep my predecessors in line and quiet, the system presidents and cabinets, board members, and other University elites joined together and gave the band staff our annual Bayou Classic Bonus! The staff traditionally got bonuses after every Bayou Classic. This has been a practice since the days of Isaac Greggs. However, the bonus was not really a bonus! It was "hush money" as the band never received its just due for the Bayou Classic Battle of the Bands. During the years of 2011-2013, a decline in revenue due to lower than usual attendance, the bonuses began to dry up and became more and more political. In 2013, we didn't receive a bonus at all. Although the attendance would rise around 2015, the "hush money" politics never went away. Gratefully, I was able to reward my staff with a $5,000 bonus from the Bayou Classic.

In the video, I spoke about the leaking roof and the ceiling tiles, but my building had floors that needed replacing and walls in need of paint. The Human Jukebox deserved better than what they had. So, when I would ask Brandon about repairs, he told me that it would come out of the band's budget. What budget? We didn't have a budget! We had a small amount of revenue. The revenue from the high school band and dance team camp. That revenue was being used to pay a $45,000 salary to Kedric Taylor, which really was $60,000 due to the fringe benefits of a pension, vacation, insurance, etc. Instead of using the revenue to make things better for the band, I had to use it to cover expenses that should be paid by the school. I'm not just talking about Mr. Taylor's salary, but everything! Essentially, all the band's profits from band camp went to cover expenses that are the responsibility of the University!

I felt helpless in the moment as all our problems were ignored by the University and thrown on my back to solve as if the Human Jukebox was its own private entity and the director was the

Juked

CEO. To help provide insight to the situation, I began to privately study subjects such as accounting as it relates to budgets and salaries, economics, and business administration. Finally, the light shined, and I realized that the University's failure to provide me training in my fiduciary obligations was not an oversight but intentional!

I didn't know who I could trust so I began to keep a lot of things to myself. I had a mole. The things I would tell my staff would somehow find its way to the MBM team and eventually to Brandon. I knew that I was on my own to try to figure out the band's problems. I had hoped that the MBM and Media teams' use of social media would bring in support but hope alone isn't a strategy. I had a plan!

I had inside information from a very reliable source, and I had to wait until the politics were right to fight for what the Human Jukebox deserved. I've become so obsessed with making the University do the right thing that I didn't think of myself and how I was walking into a political landmine! After sending my video to Brandon, he sent me a text message. Although he had no problem with the video, it was controversial, and he wanted to pass it through McClinton.

McClinton called Brandon and me to his office. We discussed the video and my reasons for recording it. After being to his office for the Bayou Classic Marriage Proposal Performance, I wanted no more problems. I really wanted them to tell me not to post the video and they would help me solve the issues that I highlighted, spotlighted, screamed, and shouted about in the video. I was attempting to call their bluff. Southern University is a very proud place with individuals who often turn their noses up at other universities by bragging that we are the only HBCU system, making fun of the facilities of other HBCUs, etc., while ignoring our own problems. I knew that my video would be the "slap of reality" that the alumni and fans needed. I also knew that the video would make the "uppity" and "cultish" crew upset. Either way, I knew the reactions to the video would be polarizing. McClinton and

Brandon watched the video during our meeting. I watched their body language and was prepared for them to grill me. McClinton boldly started the conversation.

"If you want to put that video out there then it's on you. I wouldn't advise it, but it's your choice. Also, after seeing the video, I wouldn't be compelled to give anything! "How's your predecessor doing?"

"Oh, he's doing fine! As a matter of fact, he's playing a lot of golf and looking a lot younger these days since he no longer has to worry about the problems that I am stuck with!"

"I always liked Lawrence. He never asked me for anything!"

I didn't respond. I knew that expressing my sentiments, even watered down, would lead to nothing but a pink slip! I simply thanked both gentlemen for their time and told them that I would post the video and accept whatever consequence or public backlash that would come because of doing so.

Hindsight being 20-20, clearly the meeting with McClinton and Brandon and the posting of the video would officially become the "beginning of the end" for me. The YouTube video got much attention on the band's platform. Thankfully, Sonja Norwood interceded by asking Garrett to remove the video from The Human Jukebox Media's YouTube Channel to a new platform that she created designed to increase awareness of the state of our beloved SU Band. Both the YouTube Channel, The Human Jukebox 5th Quarter and the video, *A Message from Nathan Haymer*, are still active today. Sonja's mission with the band would shift over the next year as the persecution, problems, pressure, and politics will demand her to go into a direction of larger influence.

As you continue to read all the challenges I faced, it will be evident that it was easier to get rid of me than to fix the underlying problems that plagued the institution! Although I accomplished much, success was obtained by either forcing the University's hand or by doing things my way. The political backing and cover that I would need from campus administrators never materialized, therefore I made several costly mistakes. While some mistakes were because of ignorance, I admit that others were the result of "doing what I had to do!"

Chapter 13

Jabari persuaded me to participate in a strategy meeting over Christmas break in Houston. While I'm always happy to go to Houston as a quick getaway trip from Baton Rouge, the strategy meeting designed to review the goals and objectives that the MBM team was trying to accomplish was a complete waste of my time. Jabari and Eric realized that I wasn't accessible to the numerous daily calls or that my schedule did not lend the time needed to read and respond to lengthy dissertation length emails. Eric soon realized that communication was best handled face-to-face. Since Jabari lived in Houston and Eric lived in Baton Rouge, Eric took it upon himself to make our communication work.

As the Director of Bands, I had a lot going on. I agreed to meet with the MBM team so they could have all the time and attention needed from me so they could accomplish our common goal of ensuring the success of our beloved Human Jukebox. Still, I kept my cool as we "strategize" about nothing!

Their contract gave them the authority as the MBM team to act on our behalf. When given the time and opportunity, there were moments they succeeded. In my opinion, the most beneficial aspect of our conference was highlighting the success of the fall 2014 marching season with collaborations through the MBM team and myself. Eric and Jabari successfully secured a $20,000 partnership and donation from a popular hamburger fast-food chain. They were also instrumental in securing Mannie Fresh to perform "Back that thang up" and "Nolia Clap" during our homecoming halftime show as we featured a throwback dance routine from 1999-2004 during the height of Cash Money Records.

However, they were not responsible for the partnership with the oil and gas company that I secured. Technically, Senator Cleo Fields secured it. Cleo Fields is a 1984 graduate of Southern University and a 1987 graduate of Southern University Law Center. He is a former US Congressman and a current Louisiana State Senator. He is the founder of the Louisiana Leadership Institute where I served as the volunteer director of the all-star band. As a thank you for getting his all-star band back up and running, Senator Fields made it happen.

"Hey man! Whatever they're trying to do won't materialize because God doesn't operate like that! Jabari is always bragging on social media talking about 'Boss Moves' and that is blocking our blessing!" Kedric Taylor expressed to me.

I must say that I agreed. Plus, it took them coming to the "photo op" during halftime and sending me an invoice for $4,000 for their services on securing something that they had absolutely nothing to do with! This "boss move" is what finally woke me up. It made me realize that the MBM team was the façade of a marketing and brand management company when really, they accomplished nothing.

But like the MBM team, the band was basically the same way. We looked good on the surface but were struggling underneath. However, thanks to Sonja Norwood, help was on the way! As I began to learn to trust Sonja, I began to realize the benefits of having an ally to teach me things as it relates to the entertainment business. Even though higher education and the entertainment business had two sets of ethical standards and governance, the operation of budgets, dealing with politics, and the administrative responsibilities are similar.

One huge accomplishment of the strategy meeting was the addition of Sonja to the team as my personal advisor. She became the glue that kept my fragile relationship with the MBM team intact. To be fair, I did not fault the MBM team for not getting the sponsorships and partnerships as quickly as we both hoped. I realized that we were doing something very revolutionary. They were taking the playbook of a Division –I Championship Athletic team and adapting it to the Human Jukebox. I understood for corporations to look at bands like athletics took time. I also understood that the Human Jukebox wasn't just a band, and if pitched right, we could be a gold mine for any potential corporate sponsor.

In all, I was just happy to have Sonja onboard. Immediately, the assistance and knowledge she brought afforded me success as an administrator. Also, she aided me in keeping the MBM team on task while her influence helped them to really begin to make boss moves!

Chapter 14

Not only did Christmas break serve as the time to have a strategy meeting with Jabari and Eric, but it also served as the perfect time for the band staff and I to prepare for the 2015 Honda Battle of the Bands in Atlanta. Even though there was always something going on, the holiday break was the calm before the storm.

January is always the beginning of the spring semester at SU. Once the students return to campus, they go through the process of spring semester registration. However, the band staff shifts its mind from football season to parade season, concert band, symphonic band, wind ensemble mode. In addition to preparing for the Honda BOTB, I would also be distracted with administrative duties regarding band scholarships. I have the pleasure of reviewing all the students grades to verify who made the required grade point average with appropriate credit hours to and who didn't.

If you recall, I mentioned earlier that the band's scholarship was $45,000 per semester. Prior to Mr. J retiring, he awarded majority of the budget to upperclassmen which left me with very little left to award the freshmen. To maintain a band with 230 members, I had to do the unthinkable. I had to gamble against a percentage of the students. I had to bet that a percentage of students would not make the required grade point average causing the scholarship to not be renewed and allowing me to stay underbudget. I lost the bet. Although I'm extremely proud of the students, it caused me a major headache and the scholarship catastrophe that I refer to as the 40k Deficit.

I had to do something quickly. I didn't want to deal with Brandon and McClinton again, but I also was heading to Atlanta for the Honda Battle of the Bands. I needed time which I didn't have so I could construct a plan and although this was serious, I had to focus on the battle first.

The Honda officials treated us like kings and queens. We were the last band to perform meaning we were the major draw to the event. Our society was entering a new era of social injustice. With the unjust shooting of black men and women by the police or those who attempted to "play police" in America, I wanted to make a political statement during our performance. Since we were the biggest name and we were saved for last, my thoughts for the performance matched up perfectly with the event's line up.

We opened the show with the band's signature logo, the "S" with the eighth note, playing "Nobody Does It Better" by Nate Dogg. Brian Simmons wrote an outstanding arrangement of Marvin Gaye's "What's Going On" and the band made a stop sign on the field to indicate stop the unjust killing of black men and women by the police. I wrote a moving arrangement to Heather Headley's "I Wish I Wasn't," the Dancing Dolls' performance was amazing, and the crowd really loved our show.

The icing on the event's cake was watching Mr. J's induction to the Honda Battle of the Band Hall of Fame. This honor is given to retired directors who successfully impacted the HBCU Band World. He also had the honor of conducting the mass band! I was so happy to be a part of this especially since I was the one who nominated him for this prestigious award.

After we arrived at our hotel, the band staff, the MBM team and I went to eat at a nearby. It was a real laid-back type of evening. We joked around about random things. Then everyone noticed how "standoffish" I was.

"Hey Haymer, you good man?" Lorenzo Hart asked.

Lorenzo Hart had become an advisor of mine. I learned to depend on him when it came to drills, formations, or just overall ideas. People think of him as a silent person because he never said much and always stayed out of drama. He was the type of person that truly operated within the scope of his duties! What people didn't know is that in addition to being an outstanding percussionist, he's also a great drill-master and proficient pianist. The man is gifted and talented and was my "secret weapon" because while everyone knew the capabilities of Brian Simmons and Kedric Taylor, they often limited the Percussion Instructor to being one-dimensional or just dealing with percussion things.

"Yes, I am fine. I am just a little under the weather! I am going to take my food to go and leave y'all here. I am tired and I need some rest!"

I was sick and tired, but it wasn't physical sickness or exhaustion. I was sick and tired of the problems, I was sick and tired of the job, and I wanted out! This "dream job" that I wanted for so long was nothing but problems for me. I never shared with the staff what was going on because I wanted them to have fun, relax, and continue to be creative. If the staff knew what I knew, then they would no longer be as creative as I needed them to be in their roles. It was my job as director to shield them and as much as I could.

When I made it back to the hotel room from the restaurant, I called Sonja. She was not only a mentor and supporter, but she was also a big fan of the Human Jukebox.

"Haymer! I saw the performance online. The band did great, aren't you excited!?"

"Thank you!" I responded in an unenthusiastic tone.

"What's wrong, Haymer?

"I'm just tired!"

"Boy! You are so stubborn sometimes! Now tell me what's going on?"

She was right, I can be very stubborn and there was a huge problem. As I began to explain to Sonja what was going on, she listened carefully and asked many questions. I didn't know if I was being investigated or if she was taking notes but whatever it was, she gave me her full attention.

"Haymer, we will have to figure something out. Let me make some phone calls and I'll get back to you."

Apparently, she must have made a lot of phone calls because I never got a call back from her that night. I woke up the next morning to a text me to check my email. I immediately responded to her text. I needed more clarity, so Sonja called me.

"Haymer, I found a solution for the $40k deficit in scholarships for the band students. I will give you the details soon, but I want to let you know that I am very upset with your supervisor, Brandon Dumas. Do you know when I attempted to address this situation with him that he had the audacity to tell me that 'the band wasn't a priority?' For him to say that is very disrespectful!" Sonja was outraged!

"I am not shocked by anything that you're saying. Although Brandon never told me that the band wasn't a priority, he did an excellent job of showing me that we weren't a priority. All the sacrifices and adjustments I had to make in my schedule and rehearsals just to support him as he used the band students on a weekly basis on the road for performances that were supposed to be about recruiting, but really were about him and his ego. I am just sick of him using us!"

"Well, I've made it clear to Brandon that he's made an enemy out of me and that I will hold his feet to the fire from this point on. I put him on notice!"

"That guy pretty much does what he wants. He was in Atlanta with us yesterday because Honda provides each participating university's president or their designee a suite. He took a picture with me and the band staff to post to his social media, but that was a front. I know that he doesn't care for me as the director; therefore, the band students have to suffer."

"Yea. Well, we will see about that! Ok, now listen to this. Not only did I find a solution to the 40k deficit, but you also have more funds available than you thought. Look at what I sent to your email."

"Where did you get this budget from because I've never been provided a copy?"

"It was in the board packet from the June 2014 meeting along with all the budgets of the university that had to be approved for the 2014-15 fiscal year! I had to go through over 800 pages just to find your budget!"

She began to further explain how she interpreted the budget. I listened and took notes. It was the first time that I was provided a copy of the budget of my department along with an explanation of how to properly interpret it. I felt so lost and overwhelmed once again as I was carrying the load of the department without any explanation or training on my fiduciary obligations. If Sonja's explanation is correct, then I have access to resources that I was left in the dark on.

On Monday morning, I went to the University's budget director to confirm if what Sonja told me was indeed true. The budget director confirmed everything. I was relieved but confused and upset at the same time.

"Why wasn't I provided a copy of the budget for my department and why wasn't the budget explained to me so that I could be more effective in my role?"

The budget director looked at me in a very unbothered manner. "It isn't my job to explain the budget or go over it with you. It's your division leader's job is to do that, and your division leader is the Brandon Dumas!"

I continued to try to understand why I was left in the dark while trying to ignore the budget director's lack of concern about my problem that she had the answers to.

"Well, I didn't know about the budget or the funds available to me. What would've happened if I never used the budget due to a lack of knowledge that I had one?"

The budget director again looked very unconcerned and unmoved. "All unused funds after specific date will go back to the division's leader to use at his/her discretion."

"Thank you!" I responded. I quickly left her office. I couldn't wait to call my administrative assistant about what the budget director just shared with me. She was just as surprised as I was. She had me complete a budget modification so that I can have funds available to do more repairs on the band building. Apparently in the Division of Student Affairs, there was a budget surplus due to the departments under the division either underspending their budgets or not spending them at all. As the budget director explained, all unused funds go to the division's leader, Brandon Dumas, to use as his disposal after a certain date. The crisis was averted, and I could not have made it over this hurdle had it not been for the assistance of Sonja! Thanks to her, we were able to get the $40k needed for scholarships through the Office of the President of the SU System, the SU System Foundation, and other external resources.

If the purposeful oversight in my lack of training on policies, procedures, and budgets wasn't obvious before, it was quite apparent now as I began to suspect that I was being targeted and intentionally set up to fail! My supervisors didn't let me down because I never believed in them in the first place. However, I've become angry with Mr. J while thinking of his abrupt departure. As much as I admired and supported him over the years, I began to question what he knew and why he didn't prepare me for the position as promised. More importantly, was his sudden departure without clear instructions in how to move a set up for me to fail?

Chapter 15

Baton Rouge is about 80 miles away from New Orleans. Being so close in proximity, the band participates in the Mardi Gras parade season. Unlike years past, the band was already in shape for the parades thanks to finishing two performances in January. Still, I wasn't satisfied. I had a point to prove and that point was that The Human Jukebox is the king of bands!

As we prepared for parade season, I had the band march around campus. It is my belief that the best way to prepare for a parade is to practice daily like you're in a parade. We marched the perimeter of the SU campus from 7:00pm to 9:00pm, Monday through Thursday. I would often march to the area of campus where the students would hang out in the front of their dormitories, we call the circle. On Fridays we didn't have classes, so we marched around campus during the day from 11:00am to 1:00pm. Using practice as a time to be political, I would lead the band on a different route through campus and stop for a performance in the front of the university's administration building as a thank you to all the secretaries and receptionists who would often help me. The performance also served as a don't forget about us to all of the "big wigs" on the upper-level floors of the building. Preparing for parades was more than just practice. It gave the students, faculty, staff, and administration school spirit while also giving me a "political victory" as I would often receive emails or texts from administrators thanking me for making their day brighter. Once I had their attention, I would also change the subject to focus on the needs of the SU Band and Dancing Dolls.

The 2015 parade season was the first for Brian Simmons as a band director. Kedric Taylor was experienced with parade season. He performed in numerous parades as a high school band director. Therefore, he knew that bands get paid for their performances and the directors receive an honorarium for each parade. Finally, he understood that my relationship with Brian Simmons was a closer relationship than what I had with him as we were still learning to get to know each other while mastering our new roles respectively.

All that being stated, Kedric Taylor showed his sneaky side by taking advantage of someone's innocence or lack of knowledge on a matter to serve his own motives. He informed Brian Simmons of the practice on band directors receiving honorariums and how it worked. He also asked Brian Simmons to ask me about it to see if they were getting paid. If he wanted to know if he was getting paid for the parade season, he had the same access and ability to ask me. Furthermore, I wanted to surprise the staff with an honorarium because of their hard work and dedication for all the events that we performed so far in the rather new year of 2015.

Brian Simmons came into my office one day. "Hey what's this thing that I'm hearing about band directors getting paid for the parades?"

"What do you mean?"

"Well, Kedric Taylor asked me to come in here and ask you about it!"

I looked at Brian Simmons with a frown. "I don't know anything about that. We'll see!"

"Ok," he said as he walked out of my office.

I received honorariums as a high school band director for Mardi-Gras parades, but I never received an honorarium as assistant director of bands. Mr. J did pay me an honorarium in the past. I received honorariums for our two battle of the bands appearances, not for Mardi-Gras. Remembering how I struggled to make ends meet, I wanted better for my staff. The long-term solution was to get them a permanent raise, but the short-term was to pay them as often as I could with an honorarium. The 2015

Juked

Parade Season would be the first time my staff would receive an honorarium, but not the last.

As we finished a successful parade season, we moved into concert season. I had the top ensemble, the wind ensemble, and I assigned the symphonic band to Kedric Taylor. I wanted Brian Simmons to continue to develop and sharpen his skills as a novice educator therefore, he was assigned the sight-reading and development band along with the pep band. Lorenzo Hart had his percussion ensemble for the concert season. We had a laid-back semester with very little problems. Unfortunately, persecution, problems, pressure, and politics would rear their ugly faces once more!

Sonja came through with an event that would garner much exposure for the Human Jukebox. The event was "The Fight of the Century" between Floyd Mayweather and Manny Pacquiao in May of 2015! This was the biggest sporting event of the year, and the Human Jukebox was invited to perform for the Grand Arrival of Floyd Mayweather. The Grand Arrival was a televised event. It is a press conference for the boxer to promote himself along with the fight. What made this event special for me was it was the first time that a band performed in such a venue. Bands are known to perform in large events such as the Super Bowl, but bands never performed for a boxing event. Especially for an event of such magnitude that it had to be called "The Fight of the Century!"

I asked Sonja to have the MBM team spearhead all efforts even though she got us in the door. It was now the MBM team's responsibility to make the relationships and connections that would benefit the Human Jukebox in the long run! The band put on a great performance at the Metro Goldwyn Mayer Grand Garden Arena in Las Vegas, Nevada. I was extremely proud of how professional the students were upon meeting Floyd Mayweather and other celebrities as they didn't act "star struck" at all. It was strictly business although some students managed to get a few pictures with celebrities after we took care of business! I stayed out of the way as it relates to building relationships and allowed the MBM team to work their magic.

We left Las Vegas happy about the connections made and the possibilities for the future. When we arrived in Baton Rouge, I was summoned to McClinton's office yet again.

"Come on in, Haymer." McClinton said. "We have some concerns. Tell us about this Floyd Mayweather fight that the band performed for?"

As I started to explain the difference between the fight and the grand arrival along with the fact that we did not perform for the fight, McClinton rudely interrupted me.

"How come we didn't receive tickets for the fight?" Then he looked at Brandon and asked, "you're Mr. Haymer's direct supervisor, did he offer you any tickets?"

"No, he didn't!"

I shook my head! At this point, I've become very frustrated. "We didn't perform for the fight, sir. So, I didn't have any tickets to give. I wasn't even offered any tickets!"

"Haymer, how much money did you get? We know that Mayweather carries a duffle bag at all times loaded with cash! How much did you get?"

I laughed in their faces. "There are opportunities that are more important than money! Artists like Beyoncé and Bruno Mars perform at the Super Bowl for free because of the international platform that it provides! Well, the Floyd Mayweather event provided us with a platform that money can't buy. It opened us up to so many possibilities for the future! Not to mention, it cost the Mayweather team over $50,000 to pay for 50 people that include the band staff, band members, Dancing Dolls, the MBM team, and the media team to fly to Las Vegas, provide ground transportation, lodging, and meals for the day and a half that we were there!"

I wanted to talk to my direct supervisor, Brandon Dumas, man to man. I didn't want him to hide behind Flandus McClinton anymore, especially since I figured out the cowardly games that he played. I left the meeting upset and went home for the day. I gave Southern University and my job too much time and energy to be disrespected and unappreciated. My anger led to rage as I called my direct supervisor a couple of hours later. I wanted to meet with him, but he texted letting me know that he couldn't due to whatever that was on his schedule. I knew he was lying and didn't want to face me one on one, so I settled for the phone call.

"What do you think of my job performance? Are there any areas that need improvement because Flandus McClinton is treating me like a stepchild?"

"I have no problem with your job performance. In fact, I think you're doing a great job!"

"Well, why does Flandus McClinton treat me so cold then? By the way, thank you for letting me know your opinion on my job performance. As my direct supervisor, I want your perspective!"

"Hey man, he's hard on me too!"

I knew that I could not trust a man who could lie so easily, but at least I had him on record with his opinion.

Now that I knew my supervisor's opinion of my work, I could focus on this year's high school band and dance team camp. With all the registration issues, 2014 still managed to have the largest camp in our history. In preparation for the 2015 camp, I was able to implement all my promises to our supporters the previous year.

Brandon approved my request to use a third-party internet-based company. I no longer had to worry about massive paperwork coming from the fax machine, dealing with an expansive filing system to keep up with all the paperwork, or the University post office not getting the band camp registration forms and payments to us on time. Everything was now in a database that I could access with my computer, phone, or tablet! I also had a new band website that the camp registration ran through. The campus' Information Technology Department could not provide a website up to our standards as a brand so the Market and Brand Management team advised me to get an independent website that could run through the University's server, and I did precisely that. I learned that potential sponsors and partners place high value on the social media platforms and websites of organizations they are considering. Therefore, I had to get the website up and running and paying for the website out of pocket was the only option to give us the high-tech and professional look that we were going for.

By solving the department's tech needs, we were able to attract a record number of students to our summer band and dance team camp. The 2015 camp broke the attendance record again, proving that our success was no accident. Students were able to register and pay using our new website with the option to pay in full or in installments. Because of our new technology, we had no registration hiccups this time.

We were changing the thought process on what a band program could and should be. The only problem with the new approach is that I was Director of Bands and not Director of Athletics. Both bands and athletics take the same drive, passion, and innovative spirit to succeed with ONE-KEY DIFFERENCE, university governance. Athletics can operate more at free will through detailed negotiations in contracts. Conversely, bands are generally under state and university policies, procedures, and regulations related to academics which usually does not align with the demands and pressures placed on the directors leading the organizations.

All profits for the band camp were to be placed in the SU System Foundation Human Jukebox account as directed by my immediate supervisor, Brandon Dumas. Also, I was still responsible for covering the salary for Kedric Taylor from the band camp account in the comptroller's office. I was upset by this and again asked Brandon for the following two things: 1) a $10,000 raise for

Juked

Lorenzo Hart and 2) the university to take responsibility for Kedric Taylor's salary.

By the University doing the right thing, it would free up much-needed funds to begin implementing my plan in securing new band uniforms for the following year. The current uniforms were deteriorating. They were the first item of things that I needed to replace with the instruments being a close second. Brandon told me that he couldn't do anything about Kedric Taylor's salary but did make a pledge to get Lorenzo Hart a raise. Even though I received this information via text, I remained optimistic.

Flandus McClinton was now the Vice President for Finance and Business Affairs for the SU System and I no longer had to deal with him. Being on the system level meant that technically he was no longer involved in the day-to-day affairs of the Baton Rouge Campus. I would soon learn that I was wrong about that too.

After the high school band and dance team camp, I went to the comptroller's office to get a printout of the account from Lisa (a fictional name to protect the employee's identity). Lisa is the employee who manages the account used for band camp profits that covered Kedric Taylor's salary. I needed to know the balance, learn the amount required to cover another year of the assistant director's salary for the 2015-16 fiscal year, and ask any other questions I may have as I read over the numbers. While there, I discovered something that forced me to reevaluate how I would operate the band's finances.

"Good morning, Lisa! How's everything going?"

"Fine! I know you got some good stuff for us coming up for the football season! I was telling my friends at church how much I love the Human Jukebox! I had to ask the Lord to forgive me because we were talking about the band and not listening to the pastor!"

I would take care of the employees that took care of me. It wasn't uncommon for me to bring Lisa a souvenir such as a Human Jukebox coffee mug, Human Jukebox umbrella, shirt, etc. She was a true band fan, but more importantly, a valuable and dependable support arm for me. Lisa revealed something to me that changed the trajectory of what would become my legacy leaving the University! It was something that I could not believe, but I knew that I could not trust anyone to help solve this problem. Out of panic, the solution that I used, although I had good intentions, would be catastrophic for me!

"I need to go over the account to see what amount is needed to cover the assistant director's salary for the new fiscal year," I told Lisa as she began to click the keys on her computer's keyboard while the smile on her face turned into a frown.

"Hmm… that's weird."

"What's wrong?"

"Oh, I just need to verify something right quick!" Lisa said then shortly after she gasped. "Uh Oh!" Lisa covered her mouth with her hand. "How are you and Dr. Dumas?"

I was puzzled by her question as I tried to figure out why she was asking me that. "What do you mean?"

"The reason why I asked is that you have enough to cover your assistant's salary for a couple more months. A deposit is needed soon, but I also see other salaries drawn from this account!" Lisa was cautious in her choice of words, but she kept talking. "I am looking at the employee codes, and it appears that supplemental salaries were paid out of this account to employees in Student Affairs! You will need to talk to Dr. Dumas about this; maybe it was an oversight!"

I was baffled to learn that band funds were used to pay employees' salaries while we had needs, with one being the salary increase for Lorenzo Hart.

"Thank you, Lisa! I will talk to Dr. Dumas. Please print out everything for me, and I need the debits highlighted along with the employee codes from the account that went to all the salaries other than the assistant band director."

"No problem. I want to make sure I don't miss anything, so can you come back and pick it up in an hour? I'll leave it at the front with the receptionist, so you won't have to wait for them to let you come to the back where I am."

"Sure, I'll be back then!"

As I got up to leave, I thanked Lisa and went to my office to talk to Ms. Byrd, the band's administrative assistant. When I told her the news, she was so livid! As a long-time employee of Southern University, she was familiar with this practice.

"Nate, until you find the right person back there that you can trust you got to keep this to yourself for now!" We often referred to the administration building as the back of campus, so the phrase "back there" was in reference to the administration building. "Take that printout home when you get it. Please do not leave it in your office. There's no telling what these people are capable of around here!"

Ms. Byrd was very concerned for me professionally, but she was also concerned for my safety. I knew that she was correct, and I had to be very careful in how I would approach this situation to solve this problem. There was no campus administrator or board member at that time who would have taken on Brandon Dumas, including the new President-Chancellor. Even more insulting was Brandon using funds that my staff and I worked hard to secure by working long hours, marketing, and all the innovative things we had to do to get students to come to band camp. This wasn't a budget allocated to us by the state or federal government that Brandon was using to pay the salaries of his cronies. It was BAND MONEY or funds that wouldn't have existed without our pursuits and extra efforts. It belonged to the band! The Human Jukebox brought that money in, and the university partnered with us on NOTHING!

Additionally, I've been accused of receiving kickbacks twice while Brandon Dumas was giving his cronies kickbacks from band funds brought in by MY WORK. I've had enough! From the Bayou Classic Battle of the Bands profits to the High School Band and Dance Team Camp profits, we were officially "pimped," and enough was enough!

The first order of business was to take the printout of the band camp account from the comptroller's office and secure it in the privacy of my home. Next, I needed to play the game with Brandon to get the raise that I needed for Lorenzo Hart. Finally, I had to reinvent the band's finances.

I had permission to deposit band camp funds into SU System Foundation therefore, I knew that I would no longer have to cover anything else in the account that Lisa managed other than Kedric Taylor's salary. I also had a plan to get the University to own up to its responsibility of covering this salary. Now was the time to tap into my network. I planned to reach out to my guardian angel that resides on the SU System Board of Supervisors to ask if she could use her influence to schedule a finance meeting between the new President-Chancellor and myself. Unfortunately, as life always teaches us, things don't always go as planned. Flandus McClinton was now the new Vice President for Finance and Business Affairs, and he threw a wrench into my plans to move forward.

At the close of the Summer High School Band and Dance Team Camp, I received a text from Brandon stating that Vice President Flandus McClinton sent a directive that I couldn't deposit camp funds into the SU System Foundation. His decision left me puzzled because the Vice President of the SU System's job wasn't to micromanage the day-to-day activity on an individual campus. I was also concerned that if I put all the camp funds in the account that Brandon told me to use in the comptroller's office, all our resources would continue to fund the salaries of his cronies and others not affiliated with the band program. As a result of this, I decided to transfer the band camp funds to the comptroller's office, as I needed to continue to cover the salary of Kedric Taylor. Then, I directed all new deposits from the online registration company to a bank account that I designated for the band's travel for away games, which was an account that I oversaw.

In 2014, I walked into the stadium with the band for the Boom-Box Classic (the unofficial name of the SU vs JSU football game) with a briefcase containing over $15,000 in cash. I felt very unsafe walking around with a briefcase of cash to watch while at the same time performing my official duties as Director of Bands. I remember in 2012 when I was assistant director, Mr. J had $14,000 in cash on him in a briefcase when we were at an away game in New Mexico. While we were in the hotel getting settled, he inadvertently put the briefcase down to tend to students, and the briefcase was stolen. After experiencing feeling unsafe with large sums of cash and the experience that I witnessed with Mr. J, I complained to the university. I was told by the travel office that it was okay to open a bank account to deposit funds and use a debit card to avoid the unsafe practice of having a briefcase full of money in packed stadiums. I became comfortable with this style of management, so I convinced myself that I could manage band camp funds like I managed cash advances.

I wanted to make sure that Brandon or any other administrator would no longer misuse the band's funds generated from our work and efforts. I viewed the funds from band camp as "private funds" since it was funds generated from a service that we provided, and I would have been correct in my assumption if I was contracted like a coach.

As a result of wanting to protect the band's finances, I made one of the worst decisions I've ever made in my career. I knew that I couldn't trust anyone for many reasons, so the unilateral decision that I made was detrimental to my career as it questioned my judgment and my character. The decision to fund Kedric Taylor's salary with band camp revenue led me to treat the band program as if it was my own private enterprise. Although the administrators left me to fend for myself as if the band was my own private enterprise, it wasn't.

To the band directors or those who aspire to be, never allow an institution to put all the weight and problems of the program on your back. If they aren't willing to partner with you and have some skin in the game through guiding you along the way with competent supervision and training on school policies and procedures, walk away! Your life, your sanity, and your freedom are worth more than trying to be a superhero with the mentality I alone can fix this! When times were tough, I was left alone to fix the problems on my own. When the money and solutions to the issues that plagued the Human Jukebox started to come in, suddenly the administration wanted to question me or help themselves under the guise of helping me!

Chapter 16

The 2015-2016 academic year brought change to the campus. Southern University is a system and is the nation's only HBCU system. The President of the Southern University System oversees the entire system comprised of five campuses which are The Baton Rouge Campus (the flagship campus), The New Orleans Campus, The Shreveport Campus, The Law Center, and The Agriculture Center. In contrast, each campus is led by a chancellor who runs the day-to-day operations. This academic year the system would merge the president and chancellor positions to create a President-Chancellor. The merger combined the positions of the System President and the Chancellor of the Baton Rouge Campus. The other campus chancellors would report to the President-Chancellor.

Who would become the first President-Chancellor? The Board of Supervisors had a choice between two men. The first choice was a young man in his mid-40s who had served as the executive director of President Obama's White House Initiative on HBCUs. This position allowed him to work with the U.S. Secretary of Education on national strategies to garner more federal support to HBCUs. The second choice was an older gentleman who was a long-time employee of the SU System, with his latest appointment being Chancellor of Southern University-Shreveport. He also was a finalist for the chancellorship of the Baton Rouge Campus in 2008 but was unsuccessful in his bid.

Reviewing the candidates resumes and listening to them articulate their vision for the Baton Rouge Campus and SU System, it was obvious who was the better candidate. However, the board wasn't seeking a leader; but instead, was demanding a follower. They wanted someone that would ask how high when they said jump. They wanted a leader that would fall in line with the agenda set forth by whoever is winning the political battle. Therefore, it was no surprise with the appointment of the candidate from Southern University-Shreveport, Dr. Ray Belton. Regardless of his questioned intellect or lack thereof, he was a far better alternative than promoting Brandon Dumas as the Chancellor of the Baton Rouge campus under the old structure. Staying out of board politics sounded like the right thing to do, but I would soon learn that if you don't play politics, the politics will play you!

My entry into the Southern University's politics was a declaration of war. I was tired of extending the olive branch just to continue to be disrespected by Brandon Dumas and his cronies! I drew a line in the sand as enough was enough! I knew that standing on my principles officially declared war between Brandon and me. I was ready because the alternative would be more disrespect!

It was August and the band was getting ready for marching/football season. We had just completed a successful week with the freshmen class and got them acclimated to how we do things in the Human Jukebox. The following week would be time to get the upperclassmen in shape and to put the band together.

HBCU graduates from all over know that we love our schools. We love the good and the bad. At this moment, financial aid and housing was a mess. I submitted the students' names and amount of their scholarships to financial aid in May of 2015, and now in August, the scholarships still weren't posted to the students' accounts. To make matters worse, campus housing would not let the band upperclassmen band members check into their dorms until they paid all fees.

Sunday, the freshman band was scheduled to perform for the freshman convocation led by Brandon Dumas. Not only was Brandon my supervisor but he was the supervisor of the Director of Residential Life and Housing. I contacted the Director of

Juked

Residential Life and Housing to discuss the posting of band scholarships and financial aid. I've grown frustrated with her.

After being frustrated with the Director, I called my supervisor numerous times just to be sent to voicemail repeatedly. I never really called him in the past because our standard mode of communication was mainly through text messages. I called and called and called to no success! I even texted him and still got no answer. While all my attempts to reach my supervisor were happening, I had students and parents frustrated at the band hall because they traveled from near and far and could not check into their dorms.

"Fuck it!" I said to my staff out of anger. "I got parents and students in the band hall with no place to go, and Brandon Dumas wants the freshman band to perform. I am tired of him using us but never coming through!"

Brian Simmons volunteered to take the freshman band while I stayed in the band hall to figure the situation out. "Nope!" I told him, "All for one and one for all! We've been disrespected, and the man won't even pick up the phone after I called him at least twenty times along with texting him. If he's too busy for us, then we won't show up!"

The staff looked at me with concern because they understood the gravity of the situation. They knew that Brandon did not care for me. Honestly, I didn't care if he liked me or not. Right is right, and wrong is wrong! I wasn't there to be liked; I was there to do a job!

I was so fired up and frustrated that I let all the tea slip. It was time to let my staff know all the battles I had been fighting and the numerous times I had compromised to assist Brandon and received nothing in return.

Looking at Lorenzo Hart, I started my rant. "By the way, I wasn't going to say anything, but I requested a $10,000 raise for you, and Brandon approved it. I didn't trust him, so I waited to give you the good news. I'm glad I waited because about two weeks later, he texted me saying that he couldn't get you the raise. What's even more insulting is I found out that people who are in his inner circle make more than double your salary got raises!" Lorenzo Hart and the rest of the staff looked at me with disappointment.

I looked at Brian Simmons and it was his turn. "I am sorry that I made you go on all of those Friday trips in the fall of 2014 following Brandon and his team with the pep band. We sacrificed for him. Every time he needed the band, we were there, and I know you hated it!" Brian Simmons nodded his head in approval and laughed.

I even allowed a pep band to travel to Huntsville, Alabama, for a recruitment trip in 2014 on the day before we got on the road to travel to Alabama A&M University to perform for the football game. We eventually met up with Brian Simmons and the pep band a couple of hours before game time. We couldn't practice our field performance on Friday because too many people were missing. What band director sacrifices his final rehearsal before game day? You wouldn't ask a coach to do this. I even sent a band to the elementary school where Brandon's wife was employed in an attempt to show my support while making him look good!

The upperclassmen worked out their housing situation on their own by allowing the individuals who could not check in their rooms to double up with friends until financial aid or housing fixed the problem. I still wasn't satisfied. Brandon Dumas wasn't going to get off this time! Although I called and texted him numerous times, I realized that those weren't official forms of communication, so I emailed him.

"It is with regret that I must inform you that the freshman band will not be in attendance for today's convocation due to the need for my immediate attention, and my staff, to focus on housing several upperclassmen band members who were denied campus housing. In an attempt to resolve this matter with the Director of Residential Life/Housing, I was dismissed, and in an effort to immediately communicate this to you, I was unsuccessful!"

Within a minute of clicking send, Brandon responded to my email. Wow! He was ignoring my calls and texts! Well, that wasn't shocking to me. Brandon responded that it was unacceptable. Within five minutes, there was a knock on my door, and one of my staff members answered. It was Brandon. I was shocked that he even knew where my office was because he never came to the band hall. I asked my staff to leave so that Brandon and I could talk.

"No, they can stay. I won't be long. What's going on? I need the band to come to the event."

I calmly explained to Brandon why we couldn't perform. He wouldn't entertain my reasoning as he kept on with, "Yes, I understand, but I need the freshmen, not upperclassmen!"

"Whether freshmen or upperclassmen, they are all our students. They are here early because of the band. Do you want to come to the rehearsal hall to see the parents and students and explain this to them?"

"Alright, man," Brandon said in disappointment, and walked out of the office.

I looked at my staff as they were "big-eyed" in disbelief about Brandon's lack of concern for anything other than what he wanted. Based on his title, you would think that the Vice-Chancellor of Student Affairs would put students first, but it has always been about his agenda. The freshmen convocation was a flop, and the upperclassmen band members were housed the following day correctly. I made my point and stood my ground, not for my own selfish purposes, but for my students. I won the battle of the day, but I was no fool. I knew that Brandon was a vengeful-whiny-little brat.

Approximately three days passed, and everything was quiet. We were having another successful week of band camp, and I knew what I was experiencing was the calm before the storm! Later that day, I heard Ms. Byrd greeting a lady that was in her office. The lady had a familiar voice, and as she approached my office, I recognized the lady as the Executive Assistant to Brandon. She had a closed envelope with gold-plated lettering titled "Division of Student Affairs and Enrollment Management." Although I had a feeling what the envelope was, I still asked the Executive Assistant, "What is that?" as she gave out a sigh.

"Mr. Haymer, I need you to sign here as verification that you've received this letter." I didn't even respond; I just looked at her in disbelief. "Mr. Haymer, before you read the letter, know your rights as an employee. He's a coward and doesn't want to face you." Then the Executive Assistant left the envelope and walked out of the office.

"I know that little punk didn't write me up," I said to Ms. Byrd.

She looked at me with confusion and stated, "I know you're lying!"

I closed my office door to read the letter. As I began to read, I went from upset to furious. I wanted to go to Brandon's office and beat the shit out of his cowardly ass using all of his expensive office gadgets to hit him with. I told the band staff to run practice, and I went home for the day to cool off! There was no need for me to be at work fussing and taking my anger out on students, and because I was no longer effective in my role due to my rage, home was the best place to be.

Brandon's warning letter contained all kinds of condescending phrases. "I let things slide because you're new to your role"; "you've taken my kindness for weakness," and all sorts of cattiness and pettiness are just a few examples of what the letter contained! While I was home, I wrote his ass back up. The next day, I came to work and went straight to the Office of the President-Chancellor. My relationship with my ally, the receptionist, got me straight to the President-Chancellor without waiting.

"Good morning, Dr. Belton, I hate to come to you with this as you and I never really had a chance to meet, but I have an emergency, and you're the only one that I can talk to about this situation!"

"Have a seat, Mr. Haymer. Tell me what's on your mind."

I began to explain the events from Sunday that involved us missing the freshman convocation. I also explained the write-up from Brandon as Dr. Belton shook his head.

"All write-ups come through me, Mr. Haymer! I will talk to Brandon, and I assure you that the write-up won't be placed in your personnel file. I'll make sure of that!"

While I appreciated his tone and the news that I didn't have to worry about the write-up, I went on to tell the President-Chancellor that I wrote my supervisor back up. As an example of how I went above and beyond my responsibilities to accommodate Brandon.

1. Altered my practice schedules and travel performance protocol to accommodate the Pathway to Prominence Initiative last fall with weekly performances.

2. Allowed parts of our band to travel separately. Greatly inconveniencing the ability to perform my job and jeopardizing the effectiveness of our performance because we were unable to have our full band for the required final practice run Friday, October 10, 2014, which was the day before the SU vs Alabama A&M Game in Huntsville, Alabama.

3. Confirmed Brandon as the keynote speaker for the band banquet held this past May. My staff and colleagues across our campus spent countless hours planning and organizing a banquet that recognized the collective and individual attributes of the band students. Unfortunately, Brandon did not show the same level of professional courtesy he is demanding from me as a leader in this division when he did not show up for the band banquet to address the students that work so hard to advance the great mission of this institution. As a responsible leader, I addressed the students and never voiced or gave the appearance of disappointment. The band

students deserve the same attention and acknowledgment as our incoming students. Three days after the event, Brandon provided an excuse, in my opinion, not equivalent to my explanation for the band's absence from the event this Sunday. His excuse for not attending was supposedly due to a spirited debate he had with a board member concerning our performance for the Floyd Mayweather event in Las Vegas.

4. Upon hiring Kedric Taylor, Assistant Director of Bands, Brandon informed me that he was going to find a way to fund his salary. Then he sent me a text message shortly after the hiring process informing me that his salary would have to be funded through band revenue. This created a major financial strain on an already underfunded band department.

5. The band performed personal favors such as performing at two elementary schools, one being that of Brandon's family member and the other being the family member of McClinton.

6. I was scheduled to travel to Lafayette and New Iberia with the Symphonic Band in April. This was a performance and recruiting trip. This trip was planned two months in advance. I had to alter our plans and disappoint my colleagues because of Brandon's request to have the band at the state capitol building.

7. The band was scheduled to be in Lafayette without proper notice. In fact, I did not find out about this until thirty minutes before the trip, and we still sacrificed to save the image of the University.

8. I have placed several calls, emails, and texts to Brandon that go unanswered.

9. Our conversations involved a promised meeting with Brandon and McClinton to address Lorenzo Hart's low salary. We have yet to have that meeting. His salary is still $25,000.

After explaining the above information to Dr. Belton and giving him a copy of the write-up that I was going to hand-deliver to Brandon, he laughed.

Juked

"Mr. Haymer, it isn't wise to write-up your supervisor. As I explained, all write-ups come through me, and you have my word that it won't go anywhere. Please do me a favor, send Branon an email and meet with him so that you two can discuss the misunderstanding further. After you meet, I will know. Then I'll talk to him about the write-up."

As I listened to Dr. Belton, I just said, "OK." I had to trust him and take him at his word that he would handle the write-up. I thanked Dr. Belton for his time and understanding. I was almost out the door when I pulled two Human Jukebox shirts out of my bag.

"By the way, I don't want my president not to have any band gear. The 2x shirt is for you, and the medium is for your wife!" I said as he shook my hand and told me that he loved the band.

I walked out and thanked the receptionist for coming through for me once again. As I made it to my office, I did exactly what the President-Chancellor asked. I emailed Brandon and asked to meet with him. I wanted to discuss moving forward together for the benefit of our students. I was cautious with my wording and didn't want to come across as angry or threatening. Brandon responded the next day and agreed to meet with me after the long registration period. Well, the long registration period must still be in process because the meeting never took place!

Chapter 17

When I took over as Interim Director of Bands, I made the decision to replace the sponsor of the Dancing Dolls from 2011-2013. The former Doll Sponsor was a Dancing Doll from 1982-1985 and a great all-around person. When I was the Assistant Director, she and I got along just fine. I found her to be very intelligent and resourceful. My only problem with her was that she wasn't available enough to manage the day-to-day activity of the Dolls. She was also a bit outdated when it came to selecting uniforms and other things that were trending in 2014. I called the 1982 Doll to my office to let her know that I was going in another direction, and it was very hard for me to tell her.

The new Dancing Doll Sponsor I selected for my administration was the captain of the 2009 and 2010 edition of the Fabulous Dancing Dolls. Furthermore, I had an extensive history with her. Her entire high school and college dance time was spent under my leadership as her high school band director and college assistant band director. Most of all, I trusted her. She was the energy that I needed to start the new era of the Southern University Fabulous Dancing Dolls.

My first decision as the director was slammed into my lap the day after Mr. J told me that I was the new director. May 28, 2014, I arrived at work and walked in the band building. I went immediately to the Director's office as Mr. J answered the door!

"Come on in YOUR OFFICE, Mr. Haymer!"

Mr. J was seriously stressing that it wasn't his office anymore. He had on some very relaxed clothes, and I saw his snap on lenses in his hand. They were sunglasses that snapped over his prescribed eyeglasses. It was a weird feeling sitting in the director's office behind the desk as Mr. J was sitting in the seat reserved for office visitors. As we began to meet, there was a young lady present who was a member of the Dancing Dolls.

"Mr. Haymer, you're now in charge, but I need a favor. I promised this young lady that if she made the team this year that she will be the next captain of the Dancing Dolls! Mr. Haymer, I don't know when you will have tryouts, but please look out for her!"

I looked at the young lady and smiled. This was going to be my first executive decision as the new director. How could I tell Mr. J "NO" especially in front of the Dancing Doll that was present. Because I believed Mr. J when he told me that he would retire in 8 to 10 years, I was already planning. I had in mind who would be the captain of the Dancing Dolls when and if I were to take the helm in 2014 or 2015. I was pleased to know that Mr. J and I were on the same page. This young lady that Mr. J asked me to appoint as my first Dancing Doll captain was already someone who I considered the "heir-apparent". She was not just a choice; she is what I considered MY ONLY CHOICE!

I looked at the young lady and gave her a smile. I could tell that she was very nervous as she waited to hear my response. Since I was very neutral with my approach with the Dancing Dolls in the past, neither she nor Mr. J knew my stance on the issue. I leaned back in the wobbly director's chair. I pretended to be in deep thought about the issue, then I responded.

"Of course! I think that she is an outstanding pick. She will do a wonderful job leading the 2014-15 edition of the Dancing Dolls. If she makes the team!" I looked at the young lady and told her, "Please don't disappoint me. I know that you have the grades but bring your A-game to tryouts!" The young lady gave Mr. J and me a hug.

"Thank you so much!" she said and walked out of the office.

I was pleased with my first decision being an easy one. Selecting that young lady as captain would become one of the best decisions that I've made as the director! Consequently, it would become a challenge as well for a much different reason.

One of the hardest things I had to do when I first took the helm was to cut the Dancing Doll Sponsor. Some of the reasons I had for letting her go, became the traits of the current Dancing Doll Sponsor, DT.

DT had a great career for a company based out of Houston, Texas. She told me that the job would require her to miss certain days, but she could balance both. I understood and supported her. I wanted to do everything in my power to make our Director-Sponsor relationship successful. Besides, Southern wasn't paying her bills as being the Dancing Doll Sponsor was a voluntary position. Although DT's absence would put me in an uncomfortable position, I had to understand. Now it was time to face one of my biggest fears: getting involved with day-to-day matters of the Dancing Dolls.

One day, the captain came to me with a very serious concern.

"Mr. Haymer, DT hasn't been around very much. I don't want to bother you, but we need…."

She had a long list of essential items needed and the first performance was less than two weeks away. I remember being a little uncomfortable listening to the captain as she went down the list of needs because I had no idea what she was talking about. I was clueless! Still, I knew that I had to do something immediately due to "the help" being 4 hours away in another state.

"Ok! What are you talking about and how quickly can I get it?"

As the captain continued to explain, I got up from my desk, "sit in my seat! Pull up what you need on the computer!".

The captain did precisely that. The Dancing Dolls needed close to $2,500 worth of essentials and supplies, but I did not panic. I realized that I had to be the sponsor and advisor. I also knew that I had to project confidence. If I panicked, then the captain would have as well and that would spread to the team.

"I charged a $25.00 audition fee for a reason! The registration fee is money for the team to get supplies and anything else needed!"

"I need to go back to the Doll Room and talk to some of the team to make sure that I have everything."

"I'll tell you what. Meet me across the hall from the Doll Room in thirty minutes. I have to take care of something right quick, then I'll come with my laptop, and we will get everything that y'all need!"

After the captain left my office, I pulled up my account with the third-party internet-based registration company. I used this company for the high school band and dance team camp registration, SU Dancing Doll tryout registration, and the Southern University band fees registration. We collected $3,000 in Dancing Doll tryout registration fees.

I met with the captain and another member of the dolls. The other member was in her fourth year and a senior.

"Mr. Haymer, there's a store that has the stockings that we need, I called them to verify."

"Ok! Y'all are free at 4:00 PM tomorrow because that's band class time every day. Meet me at the store tomorrow, and we will get the stockings!"

The captain then got on my laptop and pulled up all the items that she needed from various websites. The total cost added up to about $1,800. We had to rush shipment because we had a little under two weeks to get the supplies. To ensure that we got the items on time, I had them shipped to my house; as the campus mailing system was unreliable. Solving this problem became bonding time between the captain and me.

She began to talk about DT. She didn't say anything negative, but I can read body language well. I suspected that there was a problem. I didn't press the issue because I knew it was hard enough for the captain to tell me the little that she did.

From what I gathered, she and DT had a communication issue. It was clear that the issue mainly stemmed from DT hardly being there! The little times that she was present, she would make decisions contradictory to what the captain told the line. The sponsor is ultimately in charge of the day-to-day activity, so DT was well within her right to do so. However, when she leaves to go to Texas, it's the captain left alone to figure out the business of the organization with no instructions, money, or guidance. It's a touchy situation when DT gets upset when things are decided differently from how she would have handled it. I understood the captain's frustrations, and although she did not complain or say much to me about the situation, I knew because I observed very well.

"You did the right thing by coming to me in this situation. I am glad that you came today because it was close! The items we just ordered won't be in until three days before game day!"

I met the captain and the senior member of the Dancing Dolls at the store the next day. We purchased the stockings and other items needed. The captain only had about 11 pairs of stockings in her hands.

"How long do those stockings last? I know y'all have to dance in them for more than one performance! Get about 40 pairs so we won't have to come back here every week. I believe in buying in bulk, and I wish that Costco or Sam's sold these!"

The cashier laughed. I could see the look of joy on the girls' faces as they went back to grab more of what they needed. For the next three years, you would've thought I was the dance coach because my mailbox at home would be full of catalogs, coupons, etc., from all the various websites and stores that I had to purchase supplies from for the Dancing Dolls. Although it made me feel like a more effective leader to solve the captain's problems, I knew that if I didn't try to mend the relationship with DT and the captain soon, something terrible would happen. As usual, my instincts were right!

The first game for the 2015 edition of the Human Jukebox and Dancing Dolls was at Louisiana Tech University, located in Ruston, Louisiana. After the game, while loading the buses to depart for Baton Rouge, DT came to my bus to see me. I could tell that she was very upset about something.

I pulled her to the side of the bus where we could have some privacy to talk. DT shared with me that she was livid. The Dancing Doll captain and another senior member took it upon themselves to take a well-known Dancing Doll Uniform and had it altered by a guy who she pointed out that was by our buses. Supposably, the guy who altered the uniform took a photo with the Dancing Dolls and posted it on social media as a form of advertisement for his business. I was shocked because I just had a long talk with the captain and the senior doll member.

"DT, it's late, and we're both tired. Let's just discuss this on Monday. By that time, you would have cooled down. I do not want to make a decision out of frustration or anger."

"Ok! We can meet on Monday. Have the captain and senior Doll member stay after I dismiss so we can discuss this with them as well."

On Monday, after watching a video of the first performance and talking about plans for the next show, I dismissed the band around 4:30pm. Upon dismissal, DT and I met to further discuss the incident concerning the captain and senior doll member. As expected, DT had cooled down, but she was still insistent on a two-week suspension of the captain and senior Doll member.

"I know you have been busy with work, but I had a long talk with the captain. I told her that she had to learn to better communicate with you. I am asking that you do the same with her."

Around the ages of 24 to 28 years old, I was DT's high school band director. She experienced the younger version of myself. She recalled this phase of my life. Back then, I was hard on the band and dance team. She knew what I was capable of. However, I am now 37 years old. I had more experience, more weight on my shoulders, and political implications because of the popularity of the Human Jukebox and Dancing Dolls.

"Mr. Haymer, think about it like this. If a band member took the band uniform and altered it, what would you do?"

"I would zip their ass immediately! Not only would I zip them, but they would also receive a bill for $448.00, the price of an individual uniform!"

"Exactly! You would zip a band member and charge them for the uniform. All I am trying to do is suspend two dolls for the same thing!"

I didn't hesitate to offer a response. Altering the uniform without permission was unthinkable and inexcusable. Removing them from the band and charging them the cost of an individual uniform would be a no brainer. However, she made a valid point.

I understood the politics with the Dancing Dolls were different from the band's politics. Eleven Dancing Dolls can create way more problems, pressure, persecution, and politics than a 230-piece band.! If I were a politician, my opinion would be correct, but as an educator, DT was right! As Director of Bands at Southern University, the answer was somewhere in the middle of the two, but I decided to back DT and suspend the captain and senior doll member.

"If we're going to do this, we are going to do it my way! Although I think a two-week suspension is long enough, I am going to suspend the girls indefinitely. They won't know the length of their suspension, but I still plan to make it two weeks."

I wanted to send a message to the Dancing Dolls presently and the Dancing Dolls of the future. We would not and will not

Juked

tolerate a serious offense such as this. We met with the captain and senior doll member to tell them their fate. I was not happy to enforce the punishment, but I was convinced that no one was bigger than the organization. I gave the girls written notification of their suspension outlining the handbook rules that they violated and asked each to sign the form to indicate that they received and understood their punishment. I also gave them a copy of their signed suspension notification.

"We will call you when you are allowed to return to practice."

As they walked out of the door, I looked at DT. "Brace yourself because a storm is coming!"

I knew that this was going to be a problem and I was correct. Not even an hour had passed, and the Dancing Doll enthusiasts were already on social media calling for my head and DT's as well. Of course, the story was twisted. All kinds of rumors, spins, and lies were told. Once you pulled that trigger, there was no turning back.

The implications and effects of my decision reached the Vice Chancellor, Dr. Brandon Dumas, as expected. It also reached the Office of the President-Chancellor, Dr. Belton, which I did not expect. We were preparing for one of our biggest rivals, The Jackson State University "Sonic Boom of the South" and the Prancing J-Settes. Brandon sent me a bizarre email. I won't quote it word for word, but I will paraphrase it:

The upcoming game against the JSU "Sonic Boom of the South" and the Prancing J-Settes will be the biggest game hosted on campus. I do not want the band and Dancing Dolls to be at a disadvantage, and for that reason, I am recommending that the suspended members of the Dancing Dolls be reinstated immediately!

Oh, so now Brandon Dumas is concerned about the band program being at a disadvantage? What about the upperclassmen band members who couldn't receive their dorm assignments because he failed to intervene, which put the band at a disadvantage? What about the horrific instruments, uniforms, and equipment that I brought to his attention and how it's putting the program at a "disadvantage?" What about asking me to cover the assistant band director's pay and how it's putting the department at a "disadvantage?" What about Lorenzo Hart's low salary and how it's putting him at a "disadvantage" every time he receives a bill? What about using band funds to pay your cronies and how it's putting a disadvantaged program at a further "disadvantage?"

I wanted to respond to his email by letting him know my feelings on how he operates beyond the scope of his duties while failing to put the band at an advantage, but I didn't have time to go back and forth dealing with his catty ways. I also knew that he had a few band members and Dancing Dolls working in his office or the offices of his cronies. Finally, I knew he often attempted to get inside information from them on what was happening within my department. Instead of falling into my desires, I simply responded to Brandon's email by stating that I was the Director of Bands and had the right to enforce the band handbook's policies when students violated the rules. That's it! Point Blank, period! No need for any back and forth.

President-Chancellor, Dr. Belton, called me into his office with a more "seasoned" and diplomatic approach.

"I want you to let the girls back. I know it isn't fair, but I need you to do it for me. If anyone questions you, just say that I made you do it!".

Dr. Belton didn't know a Dancing Doll from the hole in his ear. I was aware that someone in his inner circle from the Shreveport campus was close with one of the suspended Dolls. I was upset that out of all the things that I needed to advance the program and out of all the times I tried to get help from the administration, the thing that caught their attention was the suspension of two Dancing Dolls. I put band members out for doing way less. Where's their due process? Where's their spokesman? I planned to let the girls back on the team within two weeks, and I held my ground as I ignored the order from the Vice Chancellor and the President-

Chancellor. Things got way too political, and I admit, I was upset with the suspended dolls for sharing inside information that leaked to social media and caused a gigantic headache. At this moment, I realized that this was also the consequence of my vision as the media team's innovation made the Dancing Dolls, who were already stars, even bigger stars. Still, I wasn't going to allow outsiders and administrators who did absolutely nothing but take from the program, dictate to me how to do my job!

After two weeks, the suspended members were back on the team, and the problem shifted from them not being there to why wasn't the captain in the front? This caused more political issues, but enough was enough. I reinstated the captain when I was ready as I continued to ignore the request of administrators. I'll end by stating that the captain was and is a star! She shined no matter what spot that she had in the stands or field. I will always respect how she elevated the Fabulous Dancing Doll brand, even if I didn't like the politics attached to her popularity!

I wish I could say that the suspension of the two Dancing Dolls was the only issue to capture my attention. On the contrary, we weren't even halfway through the season, and I was already tired and wanted to quit! The band was doing a terrific job, but everything else caused me to hate my job. To make the season more interesting for my students and staff, I extended an invitation to Jackson State University for a head-to-head matchup in a battle of the bands on the campus of SU. I partnered with an esteemed and popular young man who was also a promoter by the name of Terral Jackson, Jr. or as most call him, TJ.

TJ had a history of spearheading successful events in Baton Rouge for many years. He was familiar with Southern University because his father was Assistant Director of Bands in the late 1970s and early 80s. He was also a student at SU and was the drum major for the Human Jukebox from 1996-1998. He is an extraordinary leader and successful businessman. Since he's promoted many successful events at SU in the past, it was easy for me to partner with him in his project.

I asked TJ to allow me to secure the Sonic Boom to sign the contract that he had in place. Once I got the JSU Band to agree, all other logistics would be on him. I thought it was a win-win situation because he guaranteed the Human Jukebox $25,000 rain, sleet, or snow. The funds would be payable to the Human Jukebox and deposited into the band's account in the SU System Foundation.

In my attempt to get the Sonic Boom involved, I acted on behalf of TJ, with his permission, and told the director that they would receive a $10,000 check plus the cost of their bus travel, lodging, and Friday night meal would be covered as well. I thought that this was a gracious offer considering when we went to Jackson the previous year, we only received $4,900 for the event. This is not including the disastrous amenities of the Hoe-Tell-Gate Scandal along with the fact that JSU did not cover our travel expenses. The Assistant Director who spearheaded the battle of the bands in Jackson told me after all the expenses were paid that $4,900 was our half of the profit. He even gave me a copy of the spreadsheet with the appropriate signatures as proof. Although I wasn't happy with such a small amount after all that we went through in Jackson and Clinton, Mississippi, I had to understand.

The Assistant Director of the Sonic Boom received a promotion to Director of Bands in 2015. We had several discussions Director to Director, and the final offer was a $10,000 check made payable to JSU in the name of the band, travel, meal, and lodging expenses covered. It was approximately $15,000 to transport the Sonic Boom to Baton Rouge a day before the game. The lodging was roughly $4,000, and I booked them in the Holiday Inn, which was one facility compared to the many motels they had us in. The meal was to be provided by a popular fast-food chicken finger chain. The Sonic Boom's package altogether exceeded $30,000, but their director wanted half of the gate's profits.

I didn't even approach TJ with the JSU Band Director's demands because I thought he was unreasonable. The Human

Juked

Jukebox received $4,900 at JSU in 2014, and now the director wants half the gate at SU! Hell no!!

I called my friend at Talladega College and offered him the same package offered to the Sonic Boom. He took the deal. I connected the Talladega Marching Tornado Band director with TJ, and the rest was history. Because Friday night football is huge all over America and we wanted the high school crowd to attend for recruitment purposes, we agreed to start the event in Southern's own Mumford Stadium at 10:00pm and end it at midnight. The "Midnight Madness Battle of the Bands name came about because of this effort.

The efforts to host an event to bring excitement and a fresh approach to the season caused many problems. Jabari and Eric wanted to host the event themselves. They tried to steer me from dealing with TJ. Also, Brandon Dumas got involved. He asked me for a financial report of the event by the close of business on the Monday after the Midnight Madness Battle of the Bands. I emailed Brandon a document that I typed, and he sent it to several SU System Board of Supervisors members using the document as proof that I was getting money from the ticket gate.

TJ had a contract with the University outlining all the logistics Brandon requested. The contract was approved by the University's general counsel then ultimately by President-Chancellor Belton. I had nothing to do with anything related to the contract and its approval. I began to regret sending Brandon that email containing the financial document. However, the results of his game playing ended with a blessing for me later in the football season!

Not to brag but The Midnight Madness Battle of the Bands was a success and changed the landscape of HBCU college bands! While I admit that the idea came from the battle against the Sonic Boom of the South, I, along with the wisdom of TJ, perfected the approach and format for a successful college battle of the bands in the social media age!

Yes, the Honda Battle of the Bands was prominent and successful, but I listened to the people as a transformational leader. They didn't like the big corporate-sponsored style of battles. The people wanted to see the clash of the titans! They wanted to witness two marching bands going head-to-head in the stands without the interruption of referees, announcers, promotions, etc. The marketing that the Human Jukebox provided for the Midnight Madness Battle of the Bands was genius. It resulted in more social media activity, a 25-percent jump in recruitment, and more success for the Human Jukebox media team.

Perhaps the only arm of the Human Jukebox that did not receive any success due to the Midnight Madness BOTB was the MBM team. They've become obsolete as the event superseded their whole purpose. The Midnight Madness BOTB was so popular that it was a self-marketing and branding engine. Due to the politics at SU and the fact that Baton Rouge wasn't a great city for band heads, the Midnight Madness BOTB would transform in the future to the Crankfest Battle of the Bands hosted in New Orleans, Louisiana; New Orleans is one of the best American cities for parties, food, music, and culture! I am proud to have had a part in the transformation of HBCU band culture as our efforts raised the bar and shifted the culture to 21st Century relevance! Bands were still operating in the VHS era and would be forced to re-examine their strategies and move with the shift of culture to the era of instant coverage known as the Social Media Age.

Chapter 18

A couple months after being appointed the "interim" Director of Bands, I embarked on a project to record the band's illustrious history. Gary Chambers spearheaded the documentary, "The Band Plays On", and decided to bring someone in to help market the project. Enter Sharon into my life.

Sharon is a local entrepreneur. She owns an advertising agency and marketing firm in Baton Rouge. Her company is called Trapezoid Media.

Gary, Sharon, and I met a lot during the fall of 2014. We met so much that Sharon started to become comfortable coming to the office without Gary. She helped raise funds for the Human Jukebox by securing a performance at the largest casino in the Baton Rouge area. She also took interest in my social media activities and noticed me doing things like reading Dr. Seuss' books to a kindergarten class, performing at elementary schools with the pep band, and other community events.

The more she came around, the more familiar we became with each other. As we became more comfortable around each other, our professional relationship grew to become personal. Establishing herself to be a support system, Sharon called and texted me quite often. I don't use the term "friend" loosely, so I never considered her a friend, but I thought that she was an individual that could become a friend once I learned that I could trust her.

As our regular ten to twenty-minute conversations about business grew to thirty minutes to one hour or more about personal matters, I discovered we had a lot in common. We have the same birthday with the only difference being that she was a year older. I also learned that she's been through a divorce as well! I've never met anyone that I had so many things in common with. We had all the things in common that would be great for conversation pieces.

As I grew more and more comfortable with Sharon, I could tell that she wanted more than conversation. Sharon had the "hots" for Haymer-Time, and I was quite flattered. She seemed to have it all going for herself. Sharon had her own business, a luxury car, a lovely home that she had constructed in a very nice area of town, and she dressed very professionally. Yes, she checked all the boxes that a man looked for and wanted in a woman. I wasn't attracted to Sharon. She just wasn't my type.

I wasn't attracted to Sharon simply because I like what I like, and she wasn't it. I was also paranoid that Brandon Dumas or somebody in the SU Elite was trying to set me up. Sharon rolled with the same church crowd, and let's just say I wasn't comfortable with that. Now that I established my lack of interest in Sharon, I still entertained her and attempted to play dumb to her attraction for me. I knew that I could only keep this act up for so long before Sharon and I had a real conversation.

I admit, I was lonely, and all I had to fill my day was band issues. Sharon was an escape from reality. We basically had all of the benefits of a relationship without one thing, sex! I paid for everything because I was paying for an escape from my lonely-depressing-career centered life. Instead of trying to mend the relationship with my ex-wife, I sought companionship in a woman that I had no interest in sexually. Perhaps that was the biggest thing that made me comfortable with her. It was a platonic relationship, or at least I wanted it to be. I knew that Sharon was growing tired of the mixed signals. She would move in for the kill very soon as she became a hawk, and I was her prey!

One Friday evening in August of 2015, everything between Sharon and I changed. Approximately a week before the football season began, I picked Sharon up in my truck so we could go out to dinner to discuss business. We were in the beginning stages of planning an event on the campus of SU that involved the Human

Juked

Jukebox performing in concert for elementary school students from the Baton Rouge and surrounding areas. Sharon and I discussed partnering on a fundraiser that she would spearhead through her company and the Human Jukebox would perform for pay. The plan was for Sharon to generate a contract between the University for the band and her company to make the event possible.

I explained to Sharon very carefully that I'd been accused of taking kickbacks during the previous year. I wanted everything to be above board because I knew that I had to be careful dealing with the snakes on campus. I made it clear that once I agreed to the performance, the contract had to be signed by my supervisor, then ultimately President-Chancellor Belton. I didn't need Sharon. I could have hosted this event myself. However, due to my mistrust for the administrations' handling of band funds coupled with the "kickback allegations," I knew that it would be best if I stayed out of it. I thought it was best to allow a contracted outsider to come in and just pay the band as an artist.

When Sharon and I made it to the restaurant, we began talking about the everyday personal things that we always discussed as we waited at the bar while a live band played until our table was ready.

"What will you two be drinking tonight," asked the bartender.

"I'll have a martini!" I looked at Sharon to indicate that I wanted to know what she wanted to drink.

"Well, I'll have a glass of wine."

"I'll be right back; I have to go to the men's room."

After quickly handling my business in the restroom, I approached the bar near the live band. I noticed that someone was in my seat, and Sharon was gone. The bartender got my attention.

"Hey! She left because your table was ready."

As I looked around the restaurant, I saw Sharon waving to get my attention to let me know where she was located. "Do you want to settle now or keep an open tab?"

"Settle now, please!" I reached in my wallet to give the bartender my credit card.

"Thank you, Mr. Haymer. Enjoy the rest of your evening!"

Jokingly, Sharon said, "it took you long enough!"

"Well, you know, looking this fly isn't by accident!"

After my response, we both laughed, and I took a sip of my martini. I began to pick up the discussion where we left off about the fundraiser on campus. This is where the night's events became unclear, as I only remember a few details. I remember Sharon waking me up in the restaurant since I fell asleep and became very weak. I remember leaving with our food in to-go containers as I leaned on Sharon as we walked outside. It was very humid outside, and it suddenly became very hot. Sharon took off my blazer as we waited on the valet driver to bring my truck to the restaurant's front entrance. The valet driver assisted me in getting in the passenger side of my vehicle as Sharon got in on the driver's side. The lights were very bright outside of the restaurant, and they were hurting my eyes. I must have passed out because I was in the driveway at Sharon's house as soon as I opened my eyes. The restaurant was approximately 45 minutes to an hour away from her house, but it seemed like we made it there in five minutes.

Although I was inebriated, I knew something was strange. Sharon got me out of the truck and walked me into her house. My body was tired and weak. I remember leaning across the right side of her body as I stumbled into the dark house. We made it to her couch, and she laid me on my back. I was so tired. I guess about thirty minutes must have passed while I laid on the sofa because Sharon came back to wake me. I could smell fresh soap, perfume, or body spray. I just remember seeing a silhouette of her body in what appeared to be a silk negligee. The room was dimly lit,

Juked

and I was under the influence of something strong. I laid there like a fly trapped in her spider web. I became alert as I knew something was about to go down, and I was afraid that I was too weak to control the situation.

I began to panic. Still sucked in by the couch, Sharon walked closer and started kissing me. She shoved her tongue down my throat as I mumbled, "No. No!" I don't know if I was saying no aloud or in my head, but I was trying to take control of the situation while still sucked in the couch.

Sharon began to unbuckle my belt and unzip my jeans. I felt her hands in my underwear as she began to play with my male anatomy. My pants were coming down as I felt the warmth of her mouth on my male anatomy. I knew that I was fighting a losing battle. She began to open the buttons on my shirt, then laid her body on top of mine. I went from comfortable to suffocating. I remember the smell of Sharon's body spray. It was a good smell, but the pressure from her weight on top of my weak and inebriated body must have forced it to go in survival mode as I muscled up the strength to push her off me to the floor. As I heard her body hit the floor, I jumped up in a panic and grabbed my keys and ran to the door as fast as I could with my pants still down to my ankles. I managed to get outside and climbed into my truck and sped off into the night. Thank God that I made it home.

I woke up the following day around 10:00 AM laid across my bed with my pants still down. I had a severe headache. It wasn't a hangover type of headache; it was something that I'd never experienced before. I began to play in my mind the events from the previous night. I remember sipping my drink, and that's when everything faded. One sip of a martini doesn't make you pass out. As an experienced drinker, it takes more than five or six glasses to get me intoxicated, let alone memory loss or a blackout.

Furthermore, Sharon knew that I wasn't in my right mind and had to be under the influence of something. Why would she try to have sex with me knowing this? As all of the scenarios played in my mind, I became angry as I began to realize that Sharon possibly spiked my drink when I left the bar and went to the restroom. I immediately made an appointment to see my doctor and was able to see her the same day.

I lied to my doctor because I was too embarrassed to tell anyone that I was possibly drugged and date raped. I told my doctor that I was experimenting with a pill that I mixed with a shot of vodka, and it made me pass out and gave me a severe headache. I asked her to test my urine to see what the pill was because I thought it would relax me. The doctor began to ask a series of questions that made me even more uncomfortable. She did a urine test and told me that she would have the results in three days. I had to sit through a lecture with my doctor about being responsible as she knew I was the Director of Bands at Southern. She wanted me to understand the responsibilities of being a public figure. As hard as it was for me to sit through that lecture, it was easier to do that than to tell her the truth. I know my doctor would have been required by the law to call to report it to the authorities had I told her I was raped.

Honestly, I lied for various reasons. I just didn't want that type of controversy. My image as a strong and aggressive musical leader would be tarnished. For others to hear that I was drugged and date raped would make me look weak! Any complaint that I made, the headlines would have been all about the "SU Band Director" when the university had nothing to do with this. No. Just NO! I did not want this to get out because it wasn't a good look. Therefore, lying was better than the truth.

On the way home, I purchased some extra-strength ibuprofen. I needed them immediately as Jabari was constantly calling me. He was upset that Sharon was spearheading the fundraiser planned for late October/November on campus. I listened to Jabari bitch and complain, but I was not in the mood.

From my perspective, it was Jabari's fault that I was dealing with Sharon in the first place. He refused to uphold his contractual obligation by working with Gary to market the band's documentary.

Had he done his job, Gary would have never had to bring Sharon in. Now he's calling to complain!

He placed me on hold to add in the other MBM team member. Once Eric joined the call, I quickly changed the subject. I told them what transpired between Sharon and me the night before. I left out the details about going to the doctor, but I told them everything else. They responded in a way that men do. They LAUGHED! After about fifteen minutes of jokes and questions from the team about Sharon, we ended the call. I spent the rest of my Saturday in bed.

Three days later I received a call from my doctor. She asked me to come into the office. It was verified that I had traces of Rohypnol in my system. I knew it wasn't just a martini. Having the date rape drug in my system explained why I blacked out and the other symptoms.

I never felt so violated and helpless in my life. I began to fault myself. I gave Sharon the signals to do this to me. I should have never taken her out and spent time with her doing the things that couples do. It was my fault that this happened to me.

As the days progressed, I knew that I had to stop feeling sorry for myself. I also knew that I had to stop making excuses for Sharon. We weren't high school kids. We were grown-ass adults. If she wanted sex, she could have asked me. I should have been afforded the right to say yes or no! If the shoe was on the other foot the entire outcome would be different.

I became very upset with Sharon. I was still embarrassed and felt like less than a man. I ignored her calls and texts. I went a week without talking to her but ignoring a problem doesn't make it disappear. Ignoring a problem makes it worse. Unfortunately, Sharon's not the type to let things go. When she doesn't get what she wants, she's willing to destroy! I would learn this lesson the hard way as this would not be the end of Sharon and me. Sooner than later, I would have to confront Sharon.

About a month later prior to the 4:00pm band rehearsal, I realized that the new drills designed for the halftime performances had been inadvertently left at home. I did not want to go home because I knew traffic was heavy, but I had to since teaching the new drill was the day's objective. I knew that if I didn't go home to get my drill charts, we would have wasted a night's rehearsal! That couldn't happen. I immediately left campus, heading home around 3:30pm. I made it home in about 45 minutes. Soon as I walked through the back door, I heard the ding-dong of my bell.

I paused in the middle of my kitchen and came to the realization that someone was at the front door pressing the doorbell continuously. I had no clue who this impatient visitor could be. I wasn't supposed to be home and I'm never home at this time. I wasn't expecting a package. Plus, no delivery person would press a doorbell continuously in such an annoying way! Ding-Dong. Ding-Dong! DING-DONG! The doorbell kept ringing.

Suddenly, the doorbell stopped ringing. Now, annoying knocks began. Knocks that sounded as if the police were the ones at the door. Deep and hard knocks. Boom. Boom! BOOM! I stood in the kitchen upset and wondering who in the hell it could be. I knew whoever it was, that they were impatient, and they knew that I was home. Finally, as I went to the front of the house and looked out of the window. It was Sharon! I didn't see her, but I saw her car parked in the street directly in front of my home.

Like it or not, it was time to confront Sharon! I opened the door and there she is with a mean mug on her face standing in the doorway as if she owned the place.

"What in the hell are you doing here?"

"I want to know why you're not returning my calls and texts. Are you avoiding me?"

"I am never home at this time. You knock on my door like you're the got damn police! Did you follow me? Are you stalking me?

Juked

"I had to do what I had to do since you're not talking to me!" She had now taken the legendary stance of rolling her eyes and her neck. We began to argue.

"Look, Sharon. I have neighbors, and you're making a big scene! Do not come to my house ever again! I have to go back to work. I'll tell you about yourself later!"

She was not trying to end the conversation. I attempted to close the door on her.

"Oh no! We ain't through talking yet. I don't care where you have to go!" She placed her foot in the doorway in an attempt to block me from closing the door on her. "I want to know why you're avoiding me!?"

"Bye Sharon! Don't ever come here again!" I attempted to close the door again. She wouldn't move her foot.

"If you slam that door on my foot, that's assault. I will notify the police!"

"You know what you did to me!"

I was so angry that I started cursing and yelling at Sharon. She looked at me, laughing and smiling condescendingly.

"I don't know what you're talking about!"

I was so angry. I wanted to push her out of the doorway. I knew if I put my hands on her, even though she was technically trespassing at this point, it would not have ended well. I was angry as I kept asking her to leave and she wouldn't budge her foot from the doorway. After about five minutes of arguing with Sharon, I calmed down. I realized that I had several security cameras professionally installed around my house a few months ago. One camera was pointing right at her. I began to laugh, and she looked at me in confusion.

"I asked you to leave several times, Sharon, and you refuse! You're trespassing! Although I would love to slam this door on your foot, I have something even more satisfying for me! Sharon, look up and say, hi!"

Sharon looked up and noticed the camera was pointed right at her! I laughed so hard in her face. I could feel her bullying energy fading away as she realized that she was caught on camera! She removed her foot from the door and speed walked back to her vehicle in her short heels. She sped off, literally burning the rubber on her tires!

I knew that I hadn't heard the last of Sharon and I had to think of a solution fast! Before leaving my house to go back to work, I made sure every camera was working and my security system was armed! I turned it on and off several times to make sure it was in full-protection mode!

While in my vehicle, I called the Chief of the SUPD. She was not only law enforcement, but I considered her a friend and I needed her advice. I explained what just transpired at my home and how I knew that Sharon would show up to my job one day. Of course, the Chief laughed. The way I was explaining the story, I conveniently left out the details of why Sharon was stalking me. I wasn't completely honest by letting her know how Sharon knew where I lived. Even though I left many holes in my story, Chief gave me some good advice on what to do if Sharon shows up on the job.

Two days later, at 4:00pm, Sharon came to the band hall and sat on the couch directly outside of my office door. Since Sharon had been to my office several times, she was familiar with my schedule. She was also familiar with some of the band students due to her frequent visits, so students seeing her outside my door wasn't anything unusual.

I opened my office door to stand in the hall. I would often do this ten minutes before rehearsal. This ritual was an indication to the students. It let them know that it was time to stop hanging out. Go warm-up and tune-up. Start preparing to sit up and shut up! Simply put…it's close to rehearsal time!

Juked

When I walked into the hall, I was shocked to see Sharon outside of my door talking to the students as she looked at me and spoke with the most professional tone that I've ever heard come out of her mouth.

"Good afternoon, Mr. Haymer!"

She knew that I couldn't tell her what I really wanted to say. Besides being at work, I knew there were students watching! I stayed calm. I had a plan. I just prepared for this situation with the Chief of the SUPD.

"Hey, Sharon! How are you?" I responded with a very facetious tone as I addressed the students. "Hey y'all, go get ready for rehearsal!" The students scattered like ants in an interrupted ant bed.

"Hey! Give me a hug! I haven't seen you in a while."

As I spoke to Sharon, she attempted to walk past me and enter my office door. She had a startled look on her face. My positive reaction frightened her. I hugged her tightly and passionately. Then I whispered in her ear.

"The SUPD is on the way."

I backed away from her in the crowded hallway. I noticed the look of panic on her face. She calmly walked away. I went back into the office and literally laughed out loud!

Several weeks have passed. I limited my communication with Sharon to emails only. I knew I had to end the fundraiser planned with her or get a third party involved serving as a liaison. Since the MBM team wanted no part of dealing with her, I had a Plan B.

The Friday night before homecoming Saturday Marissa, the President of the Human Jukebox Alumni Association, came to my office. She and I were very good friends. Marissa is a former member of the Human Jukebox and one of my all-time favorite students. She marched in the band from 2006-2009. As a student, she was very active in various committees in the band and in the general student body. She even started her own dance line that was often featured in front of the Human Jukebox to close our halftime performances.

What made me respect Marissa the most was her ability to party with a purpose! I've never had a student who could party all night long and still make the dean's list with all A's and B's. She represented the perfect example of work hard, play hard. At the time, she was on the promotions team of a very famous Baton Rouge rapper. She and I got along so well that we never had a normal student-teacher relationship. She would always come to my office and set it off," being the life of the party. After she graduated, it was natural for us to become friends. We became real friends, not that fake stuff that most people call a friendship.

Although I considered Marissa a real friend, I never told her about Sharon. Marissa was no fool. Immediately upon meeting Sharon, she saw straight through her. To finish the fundraising project and to keep a bad situation from getting worse, I introduced the ladies to each other in hopes of discussing the possibility of the fundraiser falling under the arm of the Human Jukebox Alumni Association. I needed Marissa there for my protection. However, she made an already out of control problem with Sharon even worse! Having them meet on the Friday before homecoming was disastrous.

Sharon was in my office when there was a knock on the door. I answered the door. It was Marissa.

"Oh! You better have answered this door, my nigg! I know you be in here ignoring people!"

"Hey, my nigg!"

I gave Marissa a big hug. Sharon was in the office and gave a loud uh, um cough. I turned around and looked at Sharon,

"Oh, Marissa, this is Sharon. She's the person that I told you about that's spearheading the fundraiser."

Juked

The two women politely and falsely greeted each other. Marissa walked through the doorway and sat down in the office. Before we could begin the meeting, a student walked in through my office's back entrance.

"Mr. Haymer, they are ready for you." The assistant directors were through with their part of the rehearsal. It was time for me to give last-minute instructions and dismiss the band for the day.

"I'll be right back!"

I left the ladies in the office alone. After switching my mind to band director mode, I forgot that I left them in the office. I was busy. It was a hectic two hours. I gave the band a longer than usual speech because it was the Friday night before homecoming. There were plenty of campus activities going on such as the Greek show and tailgating, that I didn't want the students to be distracted by. We had a 5:00am rehearsal, followed by a homecoming parade. I wanted to make sure the students understood that they shouldn't partake in any alcohol or other things that could hinder their ability to perform.

Also, Marissa and other members of the Human Jukebox Alumni Association were there to present the band with a set of new marching euphoniums. The marching baritones that we were playing on were severely outdated. The Human Jukebox Alumni Association led an initiative to replace the old set of horns with a brand-new set due to the 2014 YouTube video I posted.

I finally dismissed the band. I entertained the band alumni and many other visitors. The band hall was full of alumni band members and alumni dolls from various eras. By the time I got back into my office, I was quickly reminded that I left Sharon there. I sat down at my desk and noticed that the desk calendar had some strange writing on many dates. The comments alluded to dates or activities with Sharon. October 10th read take Sharon to the movies, and October 15th read take Sharon shopping. The comments went on to about ten other dates. I quickly tore the month of October off the calendar and realized that Sharon's graffiti was in November and December as well. I threw the calendar in the trash. I was annoyed that she would do something so childish. Sadly, I was used to her antics and wanted to get the fundraiser over so that I could finally part ways and let bygones be bygones.

It was around 8:00pm. I was hungry and I hadn't eaten the entire day. I was also getting sleepy. I called Mr. Hart, percussion instructor, over the intercom. I asked him to lock up after everyone left and that I would see him early in the morning. Shortly after, Marissa came in. We began to laugh and joke like we normally do. We must have talked for about fifteen minutes.

"Hey! You know that I am an old man. I am tired but hungry. Let's get something to eat. I can go for some buffalo wings! I just want something quick so that I can go to bed."

"Ok, I'm down! I don't have anything else to do."

Suddenly, I heard a knock at my office door. Bam. Bam! BAM! Someone was knocking and attempting to turn the locked doorknob. I sighed. I thought it was a drunk band alumni trying to tell me another story that I've probably heard a thousand times. Marissa opened the door, and I was shocked. It was Sharon. She was dressed in a floral printed outfit and a denim jacket.

"I'm going with you. I know you're partying tonight!" Sharon rolled her eyes at Marissa and gave her a hand to the face. Marissa looked at me.

"I'll meet you outside, Haymer!"

I was happy that Marissa just walked out and not laid hands on Sharon. I was also thankful that I never shared everything that transpired between Sharon and me with Marissa. I stood in the office with Sharon. I was agitated and tired.

"I'm going home, Sharon! I am tired!"

"I know that you're going out to an exclusive club tonight, and I want to go too!"

"There you go again, Sharon! I am tired! Get out! I am going home!"

"You're lying! I am not leaving unless I leave with you!"

"Sharon, GET THE FUCK OUT OF HERE. DAMN!"

I shouted because I'd had enough. Sharon walked out of the office, slamming my door so hard that I thought the walls would break! I left out of my office's back entrance and the back exit to the band building. I jumped in my truck to call Marissa. I told her to meet me at the restaurant.

"Don't be all night! I have to go to sleep and be back on campus at 4:00am."

I was pleased that we arrived at the restaurant around the same time. Actually, Marissa was there before me. I got out of my truck and she was in the parking lot.

"It's about time, my nigg! Did you haul Sharon in the bed of your truck?"

We both laughed and walked into the restaurant. The hostess quickly placed us at our table, and we immediately began to talk about Sharon.

"You better be glad that I didn't want to create more problems for you. I was about to beat that hoe down when she put her hand to my face!"

"Yes, I was so nervous because I know your temper. I also saw when you tried to slam the door in Sharon's face!"

"Yes, it was best for me to leave. I couldn't take much more of her shit with that ugly ass floral romper on!"

Marissa began to school me on what a romper was, and it was in style but not the way Sharon wore it, especially with that denim jacket. Marissa was laughing very hard! She would laugh even harder when I explained what happened after she walked out of the office.

"So, Sharon came at me talking about how she knew I was going out to some exclusive club."

I continued telling Marissa what transpired. At that moment, I've known Marissa for nine years and although she and I joked around a lot and shared many laughs, I've never heard Marissa laugh so hard! It was like her soul was leaving her body as she had to fan herself and catch her breath from laughing so hard. I continued explaining what happened after she left the office. Over the course of time, we already placed our order, the food and drinks were at the table, and we had a couple of tequila shots.

"Damn! I am good!"

"What do you mean?"

"Haymer, when you left us in the office to go talk to the band, Sharon got up and sat at your desk. She began to talk to me. She told me, 'I am trying to get Nathan to loosen up. He is always so stuck in the office, and work is his life. I want him to take me out more and do more of this and that.' Haymer, let me tell you."

I continued to listen. Marissa had my full attention because I wanted to know where Sharon was going with this. I hoped Sharon didn't say too much. I was embarrassed enough by the little I did with her. Marissa kept going.

"Haymer! You know me....I put on my sophisti-ratchet voice and told that hoe. 'That's funny because Nathan and I go out to eat all the time! In fact, Nathan has taken me to all of the exclusive spots, and we are even going somewhere exclusive tonight!'"

She laughed hard again. I sat there with my mouth wide open. Marissa continued.

"That hoe ain't have nothing to say back. I could tell that she was mad because she was writing something all over your desk!"

"Damn! That explains all the stuff I saw on my desk calendar!"

"Yep!"

Marissa screamed and laughed hard. I began to laugh too. It was funny. Marissa didn't really know the lengths Sharon would go. She didn't understand how crazy, NO, PSYCHOTIC Sharon really was.

"I was wondering why Sharon accused me of going to an exclusive club tonight!"

"I don't know where she thought she was going dressed like that!"

She kept laughing. I just sat there in disbelief. Marissa was smooth.

"You mean to tell me that you got in Sharon's head so bad that she left campus, drove 30 minutes or more to her house, hopefully took a bath, found something to wear to an 'exclusive club,' drove back 30 plus minutes to campus while driving through homecoming traffic, took another 20 to 30 minutes to find a parking spot on campus just to come to the office and get mad, slam my door on her way out to repeat the process over again while leaving campus?"

I couldn't even make it through my statement. Marissa was screaming! She was laughing so loudly that the waitress thought that we were drunk!

This day would be the last time that I saw Sharon. We still communicated through text message and email because I was no longer comfortable being around her. I don't know what I was thinking by introducing Sharon to Marissa. I should have known that Marissa was going to haze her.

Unfortunately, texting as a primary way of communication is not a good idea. The intent of a text is not interpreted! While Marissa and I were sitting in the restaurant, literally laughing our asses off, Sharon-the-rapist was getting prepared to play hardball!

Chapter 19

Homecoming was over and we were entering into the latter part of the season. I was counting down to the Bayou Classic, the last game of the season. I've been through many marching seasons however, the 2015 season was the longest season that I've ever experienced, and I was tired.

Even though I was sharing the insurmountable task of running the Southern University Department of Bands, the Human Jukebox was handling business. The band appeared to run smoothly and effortlessly. However, the staff, mainly me, was paddling frantically to propel The Human Jukebox forward.

I had no problems with the students, teaching the music and drill formations, and all the things that we are formally trained to do as band directors. My band was very disciplined! I entered various stadiums around the SWAC with my director's suit on and my shades over my eyes looking like a five-star general. I was in complete control as the band's appearance, performance, and decorum were unmatched.

However, the day-to-day operations and the measurements needed to maneuver the rough and rocky road for the band to be successful was challenging. The goal I created was a self-imposed obstruction to obtainable resources with limited time and support. The financial struggles were constricted pressure with no foreseeable relief. The politics due to my vindictive and vengeful supervisor were worsening by the day. Interactions with Sharon had my personal life seeping over to my professional life.

To make matters worse, I was digging my own grave with the private funds account. Even though I was doing right by the band with these funds, I shared the information of the account with no one. It felt wrong, but because of the circumstances I was up against, I told myself that I was doing the right thing! I had to carry this burden alone since I couldn't trust anyone, including members of my staff. Regardless of my feelings, my greatest concern for my staff was a raise, but it should have been conflict resolution and team building.

Both assistant directors were becoming very popular. I purposely set it up for them to get the attention that they deserved by having the media team include close-up shots of them conducting, among many other things. I was secure in my abilities as the director, and I didn't have to be in the front all the time. I wanted everyone to know that I had a capable and competent team. Although I didn't have the team of assistants that I initially hoped for, I was over that and overall happy with our progress.

The problem came into play when one assistant felt that the media team was giving more attention to the other. I also knew that one MBM team member played a significant role in this situation with his unsolicited accusations. To help kill the issues, I met with Garrett and simply instructed him to make sure that he covered both assistants equally. If he did a close-up shot, a drone shot, or any other shot for one, do it for the other. I also talked to Mr. Taylor and Mr. Simmons individually to assess what they felt about the media coverage, and both gentlemen seemed to be okay with everything.

Each staff member brought me some pain and pleasure to the organization. We weren't a cohesive staff and the chemistry of our team under my leadership was not as good as it could have been. I take full responsibility for not being more confrontational when I should have been.

In my attempt to not be the type of supervisor to my staff that I had, I wanted them to feel comfortable talking to me. Mr. Taylor used my kindness as an opportunity to further tear our team apart. In a private meeting with me, he shared that he had proof that Mr. Simmons had a sexual relationship with a student in the band. This was a very serious allegation. I needed evidence. I was honest with Mr. Taylor as I told him that I would have to talk to Mr. Simmons about the allegations and warn him of the severe consequences that would occur if, indeed, the rumors were true. Rumors worked both ways. As Mr. Taylor was telling me about the situation with Mr. Simmons, I now had to confront him. It had been brought to my attention that he too was involved with a student. Like with Mr. Simmons, I needed evidence.

I spoke to both men. I was prepared to remove anyone if credible information was provided to me, such as a text, a recording of a conversation, or even a student or witnesses coming forward to share with me what they've experienced. Both denied all inappropriate relationship with students. But the damage had been done. Mr. Taylor had a sense of entitlement and privilege. He always wanted more even though he was better off than I was in the same position years before. Mr. Simmons guessed at the beginning that Mr. Taylor was behind the rumors, yet I denied it. I needed Mr. Simmons to stay focused. Knowing his temper, I made him promise not to let this issue affect his working relationship with Mr. Taylor.

Far from perfection, I've become so depressed dealing with everyone's issues and all the responsibilities placed upon myself that I began to overindulge in alcohol to cope. I had a severe alcohol addiction. I would wake up and drink just to prepare for work and the day's agenda.

I remember being in the office once during night rehearsal. I felt so overwhelmed with problems from potential lawsuits, being drugged and raped, issues at work, and all other things to come. I couldn't take it anymore. I drank a whole bottle of 1792 Kentucky Bourbon Whiskey in my truck, walked into the office, and passed out.

My assistants were waiting for me to come out to take the band to the field, but I never did. I wanted to end it all! I thought I would die in that office as I remembered coughing and violently vomiting in the trash can, then my memory faded. When I woke up, I

Juked

thought I was dead. I was on the floor in a dark and strange place. As I was getting myself together, I realized that I was still in my office, and it was around 4:30am. I looked at my phone and saw texts and missed calls from my assistants. I immediately started to clean my office because I did not want the janitor to see any evidence from the night before.

Suddenly, I fell to my knees, praying for God to help me! I prayed to be removed from my position because the things that I tried to accomplish, although noble, weren't worth my life or my sanity. I've never been that low, and I promised myself that I would get the treatment I needed because no problem or situation was more important than my life.

Lorenzo Hart had his act together. While he's not perfect, I could not ask for a better all-around person. I always admired his ability to stay out of the mess while staying above the fray. It was a pleasure for me to work with him for 12 years.

Individually and collectively, we faced and endured a lot. Although we managed to mend our fragile relationship as a staff, it would never be the same again. I was so upset that I allowed evil spirits to spread through the organization like cancer. If I didn't do something fast, we would self-destruct. We portrayed the image of having it all together, but there's something about jealousy; that green-eyed monster never discriminates, for once it's on the loose, it destroys all!

Through it all, we were a strong force to be reckoned with. We were in Montgomery, Alabama, getting ready to take on the Alabama State University's Mighty Marching Hornets Marching Band. As we left our beautiful hotel heading to the stadium, the SUPD had a motorcade for us equivalent to one for the President of the United States. The SUPD had the streets cleared as they blocked traffic on every intersection in our path.

As we arrived at ASU's stadium and marched in, the Mighty Marching Hornets Band was nowhere in sight. I was familiar with this tradition. They would enter the stadium and take the field to perform their traditional pregame show. When they marched in, they did exactly that. Once they completed their pregame performance, they marched to the end zone directly in front of us to create a "tunnel formation" and wait for their football team to run through.

There is a video that begins with the Mighty Marching Hornets marching towards the end zone and halting in front of the Human Jukebox in the stands. It gives the appearance that we blew on them before they started their pregame show. That allusion is false. They completed their performance and wanted us to wait three to five minutes for their football team to run through their tunnel formation as they parked right in front of us. Well, that was a big mistake on their part because I was not having it! I told Mr. Simmons to call a tune to let them know that they just FUCKED UP! Appropriately, Mr. Simmons called "No Fuckin Wit", a popular song by the rap group Migos. The stadium exploded with energy. They had to take all of that sound right in their faces.

On the video, you can see some guy and girl signaling for me to cut the band off. I conveniently ignored their request with my shades on, acting like I didn't see them. After we stopped playing, the male kept coming back in front of the media team. He walked up into the stands as if he had a chip on his shoulders. I walked down to him to let him know that I was in charge, and I didn't even listen to what he was saying.

"Hey, man! I am just going to let you know that I see you with your headset on, so you must be someone of importance! If you think that you're going to stop us from playing tonight, then I am afraid you're going to be disappointed. I don't know you, and you don't know me, so it's nothing personal, but I rather piss you off than to piss them off!"

Apparently, Mork and Mindy with their headsets got in touch with someone who knew my supervisor, Brandon Dumas. At halftime, Brandon decided to approach me with his cronies behind him looking like The Get Along Gang!

"Hey, man! I am getting reports that you're playing out of turn. Furthermore, I heard that the band got new instruments, and I did not authorize that!"

"The instruments were paid for and donated by the Human Jukebox Alumni Association. Before we even touched the instruments, they were processed through campus inventory control and properly tagged with 'property of the state of Louisiana' sticker on each instrument."

At this point, I went from unbothered to rage. The noise level increased in the stadium, and I grew even more impatient with Brandon. Alabama State just completed their halftime performance and Mr. Simmons gave the signal to the band to play "If I Ruled the World" as the Human Jukebox was cranking on full cylinders. I could no longer hear Brandon, but I could tell that whatever he was saying in response to my previous statement wasn't good. Finally, I saw the band turn towards the crowd to blow the "crank section" of the song as the crowd went wild! I was missing a moment in history dealing with him operating beyond the scope of his duties. As he was in the middle of saying whatever he was saying, I had reached my limit, had enough of his shit, and no longer cared. I interrupted Brandon.

"Hey, listen to the crowd! They love us! I have a job to do, and you're getting in the way. It is not the place or time to have a meeting about this. I guess that registration is finally over because you've been avoiding me for two months. Do what you got to do. I'm going back to do my job! I can't interrupt you in the middle of registration, and I am in the middle of my 'registration' right now!"

I walked back to the stands leaving Brandon and his "back-ups" on the sideline of the field. I was more upset at the fact that Brandon knew that he was a coward. He only wanted to talk to me when he was in the company of other people so that he could show off. Whatever it was, I no longer cared as he was not about to consume my thoughts anymore. I tried the diplomatic approach as recommended by President-Chancellor Belton, and it was unsuccessful. I no longer had confidence in Brandon's abilities as a supervisor. The other reason I was short-tempered with him was the cronies that he had as back-ups were the same individuals who were receiving a hefty supplement from the band's account in the comptroller's office.

The following day, we left Montgomery and stopped in Mobile, Alabama, to perform at a high school battle of the bands. The local Mobile high school band director was a fellow Southernite, my classmate, and former member of the Human Jukebox. Moreso, he was the brother of Mr. Taylor.

I didn't want to be selfish. I knew that it was a good look in the community for my classmate to be responsible for the Human Jukebox performing in his hometown. I also knew that Mr. Taylor would look good coming home as a college band director. To ensure that one of Mobile's very own shined in his hometown, I told Mr. Taylor to conduct one of the best ballads that he's ever arranged as a feature during our field performance. We usually charge a fee to perform at a high school battle of the bands, but as a favor to my classmate, we performed for FREE!

On Monday, I received a threatening email from Brandon. He was still in his feelings from the events at Alabama State University. He also interjected that he wasn't aware that the band was performing in Mobile, Alabama. He wanted to know where the money from the battle of the bands was deposited then he implied, once again, that I received a kickback!

This song and dance of his was getting old and worn out! I also knew that two or more of my students would inform him of our every move, and I was already aware of who they were. Not only did we NOT receive an honorarium for being in Mobile, but

Brandon should have been aware that we were performing. If he didn't, that is his fault.

As an administrator, I was very organized and fluent in my communication. I traveled with 250 people on the road along with the SUPD. On the Tuesday before any away game, I would email a detailed itinerary with the time of departure/arrival at every stop along the way to Brandon Dumas, the Chief of the SUPD, the bus company, the various restaurants where we would dine, and any other appropriate entity. Brandon received the band's itinerary for the Alabama State University game four days before the trip. The itinerary included the high school battle of the bands on the Sunday following the game.

I forwarded Branon's threatening email to Sonja. I let her know that I was sick of his shit. She called me a couple of days later, informing me to get ready for some good news and that I should expect a call from a key SU System Board of Supervisors member.

On Thursday evening of the same week, I was summoned to what used to be the president's house on campus to meet with some important people. I was already warned by Sonja what was going to happen at this meeting. She was already upset with Brandon and warned him that he'd met his worst enemy. She never forgave him when he blatantly told her that the band was not a priority. Unlike Sonja, I had no problem with Brandon stating that the band wasn't a priority. It was the only real thing he said since he's been my supervisor. However, Sonja wasn't having it! She would make sure that from the point that Brandon made that statement to moving forward, she would hold him accountable!

As I made it to the old president's house on campus, everyone sat in the backyard at a patio table. I tried to stay focused on what was taking place, but I could hear my band outside on the practice field about a mile away, and that was where I wanted to be. Present at the meeting were five members of the SUS Board of Supervisors, President-Chancellor Belton, Brandon Dumas, and a gentleman I've never met. I would later find out that the unidentified gentleman was the new Executive Vice President-Provost and was now responsible for running the day-to-day operation of the Baton Rouge Campus.

As we began the meeting, I noticed Brandon standing off to the side with his arms folded, looking like a 12-year-old kid on punishment at recess. A board member asked me to sit down. I noticed that all the gentlemen in attendance were drinking alcoholic beverages.

"Have a drink," said a board member to me.

"No thanks!"

"What? Are you too good to drink with us? I told y'all this nigga was uppity, " interjected another board member.

They all began to laugh. I laughed along with them. I knew that they were lightly hazing me.

"No, I'm not too good to drink. I know y'all hear the band from afar. Although my body is here, my mind is with the band. I have to get back to work after this meeting."

The board members took turns grilling me about money and Brandon's accusation of me making a unilateral decision to host a battle of the bands on campus. I knew that this was not the time to defend myself against the unwarranted allegations. This was a time to shut up and listen as they took turns fussing and cussing me out. Finally, the board member who used to be the SU System President when I was a student, pulled me to the side and talked to me sensibly. He verified that they knew about the Midnight Madness Battle of the Bands contract, and the proceeds were placed in the SU System Foundation in the band's name. He also told me they were just shaking me up as a political favor to Walter and Brandon Dumas, but they realized that things had to change. He walked off as another board member approached me; this board member currently serves as District Attorney in a neighboring Louisiana Parish to East Baton Rouge Parish. I liked this board member the most because I knew that he was sincere and genuine with me.

Juked

Although he fussed about contracts, among many other things, I could tell that he had my best interest at heart. I came back to the patio table again just to listen to another board member from the central Louisiana area talk about Isaac Greggs and all of his quotes and sayings. He wanted what was best for me as well. The DA Board member spoke.

"This is the unofficial meeting before the official board meeting tomorrow. We called you to tell you that we are concerned about your ability to work with Brandon. For both of you to move forward and continue to do great things for Southern, Haymer, we will move you from Student Affairs and place you under Academic Affairs. This gentleman right here is your new supervisor!"

We shook hands and I told myself that finally, the war was over. I couldn't have been more wrong. Now that I was no longer under the Division of Student Affairs, Brandon Dumas would become even more dangerous as he no longer had to play the game with me. I didn't care. I was just happy for a new beginning.

We were getting closer to the fundraiser that Sharon-the-rapist and I scheduled together. By this time, I was over it and wanted no parts of daring Sharon. She and the fundraiser were part of the past. It was a new day with a new supervisor at the helm. Unfortunately, my new beginning was a work in progress. Even though Brandon Dumas was no longer my supervisor, I was still feeling his presence and the actions of his cronies were casting a shadow on my brighter day.

I remember being in Houston, Texas, in the latter part of the 2015 season. We played Texas Southern University the day before. I took the band to a church service on Sunday before we departed for Baton Rouge. Not only were we in attendance, but part of the band also performed a musical selection during service. We just finished a moving performance of "Total Praise," and as I began listening to the pastor preach a moving sermon, my phone kept vibrating. It was Sharon sending me threatening text messages. I responded to her text messages as if someone like law enforcement would read it because I knew Sharon's capabilities.

She responded inappropriately and threatening. I responded for the last time, letting her know I was in church and repeated my previous message. Sharon replied that she didn't give a fuck if I was in church. She continued to send more threats. Finally, I just powered my phone down. By then, I already let the enemy win as I was no longer able to stay focused on the sermon due to my anger. I was mainly angry at myself for once again allowing evil spirits into my inner circle.

Sharon eventually emailed me what she called a contract. But a contract it wasn't. It was a document stating what I was responsible for with 12 items on what she claimed was a verbal agreement. There was no place for a signature nor anything on how the profits would be split between the band and her company.

Due to previously being accused of getting kickbacks and having some members of the SU System Board of Supervisors chewing me out because of the allegations of my former supervisor, why would I agree to a shady contract and jeopardize the good relationship with my new supervisor? Furthermore, I did not have the authority to sign the contract. I had to send it to my direct supervisor and allow the contract to go through the University's bureaucratic system.

I called Eric and Jabari again with Sonja on a conference call. Without going into great detail, I explained what transpired between Sharon and me. Eric and Jabari advised me to cancel the fundraiser. On the contrary, Sonja advised me not to cancel the fundraiser. While she understood my frustrations and empathized with what I was feeling, she understood better that Sharon was a woman scorned! Had I followed the advice of Sonja, I would have been in much better shape today, but I believe that things happen for a reason.

I reported to my new supervisor that I was canceling the event. I shared with him the embarrassing personal matter that

Juked

Sharon did to me. He laughed and advised me that she sent the contract to my former supervisor, Brandon Dumas, and the General Counsel for the President-Chancellor approved it. The General Counsel for the President-Chancellor ran in the circle with Brandon, and her allegiance to him clouded her judgment as an attorney. I felt betrayed by this. I told Sharon some of my struggles with my former supervisor, and she knew that he and I did not work well together. I never talked much about Brandon to Sharon because I always suspected her of being a mole of his. I always felt that she was getting close to me to relay information to Brandon.

I often told Sharon that I thought she was a spy, and although I had no evidence, my instincts just picked it up. She would just laugh the accusations off, but my instincts were true. She did know Brandon through church, and she was reporting information to him about me.

Since Sharon went around me and had the contract approved, I told Mr. Simmons to take the pep band and a few Dancing Dolls to the event. I also made it known to my boss, Dr. M. Christopher Brown, that I wouldn't be in attendance because I could not support something that I didn't agree to and what I felt was evil! Besides, Sharon's poorly written contract guaranteed a performance by the band and dancing dolls. It did not outline a specific number, nor did it require the Director of Bands to be present.

Mr. Simmons and Eric told me that when Sharon saw the pep band, she went crazy! She began to curse and act a fool for the whole event. Eric also told me that the event was a flop! It was her job to control the marketing and ticket sales, not mine. Even if I had fully cooperated and attended with the entire Human Jukebox and Dancing Dolls, the ticket sales would have still been the same.

The event was over, and I no longer had to worry about Sharon. I no longer had to worry about her, or so I thought. Sharon-the-rapist sued me. She alleged that I refused to do the event because she wouldn't give me ten percent of the profits. Not only was that a lie, but I was also never given a projection of what the profits would be. From what I heard, the event flopped so bad that had she given me ten percent, it would've been ten percent of NOTHING!

Sharon filed a lawsuit against me in 2017, then dropped the lawsuit the same year. She sued me again in 2018 with more salacious allegations so that the media would cover it. The baseless lawsuit was all about convicting me in the court of public opinion. No matter how scandalous these lawsuits were trying to be, I knew this was what she wanted for a while. Thanks to Brandon's loose lips, I was aware of Sharon's intent to file a lawsuit since 2016. Unbeknownst to her, Brandon revealed to a source that he and his rapist-church friend were cooking up something that would stick. I guess the adage is true; misery loves company as hurt people really hurt people!

If fighting off lawsuits from an attempted rapist wasn't enough, I also had to maneuver through the aspirations of hopeful future appointed board members. In the state of Louisiana, the governor ultimately decides the board members for the state's public university systems. Uninterested and unconcerned with the matters of other university systems, the board members of the Southern University System usually contribute the maximum amount to the governor's election campaign or provide other ethical favors to get the desired seat. Although I wasn't privy to this information in 2015 when Louisiana elected a Democratic governor, I soon figured it out when demands were placed on me and the Human Jukebox.

One day on campus in early November, a gentleman approached me who I didn't know, but by analyzing how he dressed, spoke, and his overall swagger, I could tell that he was someone of importance. Although I didn't recognize him, he recognized me.

"Hey, Haymer! I need you to put the initials of the governor-elect on the field during the Bayou Classic halftime!"

He didn't ask. He told me. While I had no problems doing this, I had a flashback to Bayou Classic 2014 and the marriage proposal.

"I don't have any problems doing it. I just need to get clearance from Dr. Brown, who is now my direct supervisor."

After my comment, I noticed that the gentlemen looked at me mysteriously. I guess he finally figured out that I didn't know who he was. He introduced himself. He let me know that he was the past SU Alumni Federation national president and was currently on the SUS Foundation board. Eventually, I would learn that he was a very powerful individual with many connections in the city of Baton Rouge's local, state, and federal levels of government.

"Don't worry about your supervisor. I'll handle that. Just make sure you put the governor's initials on the field! I want all three letters."

"No problem."

We ended the conversation. I didn't know him, but after he introduced himself, my vibe was right. He was someone of importance because I heard his name many times. I was quite disturbed by his demanding approach and found it disrespectful, but I was no fool. I had enough problems on my plate and didn't want to create a new one.

Perhaps, I was just tired of powerful people using the Human Jukebox for their purposes, but when we needed something, we were on our own. I later learned that the same gentleman who approached me to put the governor's initials on the field became a SU System Board of Supervisors member and eventually worked his way up to the board chair. Although I cannot prove it, I know that the band's Bayou Classic performance was the cherry on top that got him his board seat as I already suspected that he and the governor had a good relationship.

This would not be my last run-in with that gentleman and his rude and demanding approach. Again, I ask why everyone else got ahead using the band, but all eyes were on the director for being accused of doing the same thing? I didn't know if it was people coming after me or just my imagination or my conscience talking to me due to my secret of running band camp funds through my bank account. Although there wasn't any personal gain from this, I still knew that my skeleton would fall out of the closet if I didn't fix this situation.

Chapter 20

When the SU System Board moved the Department of Bands from the Division of Student Affairs to the Division of Academic Affairs, I lost an incremental part of my staff. It seems that changing my supervisor provided a reason to have the University let go of the band's Academic Advisor.

My first year as Director of Bands, I was assigned an academic advisor/tutor for the freshman class by the Executive Director for Student Achievement and Retention (EDSAR). I was very excited as I knew that I would be very demanding of the students because of the benchmarks I set forth for myself and the organization. More importantly, the overall success of the organization depended heavily on our ability to retain students in the band program. Although I never asked for this type of support, it was exactly what I wanted and needed for my freshman students. This would teach them good study habits and how to prioritize their time. It also gave them an outlet to voice their concerns without fear of coming to me, or the fear of backlash.

In our initial meeting, the EDSAR introduced herself to me and also introduced me to the Academic Advisor, the young man who would be responsible for working with the band students. He was the band's first official Academic Advisor. Prior to his first session with the students, the Academic Advisor and I met to discuss the goals and my expectations for him with the students. Since we had a 4-and-a-half-day week, I wanted to give him one to two hours on Fridays to meet with the freshman class and provide essential information such as study habits and time management that would help them to become successful academically. I also wanted him to address whatever issues the students had individually or collectively.

During the meeting, the Academic Advisor took notes and provided some information about himself. He was a recent graduate of Alcorn State University, and a member of the Sounds of Dyn-O-mite Marching Band. We joked around a bit when he told me that he respected my work and the history between my band and his band. I was very happy and relieved to hear this information. I was happy to have someone who understands the culture of HBCU bands to work with me to ensure the success of the freshmen students. I really was happy to have him onboard.

Due to the genuine efforts of the Academic Advisor, I saw much success and improvement with the freshman classes of 2014 and 2015. Although we couldn't save everyone, he was a tremendous asset to the band program. I really wanted his position to be placed under my department as I felt that all University bands needed an academic advisor. The major item that impressed me the most, was his ability to connect with the students. He grew to be more than an academic counselor. He was a true mentor to whom students could turn to with their problems. Periodically, we would meet, and he would tell me what I needed to know about certain students while keeping other things confidential. I respected this about him as I discovered that he had all the qualities that I needed around me as a professional.

Fall of 2015 I learned that the Academic Advisor was terminated. Since I saw less and less of him, I wasn't clear when his termination occurred. When I finally realized he was gone, I sent him a text expressing that I heard what happened and how sorry I was to hear it. Furthermore, I let him know how intelligent he was, and I knew that he would land on his feet because any university would be lucky to have him. His response was something that I wasn't prepared for.

"Thanks, Mr. Haymer. The process of them letting me go started with you!"

What! I needed more clarity. I replied to his text. We agreed that I would call him in about thirty minutes. At that moment I was busy giving a quiz to one of my music education classes. I couldn't wait for the students to finish. My mind was really in a wander thinking about what the Academic Advisor could have possibly meant by the statement. Finally, the last student finished his quiz. How does one take the whole 50-minute class period to answer eight multiple-choice questions!

I walked out of the building to my truck. Thanks to my mistrust of people at Southern University, I always made personal phone calls in my vehicle while driving. I never talked longer than one to two minutes in my office on the phone if it was a personal call. I called the Academic Advisor, and went straight in.

"Hey, man! Your text got me puzzled. What did you mean about you being let go from SU started with me?"

"Well, you know that the Executive Director for Student Achievement and Retention reports to your old boss, right?"

"Yea, OK!"

"I am just going to tell you the truth! They didn't care about the academic success of your freshmen. Your old boss directed my boss to assign me to the band at the beginning of the academic year. About midway into the semester, my boss asked me to create a report while in that role. They wanted me to note how you interacted with the students. They also told me to evaluate how students felt about you and their experiences in the band program. However, they never asked for my tutoring and mentoring work with the band, nor the band students' experiences outside of the band. They wanted me to document everything related to you, in hopes that your old boss could find something negative on you. They wanted me to do that under the guise of being the band's academic advisor. Man, I don't know. It's some really messed up people on that campus in leadership. I developed a relationship with your students and really wanted to help them. Finally, I'm sharing with you the evaluations and report that I submitted. It proves that you're doing an outstanding job, and all the students I interviewed really respect you. Some thought that you were crazy but not in an insane way. They thought you were crazy in the way of respect and fear of disappointing you. Well, our bosses didn't like my positive report. After that instance, we never saw eye to eye again, so I was let go!"

I appreciated the honesty, but I couldn't even respond. I remained calm as I thanked the Academic Advisor for sharing that information with me. I also thanked him for telling me the truth and for his work with the freshman band students.

"I really hate this man! I am happy that you're getting out of this hell hole. I feel stuck!"

When we ended the conversation, I was very upset but not surprised. Not including the band students that Brandon attempted to use to report inside information, this was the second mole sent my way. The first was Sharon-the-rapist!

I knew that things would worsen before they got better as it is my belief that Brandon Dumas is a psycho-maniac! I don't understand his problem and sense of entitlement! If he couldn't control a situation, then he would do everything in his power to destroy it. Never have I vested this type of hatred for someone or something. It is a hatred that was more personal than the "little run-ins" that we had. I've never let someone consume me to this manic level of hatred. It made me question information provided to me in 2014 before I've ever met that little runt.

Our fathers were business partners. I wondered if his attitude was the product of something that stemmed from them. I still don't know. I do know that whatever fueled his obsession with my demise was not normal or natural and I was over the moon excited that he was no longer my boss.

The 2016 year was ringing in, and I was ready for new beginnings. With a new supervisor, I had high hopes that change was on the brink. The staff and I prepared for another concert season and parade season, yet there was another rough registration process in session. Although I didn't have the scholarship financial deficit like the year before or preparation for a big performance, I did have some politics to maneuver through.

Mr. Pugh, the Vice-Chancellor for Finance and Administration, was in his second semester on the job. Previously an employee from the Shreveport campus, he came in with President-Chancellor Belton. Mr. Pugh was a middle-of-the-road type of guy. You never knew where he stood politically, but he was always fair and honest with me during our short interactions. One day in early January, I got a call that Mr. Pugh wanted to meet with me. Not knowing what he could possibly want, I went to his office to meet with him immediately.

"Good morning Mr. Haymer! The President wants the band to perform in Shreveport's Martin Luther King, Jr. Day Parade. What will it take to get the band there?"

I knew that the parade was less than two weeks away. I didn't particularly like performing for events without proper notice. I usually schedule all parades in the months of November and December. I didn't want to go to Shreveport, but I couldn't tell President-Chancellor Belton and Mr. Pugh no, so I knew that I had to make my face appear as if I was very interested.

"I would love to go. It's the least that we could do to support Dr. Belton. I've meant to schedule a meeting with him concerning one of my assistant's salary anyway!"

"OK! What's wrong?"

"Well, I am going on two years of paying his salary and fringe benefits out of the band camp revenue, and I don't think it's my responsibility to cover an employee's salary. It's the University's."

"Well, I can assure you that Dr. Belton didn't know about this because I didn't know. I oversee all accounts on the Baton Rouge Campus. We will investigate this and get back to you!"

"Thank you. I'll wait to hear back from you concerning that matter. In the meantime, I'll send you a bus quote by tomorrow for our travel to and from Shreveport. We will also require a meal after the parade."

"I will be waiting for the quote, and don't worry about the meal. The cafeteria on the Shreveport campus will feed you before and after the parade."

I kept my word and emailed the bus quote to Mr. Pugh the next day as promised.

"Dr. Belton would not require the band to go to Shreveport this year because of the cost, but you should prepare for next year (spring 2017) because he is going to make sure that he has the cost covered in the budget. We are also working on scheduling you a meeting date later this semester to speak to Dr. Belton, Dr. Brown (Executive Vice President and Provost and my direct supervisor), and Mr. McClinton (Vice President of Finance and Administration). I'll keep you posted, Mr. Haymer."

I literally laughed out loud from his response; He had no idea that it costs so much to move the band from point A to point B back to point A.

"Yes, sir! Now you see and feel the pain that I feel every weekend when we have an away game!"

Although I didn't want to perform for the parade, I knew that I had to if the president-chancellor mandated it. I also knew that if I had to then I might as well get something that we need. I've learned never to waste a good opportunity when you have the attention of the people who can do something for you. To all current and aspiring band directors, please remember when you have the attention of your administration, never waste the opportunity consumed with only what they want. It is a partnership, meaning it is a give and take. Give them what they want while you tell them what you need! The news of the meeting with senior-level administrators was what I needed to hear to get me excited and I immediately began to prepare my paperwork and slide presentation for the meeting.

Although it was decided not to support the MLK parade in Shreveport, I wanted to start on the good foot with my new supervisor, Dr. Brown. I scheduled regular meetings with him to create a trust and open dialogue where we could feel comfortable talking to each other about any issues. I've learned nothing but negative things about what not to do with my past supervisor's relationship or lack thereof. I just wanted a positive change and a positive vibe with my new supervisor. It was an unusual first couple of months as I had to get used to his leadership style.

I would often come to the meetings with a printed agenda of items that I wanted to discuss. I always gave him a copy. I would begin the meeting just to be interrupted by his talking about current events in the news constantly. Dr. Brown would often have his office TV on CNN or channels that highlighted pop culture. He was very in tune with current events.

At first, I found it very annoying. Then I picked up on what he was teaching me indirectly. Dr. Brown was teaching me to slow down and breathe. We developed a good relationship, and I was finally happy to get the support that I needed. Eventually, I started opening the meetings with current events such as The Presidential Campaign of 2016 season, which was just getting started, Hillary Clinton being the next President of the United States to things happening on the shows on the Bravo and BET networks. These were good conversation starters then we would go through my agenda within a matter of ten to fifteen minutes.

Under the leadership of Dr. Brown, most of the goals I set for myself, and the organization would turn from a dream to reality. His leadership and knowledge with a twist of comedy was genius. While I had a few allies who warned me that he would be worse than my previous supervisor, I learned to go in any situation with an open mind. My supporters meant well, but they were wrong! Dr. Brown was the band's best friend. As my backup, Sonja made sure to tell him everything that I couldn't or wouldn't be due to the political tightrope that I had to walk. Dr. Brown and Sonja had their differences at times, but they worked well together overall. This positive relationship brought about a positive change with the Human Jukebox. However, Brandon Dumas was not done yet. Although he was quiet for an extended period in the spring semester of 2016, I knew that he was cooking up something to come take another swing at me.

In April of 2016, I received the opportunity to meet with the highest-level administrators in the Southern University System. The meeting included Dr. Belton, the President-Chancellor; Flandus McClinton, the Vice President for Finance and Business Affairs; Dr. Brown, the Executive Vice President-Provost; A SU System Board of Supervisors member from Natchitoches, LA was present via conference call; and me.

Even though Sonja wasn't a part of the actual meeting, she was my secret weapon. Several weeks before the meeting, Sonja and I created a game plan of what we wanted to achieve. I wanted everything such as increased funding for scholarships, new instruments, new uniforms, and funding for increasing salaries. Together, we strategized scholarship and salary comparisons to other schools in the Southwestern Athletic Conference (SWAC). We also had facts about the outdated instruments and uniforms. Hell, I wanted it all, including the kitchen sink!

Since Sonja wasn't going to be in the meeting, she made sure that I had someone to watch my back. The board member from Natchitoches attending the meeting would serve as an ally. Sonja informed him on everything I needed. He was going to say everything that I couldn't say. He was in, all the way in!

I entered the meeting prepared with a plan but ready to discuss any and everything while being distracted in the process. As the meeting began, Dr. Belton thanked everyone for attending and told me that the band was a priority to him. After he was through with the formalities, I began with the show. I started with an accurate

PowerPoint slide that compared all the scholarship packages of the top five bands in the SWAC. Alcorn State University was among the top, and that was because of Dr. Brown, who was their former president. He was happy that I included his work in the presentation as he also verified that my chart was accurate because he just worked on the same problem about two years prior at Alcorn. After I finished a very compelling argument of why we needed more resources, McClinton made the most bizarre comment that I've ever heard from an "expert" in the area of finance.

"Mr. Haymer, I am looking at a printout of the last ten years of the band's financial report from the SU System Foundation. It shows that the band has over 1 million dollars!"

"The SU System Foundation is a support arm of the University. All monies deposited in the band's name usually come from events, fundraisers, and donations that the band either performed for or earned through partnerships/sponsorships. These funds do not let the University off the hook for their fiduciary obligations to an academic program. Furthermore, if I made 100 thousand dollars a year for ten years, it adds up to 1 million dollars, but it doesn't mean that I would have that amount in ten years! What I am simply saying is if I told you your yearly salary, do you really have that much leftover in a year? You have taxes, mortgage, car notes, revolving bills, living expenses, etc.! Finally, when you printed out the credits, they added up to the magic number of 1 million dollars, but you failed to print out another stack of sheets that shows the debits from the said account!"

I was upset with his statement for many reasons, but I remained calm. When I finished talking, McClinton looked at Dr. Belton as he began to stutter. Dr. Brown started to interject, but I couldn't hear anything due to the board member shouting over the conference call speaker.

"See, this is the shit that I am talking about! Y'all playing games. Either you shit or get off the pot!"

The board member spoke and then he continued with more comments. I lost focus because the meeting was out of control! Dr. Brown tried to gain control, but the board member kept going,

"I'm talking here, Mr. Provost, so you need to shut the hell up too."

He continued to ramble on. I was in the highest-ranking official's office in the SU System, and it was a "ghetto mess" there. As Dr. Belton managed to gain control of the meeting, we ended up solving absolutely nothing! I must say that I've attended over one thousand meetings throughout my career. Some were productive while others were a waste of time. Some of the meetings ended with good results, while others ended very badly. NEVER HAVE I EVER been to a meeting that was so ghetto, out of control, and resulted in one hour wasted of my life that I will never get back! The financial meeting was a disaster. We never attempted to meet again or resolve any of the critical issues that I identified.

In July 2016, the Southern University Alumni Federation (SUAF) hosted the national alumni conference in Chicago. Ms. L. Thomas, the First Vice President of the Southern University Alumni Federation and I were good friends. I would often bounce ideas off her. She worked in corporate America, and I found her advice to be very professional. Often, Ms. Thomas and I would collaborate on navigating the politics that I was up against that seemed to be non-stop! We thought it would be good to use the same slides from the "disastrous financial meeting" in April and adapt them with a little less detail for the alumni conference as I was charged with giving a state of the Human Jukebox address.

At the convention in Chicago, I noticed that most of the members were there for a party and vacation. They were not interested in most of the items placed on the agenda on any given day. On the day I presented, I saw a few administrators walking around very uninterested. I even heard a member scream a comment.

"Come on, Haymer! We don't want to hear about the lack of whatever. We want good news only!"

Every time that I tried to warn a board member, an administrator, and alumni about the plight of our beloved Human Jukebox, it fell on deaf ears! I was doing my job trying to get all University stakeholders involved, but nothing seemed to work.

The Southernites only wanted to party in Chicago while only hearing good news. I learned that they weren't interested in the truth. Although I've grown to harbor much resentment due to the negative experiences and demands placed on the band without the care to support, I decided not to give up on my mission of taking a band that achieved just about everything to the next level. Although I wouldn't give up, I decided to find another way as the board, administration, and Southern University Alumni Federation wasn't the answer. While I wouldn't find the answer in Chicago, I knew that working with my supervisor and Sonja would be the best course of action. Meanwhile, when in Rome, do as the Romans! This simply meant that I took my work hat off and joined the party in Chicago with everyone else. It truly was a party without a purpose!

Chapter 21

August 2015, I was introduced to the Queen City Battle of the Bands (BOTB) in Charlotte, North Carolina when a friend of mine attended the event. Described as the perfect marriage between the field and stand performance, he thought I should take a look on behalf of the Human Jukebox. After much research of the event, my initial thoughts of only being a Mid-Eastern Athletic Conference style band event was put to bed. Instead, I realized that the Queen City battle would be a golden opportunity for the Human Jukebox since we had never, ever performed in North Carolina. I knew that the North Carolina natives probably heard of us or saw us on YouTube. I also knew it would be a "life-changing" experience if they saw us live!

Dr. Miguel Bonds at that time was the Director of Bands at Talladega College and he gave the event's promoters my contact information as they were eager to secure the Human Jukebox for the 2016 Queen City BOTB. After talking to them and getting the projected date, I was immediately concerned that it would be difficult for us to prepare because the university's band camp is always exactly two weeks before the first day of class.

The Human Jukebox had a routine or ritual on preparing the band for the first game. The first week was just to get the freshman to get acclimated with our marching style and traditions. The second week we put the freshman and upperclassmen together and worked on getting everyone in shape. Finally, we had the next two weeks of class with practice in the evenings.

The Queen City BOTB was scheduled the weekend before the first game. This date would require us to perform a week earlier than we normally are accustomed to. Thus, participation would require us to start band camp a week earlier than usual.

Juked

As much as I wanted to participate, the schedule was an obstacle. Not the date per se, but the bigger issue was the dilemma the date created. Our band camp has a cost associated with when and how long the kids show up to how long they stay. The highest cost is the food through campus dining I was not willing to lengthen the camp an extra week due to the financial burden it would place on the students and their families. I told TJs that it wouldn't be possible for us to come because of this, and they were not trying to hear that! TJs told me to send them an invoice for the cost of one week of camp, and they would foot the bill! I wasted no time contacting campus dining and housing to email TJs an invoice. As promised, they took care of the approximately $16,000 bill. Thanks to TJs, I was now able to bring the students in a week earlier. Now we were obligated to attend the event and I thanked TJs for believing in us and assured them that we would not disappoint as the band staff, and I began to plan a very complex and entertaining performance.

As we entered our final week of band camp, I was very confident that we would have an outstanding showing for our first performance of the season. We just finished two stringent weeks of conditioning and learning fundamentals as I was just beginning to introduce to the band the drill and formations planned for the Queen City BOTB. As we began another week of practice, I knew that this was the final week before classes started and the most critical. I had just enough time to introduce the drill when band practice was interrupted.

Over the weekend, I remember being at home resting in my recliner and watching the news. I always paid attention to the weather. I pay the weather the most attention in August and September, as it is the height of hurricane season. The seven-day weather forecast was clear for the week minus a few afternoon showers.

It rained nonstop four days in the city of Baton Rouge! What appeared to be a normal shower on the weather radar was a rainstorm that parked over the city and poured continuously. Within 24 hours, schools and businesses shut down. It felt like it was a hurricane due to the panic-shopping for food and supplies, but it was just a rainstorm.

Around the second day I began to see news reports about flooding in the streets and residential areas. Kedric Taylor told me that some water was coming into his home. Not thinking much of the situation, I went to a hardware store and bought some cleaning supplies, a wet vac, and a pressure washer to give Kedric Taylor for his home.

The following day, I had nothing to do. The funny thing is that I often complained about wanting to be home because I was always at work. After being home for two days in a row, I became bored and couldn't sit still, so I went to the mall. I guess I just had an altered state of reality because while parts of the city were flooding, I was at the mall shopping. I bought a pair of dress shoes from one of the department stores and came back home. I was aware of what was going on, but there was no flooding in my immediate area. I walked into my home, placed the new shoes I had just purchased on the top of my chest of drawers, and decided to use the rest of the unplanned free time to arrange the feature tune for our Queen City performance.

I arranged the introduction of "These Three Words" by Stevie Wonder and decided to finish the rest on the next day. I saved the song to my hard drive and emailed it to myself to finish at work. I woke up the following day and noticed the water outside my front door was rising in my yard. The water at my mailbox had risen to 1/4 of its height. In denial about what was happening, I went back to sleep. Approximately two hours later, my normally peaceful neighborhood sent me into alarm when I awoke to the sounds of screaming. I looked out of the door and saw my neighbors being carried away in boats. That's when I finally realized that my house was in the path of a flood!

I had to have been in shock. My first reaction was to immediately log in to my social media and go live! After going live for about two minutes, I grabbed a few clothes that I could get to quickly, threw them in my truck, locked up, and left my house. As I drove away, I just knew that would be the last time I would see my house in its pristine shape.

Driving through my subdivision was the scariest ten-minutes of my life! I just knew my truck engine would kill due to it being flooded! The floodwaters covered more than 50-percent of my pickup truck. With my pickup sitting a little higher than the average pickup truck, the water was up to where the window and door connected. Thankfully, I didn't have a car or else I would have had to swim out of the neighborhood or be rescued by boat.

The journey from the main road to the highway involved prayer, prayer, and more prayer. The main road was a two-lane road with deep ditches on both sides. Unfortunately, the water was so high that I could not tell where the road ended and where the ditches began. To make matters worse, it was in a really wooded area and there were a lot of curves in the narrow two-lane road. I had to use the street signs on both sides of the road along with the trees to guide me as I was traveling through at 10 mph.

God instantly answered my prayers. I made it out alive, my truck didn't stall, and I didn't misjudge or overcorrect and find myself in a deep ditch. Even the highway was clear during my travels. I went to visit my twin brother and his wife as they were unaware of what just happened. Within the hour, all the roads and the highways I traveled were all underwater and impossible to drive on.

The area that I resided in was the outskirts of the city. It was located between two rivers and the rivers flooded over. After spending time with my brother and his family, I checked into a hotel. I honestly thought I would be back home the next day. Sadly, I wouldn't be allowed back into my neighborhood for five days.

The conditions inside of my home shook me to my core! Everything that I owned was ruined by 6 feet of water. Ironically the only pair of shoes that didn't get destroyed was the new pair I purchased a few days before. I didn't know what to do or how to feel.

A nonprofit organization completely gutted my house out. I had to pick up the pieces and figure out how to start over with nothing. Eight years prior to the flood when I purchased my home, my homeowner's insurance told me that I didn't need flood insurance because I didn't live in a flood zone! Suddenly, I had to pay a mortgage for an uninhabitable home and resort to living in a hotel from August to December fifteen. Once I could no longer afford to pay a mortgage and hotel fees, I moved back home and lived out of my garage while sleeping on an air mattress. I became depressed. In an effort to self-medicate, I made friends with my old friend, alcohol abuse.

Due to the flood, I wasn't sure if we would make the Queen City BOTB performance. The aftereffects of the flood left me devastated. My only ray of sunshine was the unfinished arrangement I emailed to myself. I had no inspiration to start over but hearing the introduction to my arrangement brought tears to my eyes as I listened to it over and over to draw inspiration to finish what I started.

I was so emotional. I just lost my home and the reality of homelessness seeped in. Even though my world was just turned upside down, I was surrounded by love and things that mattered. The realization of my life broke me. I broke. I cried and I cried for hours. Finally, when I stopped crying, the arrangement was complete.

Thanks to the flood I could not focus on the Queen City BOTB. The flood forced me to depend heavily on my staff to get prepared as I dealt with the gutting out of my home. As I navigated through the high demand of contractors, Brian Simmons and Kedric Taylor really came together and gave me many ideas to incorporate into the show. The performance's beginning was Kedric Taylor's idea and the performance's epic ending was Brian Simmons's idea. I knew with my staff collaborating that we would put on a show representative of the Human Jukebox's brand, but what I didn't foresee was the performance being legendary!

What made the show legendary? Could it have been the fact that the band really bought into what we were teaching? Or how about the fact that people came from near and far to North Carolina to personally experience a chance to see that everything that they've heard about us was true! It is possible that through the challenges we faced to get there, we still managed to have the perfect show that represented the best of the Human Jukebox! Although all those are factors, I truly think it was the natural disaster that made it legendary. The flood forced the staff to become cohesive. Although we worked together all the time, this was the first time I can honestly say that everyone was in it for selfless reasons! Everyone put ego aside and finally worked together. That is the key difference from being good to not great, but legendary!

TJs made a gamble investing in us by paying for a week of band camp to bring us to the Queen City BOTB. They took the risk of losing their investment due to the flood. Ultimately, they received a hefty return on their investment and to thank TJs and the audience for their generosity, we did an impromptu encore and went back on the field just to play a few more selections for the audience. As a staff, we did NOT receive an honorarium for this performance. However, the performance was good for the Human Jukebox's brand; it brought the staff together; and this moment was the healing to my soul as it lifted me out of my depression.

If our first performance was an indicator of how the season would progress, fall 2016 would be one for the records. Unfortunately, the negativity at Southern was waiting as soon as we made it back home. Technically, the flooding of my home wounded me before the season started. However, I hoped and prayed for a change from the past because I didn't have the strength to survive the dramatics that I've come to expect year after year. At the first home game of the season, I knew that my prayer wasn't going to be answered.

Even though it was the first game of the season, it was a typical home game. We were in the stands playing our standard "spirit songs" coupled with the latest in Hip Hop and R&B. The football team just scored a touchdown, and the band was jamming. Everyone felt good because we were winning the game. As I gave the cue for the band to end the song, a gentleman approached me on my left side. Although a party atmosphere due to the team winning, I considered it odd that security would allow someone to walk up to the band directors while we were working.

As the gentleman got closer, I noticed that he was the same guy that approached me a year prior about putting the governor-elect's initials on the field during our 2015 Bayou Classic performance.

"Mr. Haymer!"

I looked at the gentleman.

"Just look straight ahead and act like I am telling you some good news, and don't frown! Brandon Dumas has told me and a few others that you are using the band by placing them in performances, like the North Carolina performance and pocketing the money. Again, don't react. I am just letting you know to keep your nose clean!"

As he walked away, I stood there in disbelief. Not because of what he said, but how he approached me. No scenario would allow me to walk up to him and do the same. As an attorney and member of the SU Board of Supervisors, his professionalism should have reign over his attempt to be messy and catty. Why was he approaching me on my job with something that should have been said in the privacy of an office? This conversation was a "loaded" accusation.

Based on the rude and disrespectful matter of the newly appointed board member, I knew that it would be a matter of time before Brandon Dumas took another cheap shot at me. Since the gentleman's approach, I was left to operate in crazy-brained mode or in layman's terms: I had to allow the consistent switching of both sides of my brain's hemispheres so I could continually be able to process the foolery or politics along with the magic or creativity to keep the Human Jukebox at the top of its game. The atmosphere was festive, but my mood was ruined for the remainder of the game. No one, not even my staff, understood why I flipped in a matter of seconds.

The fall 2015 Midnight Madness BOTB held on Southern University's campus was quite successful. Our market, comprised of band heads and HBCU band supporters, began to demand more of the same in 2016. We had given the consumer a better product and they no longer allowed us to give them the status quo. Although the performance in North Carolina was legendary, it wasn't enough. Band battles during the fifth quarter at football games were no longer cutting it as well. The audience wanted the format of the Midnight Madness BOTB, and I knew that we had to improve on this model.

As a student of the band culture who became a leader, I wanted to keep pushing forward. Doing so would not only elevate our brand as the Human Jukebox but elevate the relevancy of HBCU bands in the social media age! I had to silence the nay-sayers even within my own campus such as the SU assistant athletic director.

More times than not, the SU assistant athletic director would treat the band as a tag-along or a freeloader. Many times, he would insinuate that athletics gives the band its platform. While I agree that performing for football games is a platform, a large percentage of the audience was there for the band. Since I am a man of action, I wanted to prove that we didn't need their platform because we had our own, which was bigger and way more diverse! Enter the newly, formatted Midnight Madness that became the Crankfest BOTB.

The politics at SU during the Midnight Madness was unbelievable. Therefore, I asked TJ to consider moving the event to a city that was band head friendly coupled with being a tourist hotspot. Those simple requirements pushed the event to New Orleans, the home turf and backyard of the Human Jukebox! With the self-marketing abilities that we already had in place with the use of the media team's innovative strategies along with the natural talent for the students of the Human Jukebox, I knew we would strike gold and prove that an event that was band-centered could be just as big if not bigger than an HBCU football game.

With a new venue and TJ changing the name to Crankfest to build his own brand, everything was in place except the act. To ensure the event's success, it would be only natural to have the best two bands in the HBCU band world to kick off the inaugural Crankfest BOTB! The Human Jukebox was on board, but we needed to secure the Sonic Boom of Jackson State University. Because of my failed attempt to get them the previous year, I made the decision to stay out of the negotiations.

I also had to deal with the animosity and division within my team when it came to this event. Once again, the MBM team tried to stop me from working with TJ. They accused me of getting kickbacks as the reason for working with TJ. Due to the dealings of two moles from Brandon, I've come to learn to expect any and everything while trusting no one! The more resistance the MBM team gave, the more I grew suspicious of Jabari working with Brandon Dumas to get dirt on me. In addition to Jabari, I've become suspicious of Kedric Taylor as well.

Staying out of the negotiations was a good decision. The Sonic Boom finally signed the contract and agreed to the performance. At the time, O'Neill Sandford, The Director of the Sonic Boom was an older, very seasoned gentleman who happened to be a 1965 graduate of Southern University. He also owned a home in the city of Baton Rouge. One evening he called asking to meet with me to discuss a few things concerning Crankfest. I knew that I would have to see his band twice that year, so I agreed to

Juked

meet with him on a Monday evening approximately two weeks before the big event at a restaurant.

"Mr. Sanford! Nice to see you," I said as we shook hands.

"Stop with the formalities; call me O'Neill!"

Mr. Sanford is about thirty-five years older than me. It felt weird to call him O'Neill, but I did as he asked so that things wouldn't become awkward. I passed him the menu.

"O'Neill, I've been waiting for you before I ordered. I already know what I want to eat, but what do you want to drink?"

O'Neill looked over the menu and ordered a scotch on the rocks double. I ordered the same thing. I ordered the red snapper, and O'Neill followed suit.

"I really see your growth as a professional. I was a bit concerned the last couple of years, but you really are maturing! Yeah, man, I agreed to perform in the Crankfest Battle of the Bands because my staff really wanted to do it. I've been there and done that, so these types of things really don't do much for me!"

I continually sipped my scotch while listening to O'Neill talk. I figured out early that O'Neill's biggest fan was O'Neill, and I wasn't going to get in the way of his number one fan. I just nodded my head up and down as an indication that I was listening while waiting for the right time to interject. As O'Neill refreshed his drink, I knew that he was really going to start talking now!

"You know, man, I am not a fan of the word 'Crankfest!' It implies that all we do is blow! "We should start off by playing a march to show the audience that we do more than just crank. JSU will go first, and y'all can follow with a march!"

I was no fool; I wasn't going to agree with his statement. If the Sonic Boom wanted to play a march, then that's their prerogative. I only have two rules when it comes to a battle or what I called war:

Rule # 1. There are no rules.
Rule # 2. Refer to rule one.

Well, O'Neill, you start off with your march, and we'll follow suit with something appropriate."

"I am glad that we agree, young man!"

I laughed to myself because O'Neill thought that I was young and dumb! Why would I tell him my plans? The beauty of a head to head matchup is that it is a chess match. He came to the bar ready to play checkers while I was playing chess! I was careful with my words because I knew that O'Neill would accuse me of lying or playing dirty after the battle was over. He and I ate and drank at the bar for about an hour. It was good just to relax and be Nathan because the next time I saw him, it was definitely Haymer-Time!

My best friend, Josephine, went to Jackson State University and played in the Sonic Boom. She was excited when I shared the news of the Sonic Boom agreeing to battle us in a head-to-head matchup. She was so excited that she flew down from Michigan to see it live and in living color. Josephine and I really didn't talk about the band that much outside of the drama. I would trash-talk with her sometimes, but our friendship was beyond that! Also, Josephine was not a fan of O'Neill Sandford. I let her know that the Human Jukebox would have the edge in the first round of the battle, based on my conversation with Mr. Sanford. She just laughed and said, "Welp! We will just have to see!"

It was finally Crankfest Battle of the Band Sunday! This stadium was full and at least thirty-five percent of the audience were high school band students trying to decide which band they wanted to participate in after graduation. Both bands marched in the stadium, with the Sonic Boom going first coming through the gate with their traditional stadium entrance to <u>Get Ready</u>. The city of New Orleans was happy to see them! We marched in shortly after the Sonic Boom, looking like soldiers ready to go to war! No laughing, no smiling, no nothin'! The crowd was on their feet cheering us on as I walked in waving and more confident than ever that the Human Jukebox would defend its home turf!

After the MC announced both bands and told the audience how the battle would proceed, the Sonic Boom played first. As promised, they started with a march. I was licking my chops like a lion getting ready to take down his prey! I was going to start with the 1... 2 ... punch and have Brian Simmons go in for the kill! I called <u>Lift Every Voice and Sing Fanfare</u>. It filled the stadium with the traditional Human Jukebox sound. Then Brian Simmons called <u>Tourist</u> by DJ Khaled. The first note made the stadium shake as the crowd went wild! The band gave the crowd energy as the crowd gave the band energy in return! The Sonic Boom were caught off guard because they were expecting a march! The look on O'Neill Sandford's face was priceless as he learned on that day not to underestimate and dismiss me as a young buck!

The battle would continue for a little over an hour. It was a true clash of the titans. While my opinion would be biased to who won between the bands, I will say that the true winner was HBCU bands. The Crankfest Battle of the Bands put everyone on notice that the HBCU band culture is more relevant than ever before. I tagged the assistant athletic director on social media to see the crowd size and our platform for himself! I also had a point to prove to O'Neill Sandford. I never responded to comments made by O'Neill Sandford in 2014 when I first became Director of Bands. I remember him saying, "You don't know what you're doing, but you'll learn after a few ass-kickings!"

I did receive a small honorarium, about $2,500, for the Crankfest battle. I split the money three ways between Brian Simmons, Kedric Taylor, and Lorenzo Hart. I didn't reserve any for myself as I planned to go after the "big bucks," meaning raises for the entire staff!

The inaugural Crankfest BOTB was so successful that TJ wanted to immediately host another Crankfest event in Houston, Texas, closer to the end of the season. I met with TJ to discuss the possibility of setting up a battle of the bands on the campus of Texas Southern University to take on the Ocean of Soul.

Texas was a major recruiting ground for the Human Jukebox. Due to their recent success and renovation to their campus, the Prairie View A&M University Marching Storm Marching Band was dipping into our recruits. Since we traveled 45 minutes outside of Houston for a football game to Prairie View's campus on Saturday, we could stay overnight in Houston, go to church as a band Sunday morning, then battle the Ocean of Soul Sunday afternoon. It was an excellent opportunity to take on both Texas SWAC schools in one weekend to strengthen our recruitment efforts!

Church service in Houston was becoming a tradition. The pastor of the megachurch we attended was an alumnus of Southern University and a fan of the Human Jukebox. The pastor would advise and counsel me through my personal and professional problems. He also knew about the MBM team's deceptive practices.

When we visited the church in 2015, the pastor presented the band with a $7,500 donation from the church. Upon our return to Baton Rouge, I received an invoice from the MBM team for $1,500. They were charging the band their 20 percent of the total fee for setting the church arrangement up. The pastor indicated that he talked to Jabari because he thought that he was assisting me with logistics. His invitation to attend service was not a marketing and brand management venture. The pastor gave me another donation for the band in the privacy of his study before service as he wanted 100 percent of the check to go to the Human Jukebox.

I shared with the pastor the many frustrations I had with my staff, the MBM team, and just the overall drama associated with being the Director of Bands at Southern University. He listened and began to pray. I felt the prayer. I was very appreciative, but I was also grateful for the pastor's genuine concern about me as a person.

Church service was also very moving as the pastor preached a powerful sermon, and I felt that it was tailor-made for me. I listened to his every word uninterrupted or distracted unlike the previous year. After service, the church fed us a nice meal. We had a great time praising the Lord through song, sermon, and fellowship. Now it was time for business as we loaded the buses to depart for TSU and take their campus over.

I was on social media the entire week along with my students marketing and promoting the Crankfest the Baton Rouge, Texas edition. That's right, Baton Rouge, Texas! I told the people that we were going to beat the Ocean of Soul so badly that they would rename the city of Houston, Baton Rouge! Although it was only a joke, it really got the fans and high school recruits excited about the event.

Since the inaugural Crankfest event was posted to YouTube, The Ocean of Soul was able to review the event and comprise a general idea of what to expect. Unlike the first Crankfest, I couldn't trick The Ocean of Soul into playing a march. That was fine by me! I was just happy to be on their campus to show the Houston community that the Ocean of Soul was a poor dog that couldn't bark or bite an intruder and its own backyard!

The event was packed and took place in the basketball arena on TSU's campus. We were the visitors, so we marched in first. The Ocean of Soul followed. Again, I won't insert my opinion on which band won. The band staff seemed to really enjoy it, and as long as they were having fun, I was good. Plus, it was another win for the HBCU band culture as we were not only re-energizing it, but we were also ensuring its longevity. We managed to excite the young and impressionable minds who attended the battle as well as those that watched on social media. This time we received an honorarium after the event, including myself.

Chapter 22

2017 was starting off in the worst possible way. I was still depressed due to living in my garage. I had managed to turn my garage into my very own hotel room. I mounted a television to the wall. I had a portable air conditioner/heater to combat the Louisiana Winter/Summer. I hung my clothes to a rack I mounted to the wall. For my dietary needs, I had a mini refrigerator with a microwave on top. I could no longer cook, and I never missed cooking so much in my life. I was left to either have takeout or frozen food heated in the microwave. The aftereffects of the flood caused me to completely gut the house. I did hire a contractor who managed to install a temporary sink along with a tub and toilet in my guest bathroom before disappearing.

Putting my personal life aside, business was definitely business as usual! Mr. Pugh, Vice Chancellor for Finance and Administration, called me one day.

"Mr. Haymer, I didn't forget about our conversation from a year ago. Please submit an invoice for the bus travel to me. The President has prepared a budget for the band to travel for Shreveport's Martin Luther King, Jr. Day Parade."

Somehow, I knew that Dr. Belton (President-Chancellor) wouldn't forget a conversation from a year ago. Going to his hometown was going to make him look good. But how could he remember something from a year ago, yet never mentioned anything about the finance meeting from 8 months ago!

Of course, we were going to do the parade. No matter what, I couldn't tell the president NO. However, I also needed something to take me away from my depressing garage life. I saw it as a positive situation.

At the end of the fall 2016 semester, I told myself that the next semester would be a transformational one so in 2017 I rebranded myself. I was a different type of person. I learned to stop worrying about things that I couldn't control! I also told myself that it was time to lose the dead weight around me. The MBM team didn't have to find a new client, but they had to leave the Human Jukebox. To ensure the possibility of not renewing their contract, I made plans to call up the General Counsel to the SU System Foundation. Also, I decided to give the staff more responsibilities to focus on organizational goals and recruitment.

As I moved through the process of becoming a transformational leader, we started the semester under my leadership in marching band mode. The Human Jukebox paraded around campus getting the faculty, staff, and students excited. I even continued with my Friday parade stops in front of the campus administration building as an indication to communicate, "don't forget about us because we are coming for the new instruments, greater scholarship packages, increased budget, new uniforms, and larger salaries!" I meant business, and I wasn't taking no for an answer. We practiced for an entire week before our first official performance for the semester, the Shreveport Martin Luther King, Jr. Day Parade.

Shreveport is in the state's northwest corner and is close to the Texas/Louisiana border. When we arrived on the campus of Southern University at Shreveport, we were welcomed by campus dining. As promised, they had a hot meal ready for the students before the parade and would have a sandwich type of meal afterward. I requested a portable meal after the parade because I didn't want to delay our time getting back to Baton Rouge. After all, the students had class the following day.

The Human Jukebox put on an excellent performance for the city of Shreveport. We marched through the main thoroughfares of the downtown area. The most enjoyable portion about the parade was the fact that the organizers provided an opportunity for us to give a short concert for all the high school bands that participated in the parade. North Louisiana, or Grambling Country, was a good venue to let them see and hear the Human Jukebox in action. I also used this performance to recruit for our ever-growing high school band and dance team camp. I know that we were overcrowded in the past, but I didn't care because I never thought it was such a thing as over recruiting. I must say that the event in Shreveport was better than expected as the community was thrilled to see the Human Jukebox, and I assured them that we would be back in January of 2018!

In the period between the Shreveport MLK parade and the start of our 2017 Mardi Gras parades, I received some disturbing news. My twin brother, an attorney in the city of Baton Rouge, called me.

"Nathan, who is Trapezoid Media?"

I had to jog my memory for a couple of seconds, I remembered it was the name of Sharon's company. Now, I had to relive the night Sharon became Sharon-the-rapist. However, I didn't tell my family everything that happened.

"Oh, it's a company run by some lady who did an unsuccessful fundraiser with the band. Why?"

"Well, why in the hell is she suing you? Well, not you personally, she is suing the SU Board of Supervisors, Dr. Belton, the Executive Vice President-Provost, and you! The lawsuit is very vague, but you need to be aware. I am sure that someone in campus administration will call you in about it!"

I took a deep sigh because the year was just starting, but my never-ending venture with drama remained consistent.

"Well, I'll wait for them to call me then. This has Brandon Dumas' name written all over it. I never signed the contract. As a matter of fact, I refused to sign the contract because it was poorly written, but that cow, Sharon, went around me and got to Brandon. He sent Sharon to me as a spy anyway! Brandon got the general counsel in the Office of Dr. Belton, another cow, to sign off on the contract!"

Juked

"I don't know what you mean by all of that, but you need to be on the lookout. In the meantime, I will be checking to see where this goes. Lawsuits are public information, and I just so happened to be checking for something else when your name popped up."

I told my brother to keep me posted and ended the conversation. I reflected back to a conversation with Jabari telling me that Brandon Dumas told him that Sharon was going to sue me. Although I don't put much stock into what Jabari normally gossips about, I believed him when he gave me that message.

As an employee of Southern University, Sharon couldn't sue me personally. She had to start the lawsuit with the SU Board of Supervisors and move down the chain of command to my position. Plus, a lawsuit caused by me, even though it wasn't my fault, would make me look unfavorable in the eyes of the members of the board of supervisors. Fortunately, my brother called me within six weeks to let me know that the lawsuit was retracted.

Before deciding not to agree to sign the contract with Sharon and forwarding to my supervisor, Sonja advised against doing that. Due to me not being completely honest about what transpired between Sharon and I, she didn't fully understand the gravity and toxicity of the situation. Often, I shared how she was right. I've learned the hard way that I did not want to get in any more legal trouble or political battles, and in order to do that, I was going to have to seek her advice on renewing the contract of the band's Marketing and Brand Management team. I told her my plans.

"I don't know, Haymer! Listen to me on this. You don't want to allow your personal opinion to influence your decisions on this matter!"

"I can understand where you are coming from. The fact that I never liked Jabari, but still gave him a chance to succeed should let you know my decision not to renew the contract isn't personal. If it were personal, he would have never got a chance in the first place because I never liked that snake!"

"Haymer, I hear you, but I think you are making a premature move by getting rid of them now!"

"If I had listened to you in 2015, I wouldn't have been in the mess that I am in now with Sharon. Even though wanting those backstabbers gone was personal, the MBM team still hasn't fulfilled their professional obligations. They are taking credit for everything positive achieved under my leadership while blaming me for all of the negative. They advised against the Midnight Madness and both Crankfests BOTBs, while still trying to attach themselves to the success of the events. They trash-talked and made personal comments about the director of the media team while attempting to take credit for his innovative strategies that changed the game. They talked about Brian Simmons and caused a divide between him and Kedric Taylor. They even talked about me! As I sit here and attempt to make a sound business decision, I have 10 percent assets to 90 percent liabilities that they brought to the organization!

"You may have a valid point, but you still are moving too fast, Haymer! I understand your frustrations, but your frustrations are exactly what got you in trouble with Sharon. Can't you see that you are repeating the same mistake?"

"OK, this is what I am going to do. It is March 2017, and I will give them another year. By March of 2018, I will evaluate the benchmarks, and if they still are doing the same thing, I must let them go. I also want to prove that although I don't like them, my decision is not personal. Finally, I don't want to have another 'I told you so moment' if I didn't listen to you this time!"

Sonja laughed. We continued laughing and joking about other topics. I never took my relationship with Sonja for granted. She is a second mom to me and a beast in the entertainment industry. If she could stand up to those monsters in the entertainment industry as a black woman, then I knew that I'd better listen to her advice because she's really been there and done that!

Chapter 23

Sonja started a group page on social media initially entitled *The Human Jukebox 5th Quarter* Fan *Club*. The page was designed to educate and inform Southernites near and far about the needs of the SU Band. To call Sonja Norwood an influential alumnae is an understatement. Not only did she have first-hand knowledge of my struggles with Brandon and all of the day-to-day problems I had in developing a relationship with him, but she also had first-hand knowledge of the band's operating budget, scholarship budget, and other issues.

When the social media page grew to become very popular, Sonja dropped the name "Human Jukebox" from the title, and the page became known as *The 5th Quarter Fan Club*. The page's popularity gave it the ability to get the attention of the "who's who" among Southernites. While she had insider information about the band, she began to learn of more problems that plagued the University due to her numerous sources in high places in various departments around campus.

The expansion of the original mission was just one reason for changing the name of the page, the other reason was to protect me. Sonja didn't want lurking administrators and their cronies associating her words and actions with me. I appreciated that, but it was too little too late. Everyone knew her love and passion for the Human Jukebox is what triggered her to get involved in other campus matters. The topics covered on the page were controversial as they were real issues in various divisions, colleges, and departments.

The official newspaper of Southern University is *The Southern Digest,* which reports the news that administrators wanted the public to know. The unofficial digital newspaper of Southern University was *The 5th Quarter Fan Club*, which revealed the news that the public needed to know! The 5th Quarter was powerful and had everyone talking. One day, I had to call Sonja to relay the scene I witnessed at the foundation office when I went to make a deposit.

No one at the front desk greeted me, which wasn't unusual because they were swamped in the foundation office. On the front desk was a bell that you pressed, and usually, someone would be there within a matter of seconds. I must have pressed the bell three or four times. Finally, two employees came out. One of the employees spoke as she gave me a form to fill out for the deposit. As I filled out the deposit form, they started talking to each other.

"Girl, I need some popcorn. I am reading *The 5th Quarter*, and I can't believe my eyes!"

"Girl! I heard about that page. I don't know who be giving her that information, but she is telling the truth!"

They must have figured out that I was eavesdropping as they started whispering more "hot tea" and laughed at each other. The employees in the foundation office had me laughing so hard at their reactions from *The 5th Quarter* Fan *Club*.

Sonja laughed at the story, but she let me know that they hadn't seen nothing yet. She had uncovered another scandal. The newly unfolding scandal was about the homecoming concert contract and the shady business of Brandon Dumas with a promoter. She had a copy of the contract and receipts of who received what amount.

Although I've read *The 5th Quarter* for entertainment purposes only, I had no parts in the content and comments. Unfortunately, the administrators thought otherwise. They sent a friendly face to see if I was involved in any way, shape, or form in giving information to Sonja.

Dr. Belton's Chief of Staff at the time was a woman who I was familiar with. I remember meeting her 20 years prior as an incoming freshman. My father needed help in getting an out-of-state fee waiver for my twin brother and me. We ended up in the office of a young lady who was very helpful and gave us the assistance we needed. Well, fast-forward twenty years later, that very young lady was now the Chief of Staff to Dr. Belton. She and I were always cordial. I was very interested in meeting with her because I knew that she would listen to my concerns about the band. The First Vice President of the Southern University Alumni Federation, Ms. L. Thomas, set the meeting up for me with the Chief of Staff. Ms. Thomas was in the beginning stages of partnering with me to replace the band's uniforms and began to have other concerns as well, so I was grateful that she got the attention of the Chief of Staff on my behalf.

I met with the Chief of Staff for about thirty minutes at a restaurant off campus. During that time, I went through all of the band's issues. I thanked her for her time and thanked her for being a listening ear. The Chief of Staff's response was something that shook me as she quickly flipped the script!

"So, what do you know about this 5th quarter page?"

Suddenly, I realized that although she was meeting with me to hear my concerns, she had to bring some intel back to the people she reported to.

"I don't know much about the page as it relates to the sources that provide inside information. I've skimmed through it a couple of times. As you already know, based on the information I told you today, I have enough problems with my department than to worry about others!"

"Some people believe that you are talking to Sonja Norwood regularly, and you are her source of information on the inner workings of campus matters."

"The problem with people at Southern University is that they are secretive, which gives the appearance that they are hiding something. To answer your question, yes, I talk to Sonja Norwood regularly concerning the issues I just covered with you in this meeting. To insinuate that I would know anything about a homecoming concert contract, speech pathology, or any other problems that she addresses on her page is crazy to me. I can't even figure out how to get new uniforms, so how can I figure out how to get information on campus that's 'top-secret?' Let me also add that when Sonja calls me, I pick up the phone and talk to her. Why? Because I'd rather be on her good side than her bad side. When she calls all of you, y'all ignore the call. If you want favorable coverage on her platform, start picking up the phone!"

We ended the meeting on a positive note. Although the meeting accomplished nothing in terms of the band's agenda, it eliminated me as a prime suspect in the "5th Quarter Club-Gate Scandal."

Keeping to my word of speaking to Sonja regularly, I called her as soon as I left the meeting. She laughed at the news that I shared with her. The meeting was comical to Sonja. The accusation of being her source of information was funny but the punchline to the joke was knowing that she had the administration shaking in their boots not knowing what to expect on any given day as more and more alumni began to depend on *The 5th Quarter Fan Club* as their number one campus news source.

While lurking on *The 5th Quarter Fan Club*, I learned that Brandon Dumas was a finalist in the presidential search for Paine College. I'd never heard of the school, and through a quick Google search I found out that Paine College is a small private HBCU located in Augusta, Georgia. Even though I didn't care for him, I still was happy for him. Plus, I wanted him to leave and get the executive experience he needed to reach whatever goals and aspirations that he had for himself. I also knew that if Paine College hired Brandon, it would be less "pain" for me as his many swings and misses at me were becoming quite tiring and repetitive. Several people made comments on *The 5th Quarter Fan Club* stating that they contacted Paine College in an attempt to derail Brandon's presidential bid. While I despise him, I still thought it was wrong to attempt to block someone because of not liking them. Unfortunately, he did not get the job at Paine College. I do not know what factor *The 5th Quarter Fan Club* or its active members played in the officials at Paine College's decision. I just know that it was very wrong for the *5th Quarter Fan Club* members to participate in Brandon Dumas' demise.

Even though Sonja's social media page was bringing several issues to light at Southern, my department was still having financial problems. I struggled with the administration to expand the budget. I used high school band and dance camp money to cover a debt the university should cover. Truly, I had exhausted every possibility to update resources within my department, or so I had thought. I had one more option known as The Human Jukebox Fee.

Since 2012, the Southern University Human Jukebox's survival was due to a student referendum listed as The Human Jukebox Fee. The fee was $10 per student with the breakdown being $5 per semester. As a result of the fee, the band received an annual travel budget of approximately $60,000. My answer to the problems that plagued the band was through an increase of the fee from $10 per year to $100 per year by student vote. I found myself leaning on Ms. Cousby, the Assistant to the Assistant Vice-Chancellor of Student Affairs (AVCSA), in this endeavor. I met Ms. Cousby in the student union during my second year as Director of Bands while preparing for the band banquet.

"So, you're Nathan Haymer! I've heard a lot about you!"

"Yes, I am the one and only Nathan B. Haymer, and I don't know what you've heard, but don't believe it!"

"I am Tanisha. Cousby, the new Assistant to the AVCSA, and I've heard of you through my many conversations with Gramblinites. I am also a graduate of THEE GRAMBLING STATE UNIVERSITY!"

"Oh, hell nawl! Who in the hell left the gate open and let this intruder in the house!?"

While our first encounter included a few jabs, we built a friendship and friendly professional relationship. Ms. Cousby began to schedule the band banquet a year in advance because I would often forget to do it on time. She would also assist me in administrative policies and procedures with the high school band and dance team camp and advise me on matters with staff relations. She was a godsend, and I could feel her genuine spirit through her help and assistance. She was efficient and effective. It was natural for me to go to her once again to seek advice on my strategy to get more student support for the Human Jukebox.

"Ms. Cousby, you know that I am tired of complaining about the problems that plague the band. I want to propose to the Student Government Association an increase in supporting us by placing $100 per student on the ballot for the Human Jukebox Fee. What are your thoughts?"

Ms. Cousby's eyes grew larger from the shock of the amount that I requested, but I knew she would be honest in her opinion.

"Are you crazy? I think that you have a good idea, but $100 per student is way too much! I don't think that amount would even be approved by the Senate for the Student Government Association (SGA) to place on the ballot for the students to vote."

"What do you mean?"

I looked at Ms. Cousby confused. I didn't understand the procedures of the SGA. Ms. Cousby began to explain the functions of the SGA to me. Ms. Cousby ended our conversation telling me to request a meeting with the SGA Vice-President to be placed on the agenda to make my proposal of $30 per student to the SGA's Senate. Yes, Ms. Cousby TOLD me that $30 per student was a more realistic number. For the sake of not arguing, I agreed with her as she had no clue that I wasn't going to budge from my stance of the band receiving $100 per student.

I met with the SGA Vice President. She agreed to place me on the agenda for the next SGA Senate meeting scheduled for the following week. She also gave me some pointers on what to present and told me to be prepared to answer any questions that the members of the Senate may have.

Ms. Cousby also informed that once approved by the Senate and passed the general student body vote, funds could be used for raises! When Ms. Cousby told me this, I wanted to jump through the roof. She and I sat down to put a plan of action on paper. Out of respect for her, I confessed that I was going for gold by asking for the $100 per student. She shook her head. She told me that she didn't think it would pass the Senate even to be considered for a vote. I trusted her judgment.

"It's not that I think that the Senate would agree to $100 per student. If I ask for $100, I think they will meet me halfway and pass $50 at best and $30 at worst. Either way, it is worth the shot!"

Ms. Cousby laughed and continued to shake her head. She told me that my strategy, although crazy, may work. That was all the confirmation that I needed to move forward with my strategy.

It was now the next week and time for me to approach the Senate. I had my PowerPoint slides ready as a visual. I made a comparative analysis with other universities that we compete against. I didn't need any notes. I've lived the data that I presented. I knew the troubling effects that data had on the program, but I effectively communicated it through the passion in my voice. I boldly went in, asked for $100, and answered a few questions after my presentation. After my time was up, I thanked the Vice President and the Senate for their time and consideration. Then, I went back to my office and awaited the verdict.

After thirty minutes or so, Ms. Cousby and the SGA VP came to my office. The VP started the conversation.

"I apologize, Mr. Haymer, but the Senate thought that $100 was too much to ask the students to pay. But they agreed, and I think that it's fair, to allow $60 per student to be placed on the ballot for the general student body to consider. Now it is up to you to put your campaign together and sell to the students for the vote to pass."

"YES! YES! YES!! Thank you! Thank you! Thank you!"

I knew that if I asked for more than I wanted, I would get what I needed. Running a campaign was second nature. My students and I were the kings and queens of marketing. There was no doubt in my mind now that the referendum's fate was in our hands, that the vote would pass the general student body.

The following day I called a marching band meeting. During the meeting, I explained to the band members what was at stake: the new instruments, more funding for scholarships, and a bigger travel budget. I told the band that by next fall, we would have the holy trinity (new instruments, uniforms, and more funding for scholarships) if they did their jobs by voting and making sure to bring two people with them to vote "Yes" for the Human Jukebox referendum.

"Don't worry about explaining to the general student body what the 'yes' vote means for the Human Jukebox. Just make sure they vote 'yes!' It is my job and the job of the media team to put together a mass promotion campaign to explain why they should vote yes!"

As usual with everything that I attempted, there was opposition. A group of students, encouraged by Brandon Dumas, began to speak out. They started calling the referendum a tax increase and worked to make sure that the referendum didn't pass. Fortunately, they were no match for the Human Jukebox. Grateful for our massive, already established social media presence, we were a well-oiled machine. We promoted the referendum's passing so well that students who attended other HBCUs wanted to vote "Yes!"

It was election day, and I was assured as ever that the referendum would pass. I put out one final mass text to the band to make sure they voted and brought two friends to the polls. Finally, I got the message that the referendum passed by 88 percent of the students voting "Yes!" I was so excited about the news that I told the media director to immediately put out a Thank You on the band's social media platforms. I went to my personal page.

I want to thank the students of Southern University for passing the referendum to increase the funding for our beloved Human Jukebox. Because of your vote, we can now equip the band with new instruments while giving our deserving students a better scholarship package. The students of Southern University took on a responsibility that they weren't obligated to do in order to teach our administration how to take responsibility for the University's greatest ambassador. The students also taught the administrators that our beloved Human Jukebox isn't to be taken for granted!

My post got me in more hot water with the administrators, but I didn't care. After three years of begging and pleading, you're damn right that I was going to spike the ball in the end zone after finally scoring a touchdown! I was called into the Office of Dr. Belton along with his General Counsel, The Chief of Staff, and my supervisor, the Executive Vice President-Provost (Dr. Brown).

After being congratulated on getting the referendum passed, the administrators scolded me for making the post on social media. Dr. Belton threatened to have his General Counsel come up with a social media policy for employees of the University. I agreed as I told Dr. Belton that his proposal of a social media policy for faculty, staff, and administrators was a good idea. As predicted, Dr. Belton was "blowing hot air" because no such social media policy ever came to pass.

My plans for the referendum were to utilize the funds for raises. However, Dr. Belton had to sign off on all raises. For salaries that were $60,000 and above, it also required the approval of the SU System Board of Supervisors. I was confident as ever that I wouldn't have a problem with the support of the increase since the university technically wasn't funding it. In other words, the base salary listed above would still come out of the University's general funds account, while the increase would come from the referendum.

My direct supervisor, Dr. Brown, agreed to accompany my staff and me on a trip to Indiana to the Conn-Selmer Headquarters. It was time to make the rubber meet the road. I wasted no time in setting up our visit to purchase over 1 million dollars in new band instruments. I've made plans to overhaul all of the marching band, concert band, percussion ensemble, and all other ensembles with brand new instruments. To be inclusive, I had the whole staff give their input so that we would all have a stake in planning the future of the Human Jukebox and every other ensemble in the department.

We had a few weeks before we went to Indiana. In the meantime, I was in the process of putting the band's budget together for the next fiscal year. By using the projected number of students for the 2017-18 academic year, I was able to determine how much we could afford to spend on scholarships and salaries. I already placed in the budget $150,000 per year for the next five years to pay for the instruments as Conn-Selmer awarded us a $350,000 grant! This was huge as it knocked a significant amount of the price down. We were getting 1.1 million dollars' worth of instruments for $750,000.

I submitted the projected raises to Mr. Pugh, Vice Chancellor for Finance and Administration, and received some pushback. Flandus McClinton (System Vice President for Finance and Administration) didn't want to approve the raises stating that it was too much! I told Mr. Pugh that the administration wasn't funding the raises.

"It's just not right! I've been told No for three years! Now that I went out and found the funding, Flandus McClinton still wants to say No! Well, it's not his damn money, and I am tired of the games that he plays!"

"Brother Haymer, calm down. I am on your side here. I have a feeling that one of your haters is behind this. They don't want you to make more money. I'm only giving you an update. Let me work on this. I'll get back to you as soon as possible!", Mr. Pugh stated.

Juked

While I expected backlash from Brandon Dumas, I did not expect backlash from a member of my own staff. I guess I should have anticipated it, considering how good of a backstabber he has been. Kedric Taylor reached out to a trusted staff member from the LLI All-Star band.

"Hey man! I congratulated Kedric Taylor on y'all getting the referendum passed. He told me that he couldn't trust you. You're promoting him to Associate Director of Bands with a $25,000 raise and something must be wrong!"

"I am so sick of that catty ass bitch! He's never satisfied, and I'm giving this dude a promotion to be second in line to the directorship plus a $25,000 increase! He thinks that I am messing over him! Well, if that's considered messing over, then someone should have messed over me years ago!"

He laughed, and we ended the conversation. I knew it was only a matter of time before I had to confront Kedric Taylor because I was quickly growing sick of his shit! Later, Brian Simmons told me that Kedric Taylor was upset with the raises, mainly my raise.

"Haymer, I just talked to Kedric Taylor, and he told me, 'Haymer can't justify giving me $70,000 and you $65,000 while he will be making $120,000! That ain't fair!' I told Kedric Taylor…"

I quickly interrupted Brian Simmons because I didn't want to hear any more.

"I had a meeting with the entire staff and told all of you that everyone's salary was based on a comparative analysis of the top paid HBCU band directors and assistants. I didn't pull the numbers out of my ass! I actually did the research, and if he doesn't like it, then he can keep his salary at $45,000!"

I couldn't believe Kedric Taylor was complaining like that. Well, on the other hand, I could believe it! I appeased him year after year, and now he felt entitled. I found ways to pay his salary because the university wouldn't cover it. His salary was funded through the high school band and dance team camp revenue, and he was still ungrateful. I went back to my first month as interim director when I didn't want to hire Kedric Taylor as he resigned from his position as a high school band director. Instead of breaking the bad news to him that we didn't have the funds, I found a way to bring Kedric Taylor on board. I went back to the times I paid him and the rest of the staff honorarium after honorarium. Now that I am trying to give him a $25,000 raise with a promotion, he was crying because of his jealousy of what my pay was set to!? Jesus! Take the wheel because I am about to kick Kedric Taylor out of the car!

Mr. Pugh called me to come to his office. By this time, I was used to him being the bearer of bad news. President Belton and Vice-President McClinton advised him on how the salary increases would proceed.

"The Vice-President called all of the schools that you listed in your salary comparative analysis, and a few of the numbers weren't accurate, but most were. The highest-paid band director was at $115,000, and you requested $120,000."

"The highest-paid is at $120,000. I assure you, but who cares? I have the best band, and I think that my job performance exceeds my salary request!"

I could tell that the tone of my voice made Mr. Pugh a little uncomfortable, but I wanted all of them to be uncomfortable. I was negotiating with idiots! Why are they idiots? Because Dr. Belton salary was $452,000 a year, and his pay exceeds his poor job performance by $452,000! As I sat there upset, Mr. Pugh continued.

"The VP wants …"

I interrupted Mr. Pugh because I've grown tired of Flandus McClinton! I knew that he and Brandon Dumas were behind this. They wanted to make the top salaries while not doing a damn thing. Still, the band staff who work 7 to 8 hours overtime every day in the fall, work weekends and holidays, and the fact that I had to compromise with people who do absolutely nothing but say "No!"

was very insulting. I sternly communicated this to Mr. Pugh. I wanted to tell them all to go to hell! I was sick and tired of being sick and tired of SU!

"Mr. Haymer, hear me out, please! Your Percussion Instructor and Administrative Assistant are fine at $50,000/year. Dr. Belton can sign off on that immediately. Everyone else would need board approval and the politics are tough. For the salaries to get board approval, Dr. Belton wants you to make the following adjustments: The assistant you requested $65,000 will adjust to $60,000. The assistant that you requested $70,000 will adjust to $65,000. I also saw that you are changing his title to Associate Director of Bands. You will need to submit the title change along with the new job description to Human Resources. Your salary at $120,000 will adjust to $110,000. One more thing, Dr. Belton also wants you to agree that you and your staff would no longer receive the annual Bayou Classic Bonus."

Mr. Pugh looked at me with caution because he had grown to expect anything to come out of my mouth. I paused to take in everything that he shared with me. I was tired of negotiating and fighting; well, at least for the semester because I was coming back to them about slaving us at the Bayou Classic Battle of the Bands by not giving us OUR profits. I knew that it wasn't the time at that moment because we made a lot of progress.

"Mr. Vice-Chancellor, although I think that Flandus McClinton is a 'Scrooge,' tell Dr. Belton that I will agree to his terms!"

"Thank you, Brother Haymer! I am glad that you see the big picture. Make sure you attend the SU System Board of Supervisors meeting at the end of the month. I know you want to be there to see the salaries get approved!"

I told Mr. Pugh I would be there bright and early. Little did I know, the board meeting would be everything but ordinary as a scandal would overshadow everything else on the board's agenda.

It was time to get on the road again to recruit for the Human Jukebox. By the spring of 2017, there really wasn't a necessity to travel through various states as we did in the past. Due to our efforts since 2014, the Human Jukebox brand has dominated the scene in the band world. That's right, the band world, not just HBCU bands, but all bands! I guess that I've been too caught up in the band's problems and my personal problems that I never took the time to count our blessings, successes, and the lives that we were touching.

We have accomplished much through our social media initiatives. Our *Jukebox-Cares* initiative gives back to the community. I made the wish of a young man with cerebral palsy come true as he desired to be the drum major for a day. I went to his high school in New Orleans and surprised him by making him an honorary SU Drum Major. Then, I invited the young man to the school during one of our parade rehearsals, where we marched around campus as he led the band. My staff and I started a tradition with the *Jukebox Christmas-Wish*. It is an initiative giving deserving children in the Baton Rouge area a Christmas gift from the Human Jukebox. The Human Jukebox staff visited their homes to surprise them while delivering their gifts that I paid for personally.

The Human Jukebox brand was really taking off. The fact that the referendum passed, I felt accomplished. I served my purpose, which was curing all the problems that plagued the band. The First Vice President of the Southern University Alumni Federation, Ms. Thomas, was working very hard on our behalf with the *Adopt-A-Juke* initiative; a fundraiser to secure new band uniforms, which was the last piece of the puzzle. If she successfully pulled off the *Adopt-A-Juke* campaign, the future of the SU Band would be bright. In the meantime, I developed a strategy to ensure that we would replace the new uniforms five years down the road and new instruments in ten years without ever having to organize or fundraise again.

Juked

    The budget I created displayed transformational leadership in action. It is the answer to the question that I asked myself on day one; *How do we take a band that achieved just about everything to the next level?* The answer is in the budget, which cured all of the problems that plagued the Human Jukebox since I took the helm. It also allowed me to achieve every benchmark I set for myself in year one, except for the 10-year plan to build a new band hall. I had a plan for that as well through our corporate sponsors/partners. We were now at the point that I described as Next-Level! We managed to take the band from operating in the red to having over a million dollars surplus throughout our various accounts. For every **NO** that I received; for every **That's too much**, for every **We will get back to you**, for every **Look at the big picture**, for every **Good Cop and Bad Cop routine**, and for every **Headache, heartache, and pain**, I finally knew that all of my efforts were not in vain!

    Although I was celebrating, Kedric Taylor and Brian Simmons weren't. I don't think they totally understood the gravity of the situation. Their *What have you done for me lately?* attitude was because of my leadership style. In addition to such things as honorariums and reserved parking spots, I shielded them from most of the problems and issues that I faced daily. Of course, they were thrilled by their proposed raises. Who wouldn't be? Still, they were also unaware of the tough negotiations I had to go through to get to the promised land. Kedric Taylor only saw that I was making more than him, and Brian Simmons only saw that Kedric Taylor would have a higher ranking than him. The only staff members who were truly content as they understood the fight due to their wisdom and experience were Ms. Byrd, Administrative Assistant and Lorenzo Hart, Percussion Instructor.

    While money was the answer to the problems that plagued the Human Jukebox, money would also be the wedge that further divided the staff. For the love of money is the root of all evil and more evil began to lurk at the front door due to my salary increase and my sense of high-end fashion. Of course, I did not help the problem due to my unorthodox practice of hiding band camp funds to pay the bands and Dancing Dolls bills and expenses. Every year, this was eating at my conscience because I was often accused of making money off band performances. While the accusations weren't totally true, as we did receive honorariums, I knew it would only be a matter of time before the cat was out of the bag on what I was doing with the submission of false invoices and running band camp funds through my account. Even though I had good reasons for doing so, I knew that no justification would matter once the public found out this information. Now that I had a bigger spotlight on me, I had to figure out how to close Pandora's box or Pandora's box would close me!

Chapter 24

It was recruitment time, and we were on the road. Although I call it recruiting, technically, we were auditioning students for the band. Due to the success of the high school band and dance team camp and Crankfest, the interest in a Human Jukebox and Dancing Dolls was at an all-time peak. We had a long line of students already interested in the Human Jukebox.

Partnering with the various chapters of the Southern University Alumni Federation made our auditions even more successful. The individual chapters would set up a one-stop-shop for us. Weeks in advance, they would inform their local band directors and students of the audition place and time in their respective cities.

Our road trip occurred the week of SU's Spring Break. We traveled through seven states that consisted of Louisiana, Texas. Arkansas, Tennessee, Alabama, Mississippi, and Georgia. I'm not too fond of regular staff meetings, so besides a great bonding experience the road trips would ultimately result in a meeting as well. Often, we would bounce ideas back and forth, plan for the fall marching band season, make suggestions for improvements, and relax and laugh at each other's jokes. I really came to enjoy our recruiting trips.

The ugly side of the trip always allowed me to see Kedric Taylor for who I knew he was. Usually, I would do most of the driving because I just enjoyed being behind the wheel. After one stop, I was tired, and Lorenzo Hart took over driving while I went to the back seat of the SUV with Kedric Taylor on the other side. I woke up from a quick nap and saw Kedric Taylor on his phone texting in plain view. Whoever he was texting, their conversation was about me.

Kedric Taylor was sloppy when it came to the way he communicated and talked about everyone on staff. I would always get screenshots from his so-called friends, but this time was different. I'll never forget the time I saw it with my own eyes. We were on the way to Atlanta from Jackson, MS. It was around 6:30pm and the sun was setting when I fell asleep. I woke up around 8:30pm. It was completely dark, so the light from Kedric Taylor's phone illuminated the entire rear area of the vehicle. As soon as I opened my eyes, I could clearly read his phone due to the angle in which he was sitting. The text message was nonsense. He texted about me messing over him by not paying him enough money. I noticed the text was a group message, so he was communicating and lying to his fan club.

I always knew that Kedric Taylor talked about me. Now, I can attest that I've seen it with my own eyes. I would never confront a grown man about what he texts to others about me. Why should I? I was sitting right next to the coward, so if he felt a certain type of way, he should be able to talk to me. To let Kedric Taylor know, *hey, I am up, and I can clearly read your phone,* I coughed and spoke to Lorenzo Hart.

"Hey! Are we out of Jackson yet?"

As soon as I made that statement, Kedric Taylor jumped from being caught off-guard and locked his phone. Brian Simmons was sitting in the front passenger seat and responded.

"I will drive if you want me to!"

"HELL NO," everyone responded.

Brian Simmons' driving was the exact opposite of Lorenzo Hart's. He would blast the music while using the speed limit as an indication for speed minimum! My driving, although not as bad, wasn't much better. Ironically, Kedric Taylor never drove.

We stopped at various schools in many states. We had a very successful recruiting trip on the road. Not long after, we were set to fly to Indiana to visit the Conn-Selmer Headquarters. We had a

Juked

general consensus of the instruments necessary for the band, but we thought it would be nice to tour the Conn-Selmer Headquarters for historical reasons and expand our way of thinking about band instruments of the future.

 I was also excited that my supervisor, Dr. Brown, agreed to travel with us. In addition to Dr. Brown, I asked Eric from the MBM team to join us as well. In the past, Eric worked at the leading music store in Baton Rouge. He was familiar with band instruments. He also understood the language regarding inventory, the ordering process, the MSRP versus the deal's actual price, and the terminology band instrument manufacturers used. We flew out of Baton Rouge airport, which was very convenient. Close to the SU campus, it is a small regional airport that didn't have long lines to go through and hassles of the TSA.

 Shortly after we were in the air, we ran into a problem. I have flown many times and never had to make an emergency landing, so I was alarmed. Leaving Baton Rouge, there were only a few places where you could go for a connecting flight, and we were on our way to Atlanta, and from the amount of time we were in the air, I knew that we were somewhere close.

 "Due to severe weather, we have to make an emergency landing! We will make our emergency landing in Montgomery, AL."

 As I predicted, our forty-minute flight had us very close to Atlanta. From Atlanta, we were about two hours away by road which meant we were about 20 to 25 minutes away by air. Once landing in Montgomery, we had to deplane and wait in the small airport until further notice. This unexpected series of events would allow me the opportunity to get to know my supervisor a little better. He was funny and quite entertaining. I don't know who caused me to laugh the hardest, Dr. Brown or Brian Simmons; they often exchanged jokes with each other. Because I was entertained with my traveling company, it allowed our two-hour wait to go by faster which seemed more like 20 minutes. The weather was still bad, but it cleared up enough to fly to the Atlanta airport, where we could still make the connecting flight to Indiana.

We finally arrived at Hartsfield-Jackson Atlanta International Airport, the busiest airport in the USA. If you're not familiar with Atlanta's airport, there are many restaurants and other entertaining things to do. We decided to eat at a restaurant and talk some more as we waited for our delayed flight. The delay would eventually turn into canceled as the weather continued to deteriorate. After spending about 9 hours in the airport, we realized that we had nowhere to go. Dr. Brown called one of his friends, a pastor in the Atlanta area, and we were invited to spend the night at his house. This would give us time to either reschedule our visit to Conn-Selmer or just go back home.

I was hesitant about going to a stranger's house. It didn't matter if he was a pastor or not, I had my concerns. However, traveling with five other people helped me realize that this was the best option. I'll admit it! I was concerned that a stranger letting six individuals into his home would be a negative experience. I don't like being cramped up in tight spaces or sleeping on the floor. I would've preferred a hotel. I knew that now wasn't the time to be a maestro. I began to let go and not worry about the things that I couldn't control.

We took an Uber to a very exclusive area of the city. When we arrived at the Pastor's house, it wasn't a house at all; it was a mansion! All my concerns were for nothing as he had room for us plus a whole army. His basement area alone was bigger than my house! After we settled in, we ate a nice meal and continued to talk and fellowship. Although we didn't make it to Indiana, we had a much-needed bonding experience among the staff, and I got a chance to see and understand that my supervisor was the real deal!

On the following day, I made a two-plan scenario. Plan A was for us to fly back to Baton Rouge. Due to all the flight cancellations the day before, it wasn't easy getting a flight back home for six people immediately. I did not want to overstay our welcome at the

Juked

pastor's house. Plan B was to rent an SUV and drive home. Luckily, we could fly back home the same day while Dr. Brown took a flight to his hometown in another state. We never made it to the Conn-Selmer Headquarters, but I was able to call them and let them know the one thing that I required for the new sousaphones. I wanted the name *Human Jukebox* engraved on the horn's bell with the band's logo, the signature "S" with the music note in the middle of the sousaphone's bell. The Conn-Selmer representative told me that it was easy to do, and the rest was history! The Human Jukebox was finally moving on up like George and Weezy!

A great recruiting trip! An amazing bonding trip! Instruments the band needed at a wonderful price! All good things but I was waiting for the other shoe to fall. My life had become this horrible reality show where I had come to expect something to go wrong after a series of good things. Like a great show cue drama entrance stage right!

The setting of our episode is the planning for the upcoming high school band and dance camp. This should have been a breeze. Registration and payment issues had been updated from the old system. We had record-breaking numbers the past two years, and I expected the same for this camp. Now, entering drama stage right in the human form of the Director of Residential Life/Housing (DRLH) and her assistant. I'd had enough of them, and they were just as upset with me.

Due to the 2016 high school band and dance team camp's housing crisis, I wanted to make sure that it was a clear understanding and a clear line of communication. We were in the middle of a dispute. The DRLH wanted to charge the band approximately $40,000 for the use of the dorms. She wanted me to be responsible for paying the cleanup fees and overtime pay for the staff to clean the rooms after the students left band camp. I couldn't get over the dirty dorm that was full of pests before the students even moved in for the camp of 2016.

It was time for Dr. Belton to do what the board member told him to do during the finance meeting in 2016. It was time for Dr. Belton to "shit or get off the pot!" as his inability to decide on the matter caused the problem to escalate.

Dr. Belton and Mr. Pugh both agreed that I should pay the cleanup cost but only in addition to any other applicable fees such as overtime pay. The DRLH wanted $15 per day per student, which resulted in a bill of up to $40,000. I was already paying $60,000 for food and $60,000 for Kedric Taylor's salary. To pay $40,000 more is not only insane, but it would also put the camp in the red. Literally, it would cost more to operate the camp than the revenue it generated.

The DRLH and her staff were bold in their approach because Brandon Dumas backed them up. Since Dr. Belton and Mr. Pugh already told me that I only had to pay cleanup fees, I assumed that they were backing up my stance on the issue. It was now time for me to see if Dr. Belton was really in charge or if he was Elmo the puppet!

A meeting was scheduled in April of 2017 to bring forth a resolution. The meeting would have Brandon Dumas; Mr. Pugh on behalf of Dr. Belton; Marcus Coleman, the Dean of Students; the DRLH and her assistant; The Assistant Provost since my supervisor was out of town; and yours truly! To get the hater on my staff to understand what I went through daily, I brought Kedric Taylor to the meeting with me. Since he likes to talk and text mess, I wanted to teach him a lesson. After all, Kedric Taylor was the benefactor of the high school band and dance team camp since it funded his salary for three years at this point, which was $180,000.

Walking into the conference room, I noticed Brandon Dumas was not physically present, but his attendance was via conference call. Mr. Pugh started the meeting.

"Thank you, everyone, for attending. The purpose of this meeting is to come up with a solution between the band and the

Department of Residential Life concerning campus housing fees owed by the band..."

I stopped listening. At this point in my career, I've gained enough wisdom and experience to know a pointless meeting when I see one. It was pointless because Dr. Belton already stated that I was only responsible for cleanup fees. As I continued to sit in a meeting uninterested with a blank look on my face, the DRLH began to speak.

"Mr. Haymer walks around here being arrogant and thinks the name of this institution is Haymer University! Mr. Haymer owes us $40,000, and we will not let his camp continue until he pays the bill!"

I literally laughed out loud. My laughter caused the DRLH to become even more upset. My intuition about this meeting was correct because it went in the wrong direction from the beginning. We were supposed to discuss a resolution to our dispute, not how we felt about each other. I continued to sit calmly and uninterested with a blank look on my face. Mr. Pugh had a look of panic on his face as he interjected.

"OK…hold on! We're here to work together."

At this point, I was unphased by anything that anyone had to say. Brandon interjected a statement over the speakerphone. Since the speaker's volume was up, the room heard his voice loud and clear.

"It is expected that Housing is paid!"

I sat there unphased and Mr. Pugh continued to look confused. It appeared that the DRLH and Brandon anticipated a circus. Since I was bored, I was up for the challenge. You might as well call me Bozo the Clown because I had time, and I was for the foolishness this day. I had enough of Dr. Belton and Mr. Pugh not being able to reign in their subordinates.

"I ain't paying a got damn thing! Dr. Belton and Mr. Pugh already made their decision. Who is in charge here because it's surely not them?!"

Pretending to be appalled, Brandon asked, "Are y'all recording him?"

"Oh yea, I am recording him!" responded The DRLH.

"I don't give a good god damn if you're recording or not! I am sick of all of you. First, you want me to pay the salary of my staff member. Then he's on the speakerphone because he's too afraid to face me! How about you pay for housing with the money that is missing from the band camp account in the comptroller's office instead of paying your cronies salary increases!"

I went into full fake rage when I heard that the DRLH was recording. I stood up next to my chair. I pointed to Kedric Taylor to highlight my rage. Kedric Taylor was shocked. He's never seen me in attack mode. I am glad that he was there to see me in action as a warning of what could happen to him if he kept being catty!

The Assistant Provost, a lady I deeply respect, interjected, "Mr. Haymer, you need to calm down. You're out of line!"

"I am sorry, but you have no clue of what I've been through with these people. I would rather cancel the damn camp before they get another dime from my hard work! I'll go on social media and tell the truth about this school, starting with a lack of institutional control. I have no idea who is in charge around here! Come on, Kedric Taylor, let's get the hell out of here. I am done!"

I walked out of the meeting and slammed the door. Before I made it to the door, the DRLH shouted at me.

"Well, since you're threatening to go to social media, make sure you have your girl to put that on *The 5th Quarter Club* page as well!"

I walked through the office of Dr. Brown to exit the third floor of the campus administration building. All the secretaries and receptionists I became familiar with during my constant visits to my

Juked

supervisor all paused. They had a look of shock and disbelief on their face. Apparently, I was so loud that they could hear me outside the conference room where the meeting took place. I just kept it moving with a look of confidence on my face and in my walk. When I got to my vehicle, I looked at Kedric Taylor.

"Now you see the shit that I have to put up with! I know sometimes y'all don't understand why you aren't paid properly and why other things aren't happening as they should. Well, welcome to my world!"

I said all of this to Kedric Taylor as an indication that while he's texting and worried about the wrong things, he doesn't know what I must go through. Bringing Kedric Taylor to that meeting with me was the best decision that I could have made. I've never behaved in a manner like that before. Still, after three years of constant drama, three years of hearing NO said in many ways, and after staying encouraged to blaze my own path to success with achieving the benchmarks, I still had to fight the opposition. I've had enough! I wasn't upset. As I stated, I pretended to be mad. Still, I wouldn't allow them to bully me in a meeting while Dr. Belton and Mr. Pugh sat idly by. I was at the point where I no longer cared about the consequences of my actions. I had zero confidence in Dr. Belton's qualifications to run the University or his ability to be respected by Brandon Dumas, a want to be president.

When I arrived at my office, I immediately emailed Mr. Pugh and the Assistant Provost. I apologized to them for seeing me behave like that. I did not apologize for my words because I meant every word I said, I just wasn't directing my comments at them. A couple of days later, I met with the Assistant Provost. She had a better understanding of my fight than what I thought. She told me that some changes would happen soon.

"Mr. Haymer, you and I will work with each other more directly. Dr. Brown has assigned the band to me, and I want to make sure that I hear your concerns."

She called Mr. Pugh on the phone. She asked him to come into the meeting. Shortly after the call, Mr. Pugh entered the meeting and started speaking.

"Mr. Haymer, we were wrong to even put this on you. Dr. Belton wants me to tell you that in July, you will no longer have to pay the salary of your assistant director. That was a responsibility that you should never have had to take on!"

"Thank you! It is a huge relief for me."

"I also saw your email and I accept your apology. You cannot let people get the best of you like that."

"Don't worry about your situation with housing. We will handle it. Just start planning your camp like you normally do," stated Dr. Young, Assistant Provost.

I thanked her and Mr. Pugh as we ended the meeting. I had a feeling that my housing problems wouldn't magically go away, especially since I've been told this in the past by Dr. Belton and Mr. Pugh. I also knew that Dr. Young was positioning herself to become the next Executive Vice-President/Provost. My supervisor took the job at Kentucky State University as their next president. Even though his appointment wasn't official at the time, he reached out to me. Because he knew my frustrations, Dr. Brown asked if I would consider leaving Southern University to become the Director of Bands at Kentucky State University.

Here is the second job offer I received during my tenure at SU. Although it tempted me because of my positive relationship with my supervisor, I declined the offer. I didn't solve all the problems that plagued the Human Jukebox and put up with three years of fighting battles just to pull away when I was winning the war. It was now time to prepare for my 5th supervisor in only three years as the Director of Bands.

April was a huge month at Southern. I went from showing my ass in a meeting to seeing Brandon Dumas' ass, literally! I remember being in the parking lot at my favorite grocery store when I received a phone call from a friend.

"Hey, man! Did you see the video on social media?"

"What are you talking about?"

"Check your text message. I just sent the link."

I immediately ended the conversation and checked my text message. I saw a short video of what appeared to be Brandon Dumas with the former Miss Southern University. She was no longer a student at the time; however, she was a campus employee under Brandon's supervision. They were nude and fully inappropriate and playfully in the bed. I could clearly see the former Miss SU in the video without a doubt on top of a man asking, "You want to be in my snap?" The camera moved so fast that it caused me to question whether it was Brandon or not. If it was Brandon, as everybody I talked to thought, then it definitely would be trouble heading his way professionally and personally due to him being a married man of God!

The scandal made the evening news, and I refused to watch. My feud with Brandon Dumas was bigger than I thought because I received many texts and calls from individuals who felt that I was somewhere celebrating the fact that he was exposed in such a shameful way. I wasn't celebrating. Instead, I'd become quite irritated at the people's reaction around me. I knew if the shoe was on the other foot, he would be thrilled to see me taking a fall, but I never took pleasure in the pain of someone else.

I can only speak of the "sex scandal" from the point of view as most because although the rumors would say otherwise, I was on the outside looking in. The scandal resulted in the termination of Brandon Dumas. To make matters worse, he requested a public hearing on his termination. He was choosing his right to due process by defending himself to the SU System Board of Supervisors in an attempt to overturn his termination.

Brandon's public hearing was scheduled for the next board meeting. This was the same board meeting I planned to attend because of the band staff's salary increases. Both issues were on the same agenda.

I was concerned about how my appearance at the board meeting would be perceived. I had plans on being at this meeting prior to Brandon's indiscretion. My twin brother also knew that my presence in the boardroom would appear as if I was there to see Brandon suffer! I was also concerned due to all the rumors and lies about my involvement in the scandal. We had about a week to prepare for the board meeting, but my first priority was the annual band banquet. We had a reason to celebrate, and with everything that was happening around me I wanted to end the semester on a good note!

Thanks to the Dumas Sex Scandal, many SU alumni rushed to begin a positive social media campaign. The campaign, *Don't ask me about SU*, trended on social media for weeks. It was geared towards friends of alumni who would often ask or comment on the scandals at SU but never attended the University. As a result of this, the alumni began to post positive memories that caused a nostalgic moment that we really needed during this difficult time!

The SU System Board of Supervisors meeting was finally here. It was a packed circus with no room for any bystanders. There were many Who's Who present along with the local media due to the constant news coverage of the scandal with Brandon. Among the influential who's who present was Sonja. She was the University's most influential critic as her *5th Quarter Fan Club* page grew in popularity by the day. Unlike most of her campus sources, I was never afraid to be seen with her in public. I don't know where I would have been without her help and support. I was never ashamed of that. I never denied knowing or communicating with Sonja, even to the Office of Dr. Belton. I didn't deny her then, and I definitely wouldn't deny her at the board meeting. I made sure to sit close to her. My twin brother and I sat directly behind her during the meeting.

Juked

    Initially, the meeting consisted of boring procedural items and other minor campus matters. Finally, the time had come for why I was there. The board quickly went through and approved the raises for the band staff and me that I barely had the time to celebrate. The raises were highly important to me. It gave the band staff their deserving salary and it provided me the cushion needed to pay the rent for my apartment and the mortgage for my flood-damaged uninhabitable home! Although the raises were my top priority, the main event of the meeting that brought the onlookers was the termination hearing of the Vice-Chancellor of Student Affairs, Brandon Dumas!

    Before Brandon took the podium to present his side of the story, the stage was open to the public so they could voice their concerns. First up to make a case on why the termination of Brandon should not be overturned was Sonja Norwood! I watched and listened to Sonja. As she was speaking, I saw the look of disapproval on Dr. Belton's face. It was clear that Dr. Belton did not want to fire Brandon for the same reasons that he was given his position in the first place, his father, Walter Dumas. Mr. Dumas was in the room, standing and looking to see when the board stood; he was looking at the opposition and taking names. Every board member would have to vote yes or no aloud, publicly, after both parties made their case. Through all of this, Sonja stayed the course as she made her case. She went into Brandon's intimidation tactics, the concert scandal, and other topics that she made public through her platform, The 5th Quarter Club.

    Sonja was interrupted by the board's chair, "I am sorry, but your time is up!" Sonja began to leave the podium and take her seat. Suddenly, the gentleman that was in line behind her to speak approached the podium and spoke into the mic.

    "I would like to yield my time to Sonja Norwood!"

    The room exploded in applause. The board chair struck her gavel on the table to regain order in the boardroom. As the people began to settle down, I looked at my phone and noticed I had many text messages from Jabari. He tuned into the meeting via YouTube live stream. I didn't even respond to his text messages; I was too consumed by the action taking place before my very own eyes. The boardroom attendees finally settled down, and Sonja continued to make her case. I could see the look of disapproval on the faces of Brandon and his father. Finally, it was time for Brandon to make his case.

Brandon and his attorney approached the podium with a stack of papers. Brandon began to distribute the stack of papers among the 16 members of the board as the chair read the rules of the appeal's process aloud. It took the board chair approximately three to four minutes to read the required, long passage aloud. Brandon was circulating the papers to the board members and to the board's General Counsel to glance over. The board chair finished reading.

"I am sorry, I didn't catch everything that you stated," stated Brandon.

Brandon's statement required the board chair to read the passage over. This gave the board members additional time to glance over their thick document that Brandon passed out in his defense. Once the board's chair read the long passage for a second time, Brandon attempted to speak on the document that he distributed. However, before he could start, the General Counsel objected.

The objection was because of the document that Brandon passed out to the board. The General Counsel communicated to the board chair that the document contained an employee's alleged actions and activities that Brandon Dumas supervised and not about him or a valid reason for appealing his termination.

As soon as the General Counsel made his objection and stated the reasons why, my brother turned to me.

"Nathan, I bet whatever is in those papers is about you!"

"I know he ain't that crazy. Although I know that he hates me, this moment is not about me. It is about keeping his job. If he made it about me, then why would he appeal? He's conceding and trying to burn the house down!"

My brother continued to look at me with concern in his eyes. "I don't know Nathan. I still think it is about you!"

Sonja turned around and joined the conversation. "That's typical of him! Blaming someone else for his failures. What employee made him get in the bed and make a video with the former Miss SU?"

I was in disbelief. I continued to pay attention to the clown show that was happening in front of my very own eyes. Suddenly, one board member threw his document to the table.

"Man come get this. I am not reading the rest of this!"

The board chair immediately jumped up to approach the audience. I was familiar with the chair. I often referred to her as my guardian angel. Never had I seen her with the look she currently has upon her face. It was a look of panic as she approached the audience to determine if any of the papers made it out to them. She was relieved when she found out that no one in the audience had a copy. My brother didn't change his stance.

"Nathan, I am telling you, that document is about you!"

Still, I was in disbelief. I began to wonder what was in the document that was so bad that a board member threw it to the table while the board chair had to approach the audience? What was so bad that the General Counsel had to object not once, not twice, but three times to Brandon Dumas and his attorney's rationale for presenting it. Whatever it was, I wanted to find out. It seems like we weren't going to find out anything as Brandon and his attorney requested to move the hearing to an executive session, closed to the public, and the board agreed. While the board members and Brandon moved to another room for the executive session, the audience was left behind to wonder and gossip about what could have been in the papers he distributed to the board. The public meeting was now in recess until the board's return.

Tired of sitting in the boardroom, I went outside. Truth be told, I wanted to leave. I didn't care about the outcome for Brandon Dumas. I got raises for my staff and myself, so I was satisfied. However, I promised Sonja that I would stick around with her. About an hour or so later, the board meeting resumed. The only item left was the termination of the embattled Vice Chancellor, Brandon Dumas. The vote resulted in upholding the termination of Brandon!

Approximately 2 hours later, I was on the road driving to Houston. The Human Jukebox Alumni Association had a battle of the bands with the Alumni of the Prairie View A&M University Marching Storm. As Director of Bands, I wanted to go and show my support. My phone began to ring as I was driving west on the dark interstate. I noticed it was my Guardian Angel, the chair of the SU System Board of Supervisors. I thought that she called me to congratulate me on the raises for the staff because she was aware of everything that I was up against over the years.

"Hello Madam Chair. How are you this evening?"

"Hey, where are you?"

"I am on the road headed to Houston to attend an alumni battle of the bands!"

"OK! Are you alone?"

"Yes, I am by myself. What is going on?"

"Well, Mr. Haymer, this is a confidential conversation..."

Our conversation consisted of the board chair revealing to me the details of the 15-page document that Brandon Dumas handed out to the board. The entire document was all about me! It started with my years as a high school band director when I was arrested for the alleged theft of band funds, moved through the time Brandon wrote me up and Dr. Belton told me that he would discard it, to finally ending with other allegations from various moles he had infiltrated through my department. She advised me to get a lawyer because she was confident that Dr. Belton would call me in.

I thanked the chair for sharing the information with me and we ended the conversation. Instantly, I pulled to the side of the road. I required a moment to pause and take it all in. My first reaction was to stop at the nearest gas station and buy the strongest bottle of whiskey that I could find. Thankfully, I didn't give in to that temptation. I've come too far in my struggle to beat alcoholism. I wasn't going to give in to the temptation caused by my enemy.

Instead of falling to my demons, I reached out to my angels. I called my brother, Niles, and Sonja. I revealed to them the news I had just received. No one was surprised at how low Brandon would stoop except for me. Even my ally on campus who worked in the administration building was right the whole time. He would often tell me, "Haymer, you have to fight dirty with these people. Your problem is that you are too nice!"

Since Brandon was no longer employed by Southern University, I knew that he would be an even bigger threat. I had about three hours remaining on the trip to Houston. I spent most of the remainder of the trip thinking about the issue and digesting the words of the board chair. On repeat in my head I heard, **get a lawyer**, and **the President was going to call me in**. Finally, I shook myself loose. I concluded that I would wait to see what happened. I told myself not to get a lawyer until Dr. Belton calls me in. I look forward to talking to him because he has been avoiding me for quite some time now! My fear turned into boldness as I turned up the stereo in my truck to Johnny Kemp's "Just Got Paid." I was celebrating my raise, and it was a Friday night!

Chapter 25

The Brandon Dumas Sex Scandal and job termination was all the talk. It was like the Energizer Bunny....it kept going and going and going. For me, it was the prelude to the Dancing Doll Drama of 2017. I knew that every year I faced some challenges, twist or turn, surprise or issue and this year would be no different.

Tryouts for the 2017 Dancing Dolls were the same day I made plans to be in Dallas for the Southern University Alumni Federation-Dallas Chapter's annual Bayou Bash. The First Vice President of the Alumni Federation, Ms. L Thomas, was also the president of the Dallas chapter. I felt I had to be there to support her especially since she was the lead person for the ***Adopt-A-Juke Campaign*** that secured close to 200K worth of new band uniforms during the fall 2017 season.

Going to Dallas was non-debatable and non-negotiable. I had to figure out how I would make things work with tryouts. My flight was for 4:30pm. In order for me to make my flight, I would have to be at the Baton Rouge airport by 4:00pm. To be at the airport by 4:00pm, everything would have to go smoothly and be completed before or by 4:00pm.

DT and I were very accustomed to each other's leadership style by now and I was comfortable letting her run the show. "Everything is on you this year. I trust your judgment. You are responsible for the judges, the coach assigned to teach the quick routine for the candidates to pick up, and everything else related to tryouts. Just let me know what y'all need. I'll be in and out bringing food and drinks for the judges. I may go home for a little while to make sure that I have everything needed for my Dallas trip."

It was a typical day of tryouts. The judges were going through their usual routine of scoring candidates and making cuts each

Juked

round. I wanted everything to go smoothly, but I knew there would be a little friction. I allowed the captain of the 2016-17 edition of the Dancing Dolls, who completed her fourth year, to try out a fifth time. Fifth-year Dolls are a rare thing, but it's the director's prerogative on whether he wants to allow it or not. In this case, the captain suffered an injury that required her to sit out a large portion of the season. I expected more from the captain, but I thought she did the best that she could under the circumstances.

Allowing her to try out for the fifth year wasn't even on my radar. DT called to ask if I would consider letting the captain try out again. I wanted to take the time to think about the situation. I needed to think about the perception of the captain potentially robbing another young lady of the chance to lead or robbing a young lady her first year on the squad. I took 3 days to think about the situation. For about three days, I weighed the fact that the captain did not reach her full potential due to her injury versus how potentially making the team for the fifth year would affect the other girls who were next in line to lead. Finally, after making my decision, I called DT.

"I am trusting that our systems in place are strong enough to support my decision. After thinking about the situation for three days, I realized there are no set positions with the Dolls. Everyone must 'bring it' at every tryout to earn their spot. I will determine the captain based on the interview round and who I think is the best fit to lead. With that being said, I am going to allow the 2016-2017 captain to try out again. I may receive some backlash, but it's my decision!"

It was tryout day and DT was thrilled that I decided to give the captain another opportunity to try out again. I thought to myself that everyone was moving really slow. It was close to 3:00pm and I needed to be at the airport in an hour. Suddenly, DT came into the office.

"Mr. Haymer, just letting you know that we have a problem!"

"What is it now?"

"Well, two other girls …" DT named two individuals who were members of the team the previous year. One was a two-year member and the other was in her third year. The third-year member was also the acting captain. I thought she did an outstanding job taking the lead during the injured captain's recovery time. Because the acting captain was in place during the parade season of 2017, it was natural for "Doll fans" to assume that she would be the next captain. I grabbed my head because the news that DT relayed to me gave me a massive headache as she continued. "Well, the judges scored them low!"

"Wait a minute! How in the hell could the judges score them low? There's no way that all the remaining girls outdanced them!"

As I was responding, I looked out the window in my office which gave me a direct view of the rehearsal hall where auditions took place. Normally, I would never use that window because I didn't want the girls or judges to know that I was peeping in from time to time. I would always go upstairs to the dark studio to look in while being undetected. In this case, I didn't care. I looked out to see who the remaining girls were and also saw the two members of the team that DT referenced. One of the girls had on black and white when everyone had instructions to wear all black.

DT kept explaining. "It wasn't anything wrong with their dancing other than they weren't going 'full-out' in some of the routines. The reason why the judges marked them so low is because they laughed at some of the girls who struggled to keep up during the previous rounds. One of them had a hairstyle that was unfitting according to the instructions, and the other had on dance attire that was not appropriate!"

I began to think about all the drama I've been through. I became depressed again. I thought about the events of past Dancing Doll tryouts, along with the constant attacks from the former Vice Chancellor of Student Affairs, the drama with the DRLH, drama with the administration related to our raises, issues

Juked

with running camp funds through my bank account, and my personal issues. All of these things made me become weak and I didn't want to fight anymore. Still, I knew that being in the seat required me to stand firm on our principles.

"This is going to be hell on wheels for me! If I allow this decision to stand, you realize that I will be attacked for it, right? If you can assure me that the judges were not biased in their scoring because I already know how they can be, I will let the decision stand. I won't be intimidated by making an unpopular decision. I am just tired of going through unnecessary bull shit!"

DT assured me that the judges' scoring was 100 percent accurate. She personally witnessed the same thing.

"Ok. I realize that there will be more shots fired at me, but that's ok! I just want you to realize that once we pull the trigger, there's no turning back! If you are really sure, then go ahead and pull the trigger while I prepare myself to deal with the effects!"

DT, once again, told me that the scores were accurate. I gave her the nod as she left my office. Within ten minutes, I could hear screaming and crying in the hallway! It was at that moment I knew that the decision was out and there were some unhappy people. I opened my door to look in the hall to see where the commotion was coming from. It wasn't from the former members of the team who didn't make it. They were already gone. The uproar came from a few remaining members of the team who made it to the interview round.

I took a deep breath and prepared to quickly conduct the interview round so that I could leave for the airport immediately. The Mobile Doll (Mobile, Al) was about to begin her third year on the team. During her interview, she took a bold chance of getting cut by standing on her principles.

"I am sorry, Mr. Haymer, but I don't think it's right what happened to the two girls that were cut!"

She continued to talk about her experiences with DT, the judges, and other things. She took a huge chance by challenging my decision to my face while I was deciding whether to allow her a third year on the team. Typically, once I reach a decision, whether popular or not, I am usually "a my way or hit the highway" type of guy. In this case, I listened to the Mobile Doll. She has always been respectful and never caused any trouble as she voiced her concerns.

"DT did this a couple of years back to my captain. She has her picks and favorites, and she lies to you to get her way!"

What a bold accusation by the Mobile Doll! However, I sat behind a desk and allowed her to speak her truth. I've seen the judges' scores and listened to the justification of those scores from DT, but something told me that everything I heard from the Mobile Doll was the truth. I don't know what it was about the Mobile Doll's delivery that wouldn't allow me to cut her off and go into full band director mode. Her words resonated with me. I heard her voice full of passion as I felt her words were true. The Mobile Doll spent her interview by speaking up for the former members of the team.

"Thank you for letting me know. Now, I want you to focus on being the best dancer that you can be… if you make the team again this year!"

As The Mobile Doll left the interview room, I needed a moment to take it all in. If the girls that were cut did anything remotely close to DT's explanation, then they got what they deserved. However, if the girls were targeted as the Mobile Doll so passionately stated in her defense for them, then DT played me like a fiddle!

What had me pause and consider everything was the biggest question floating around in my head. *Why would the Mobile Doll come to her interview, take a huge chance in getting cut, and stand up for something she believed in if she wasn't telling the truth?* What I saw and heard was respectable. It was all the characteristics I look for in a captain to lead the team. She took a chance of risking it all by standing up for what she believed in. It was not a matter of whether I agreed with her or not. Her principles, integrity, and passion to tell her truth resonated with me. I grew so much more respect for her because she did so.

Unfortunately, the trigger was already pulled. I had to move forward with the decision that I allowed to take place. After I conducted the interview round, I told DT that I had to leave for Dallas, and we would reconvene when I returned to Baton Rouge. Unlike in the past, we decided to do things differently for the 2017 tryouts. Instead of announcing the team on the same day as tryouts, we decided to take professional headshots of the 2017-2018 edition of the Southern University Fabulous Dancing Dolls and post them to the band's various social media platforms!

The plane landed in Dallas and as it taxied to the gate, I turned my phone on. Why did I do that? I had so many social media notifications. Most was backlash from the decision I allowed to stand with the two former members of the dancing dolls. As I moved through the airport, I ignored most of the alerts. I rented a vehicle and drove immediately to the Bayou Bash. There were many SU alumni present from various places. They were there having a good time and I began to engage in conversation with several of them. Suddenly, a very cool and direct Southern University Young Alumni Network group approached me.

"Mr. Haymer, why did you cut …"

It was clear that they got the word of what took place a few hours ago in Baton Rouge through their social media. I turned and faced the concerned group.

"I am not here to discuss the business of tryouts. I am here to show my support for the Dallas chapter! I am aware of what's on social media, and I just ask that you don't believe everything that you read!"

A young lady in the group responded, "Well, we don't believe everything that we read because they got you all the way fucked up, Mr. Haymer!"

She handed her phone to me. I saw that I was the topic on a social media group page. It alleged that I cut one of the girls because she dated the drum major. I was jealous because the drum major and I were in a secret relationship. They even posted a picture of me next to the drum major to make it appear more believable. The only problem was that the guy in the photo wasn't the drum major!

"It's gone be alright!" I brushed it off and kept it moving.

When I returned to the office on Monday, I received an email from the Office of the Executive Vice President-Provost. I called the office to simply let him know how and why the girls were cut. I also had an email from the mother of one of the former members of the Dancing Dolls who didn't make the team. When I saw the email from the mother, it was so long and loaded that I knew that I had to read it several times to digest it before I responded. I knew that it was an emotional explosive situation, and anything that I typed could make the difference between a bad situation staying bad or turning catastrophically worse! Since I wanted to be careful in my response to the parent, I responded immediately to the email to let her know that I received it.

Good morning! This email serves as an official notification that I've received your message. Please allow me 48 hours to respond as I want to make sure to address all of your concerns with the most accurate information that I have available.

I thought the mother needed to know that I received her email, and I took her concerns seriously. She quickly responded to thank me. I read the email and it was loaded with accusations that, if true, were quite troubling. The email highlighted issues that broke my policy of ensuring that the judges were not related to or had any personal relationships with the Dancing Doll candidates. The email listed other concerns and went on with threats of the parent knowing a few members of the SU System Board of Supervisors. I wasn't concerned about that as I understood that the parent was very frustrated and probably said what she had to say to get my attention. I called DT and asked her about the accusations of the

Juked

judges and candidates' relationships. Although she told me that she didn't know anything about it, I found out through another source that what the parent told me was true.

We already pulled the trigger, and there was no turning back. I responded, addressing all of the parent's concerns as openly and honestly as I could. I let her know that changes would come in the future. While I am sure the changes would be no comfort to the parent due to her daughter still being cut, she appreciated my honesty and openness. The situation further spiraled out of control as the drum major, JT, became very upset.

I called him to my office to let him know that I was in the process of replacing him due to his graduation scheduled for fall 2017. When he entered, I could tell he was upset. He was upset due to hearing that I wanted to cut his girlfriend and him due to their social media channel. I already addressed my concerns with JT on the activity of his social media channel that I thought was inappropriate for the brand of the band, it had nothing to do with my decision to replace him as drum major. Apparently, he must have forgotten the conversation we had in the summer of 2016 when he told me that he would graduate in fall 2017. I always planned for the future, so when JT told me his projected graduation date, I immediately began to search for his replacement.

"JT, do you remember that I had you as a backup drum major two years before you even got the position?"

"Yes,"

"Then you should know how I operate. What makes you think that I wasn't looking for your replacement? I admit I didn't have a backup for you, but I was looking for one!"

"Well, Mr. Haymer. I know for a fact that you were unhappy with me, and you told TJ that me and my girlfriend were doing too much on social media!"

"Son, I did tell TJ that. It's not like I was putting your business in the street or talking behind your back. I asked him to train you for the position. I also asked him to be your advisor. Furthermore, I told you that y'all were doing too much after I saw the gender reveal video last semester with you and your girlfriend in full uniform without even asking for my permission!"

"I know that she's your girlfriend and you care about her, but I will not discuss matters of another student with you just like I wouldn't discuss your business with another student!"

The drum major and his girlfriend participated in a gender reveal for a couple having a baby that I assumed they knew. JT went on to talk about his girlfriend, asking why she didn't make the team and how unfair it was. He was there for a different reason; I didn't call him to the office to talk about his girlfriend or his social media channel.

"JT, I picked the new drum major, and he is right outside of my door right now. I called you because I wanted you to work with him!"

"Can I make a suggestion on who my replacement would be?"

"No, I have already selected your replacement, but who are you thinking of?"

"The crab that plays the F-Horn (mellophone),"

I didn't even respond to JT. I walked to the door and opened it, revealing his replacement. His eyes grew larger as he saw his replacement; it was the guy he just described as the F-Horn crab. I took a picture of the two to indicate the passing of the baton and posted it to the band's social media platforms. Then, I left them alone to talk about working together.

I went to the office to set up a meeting with the two young ladies who were cut from the Dancing Dolls. For them to feel completely comfortable talking to me in the office, I asked both young ladies to come at the same time as I set the meeting for the next day. I assured them that I would hear their concerns and answer any questions because, in my mind, it was time for closure.

During our meeting, the concerns raised had a lot to do with DT and her selection of what they deemed as biased judges. There were also accusations about the captain being allowed to try out again. I couldn't question their concerns about the judges. I just learned of the situation myself due to the parent's email;. I let them know that allowing the captain to try out again was my decision. DT asked if the captain could audition again, but I took the heat because I could have easily told her no. I thought that under the circumstances, the captain should have another opportunity.

Once the judges give a score, it is final. We do not share the scores with the candidates as that has always been the policy.

"We have never shared the scores with candidates before, but I am the director, so I am going to break that policy and let y'all see your scores. I want you to leave this meeting with the understanding that I did not make anything up, nor do I have any personal motives here!"

I printed out the score sheet and let them see it. I also had it on my computer screen so that they could see the scores of all of the candidates. Both girls were cut right before the final round, which was the interview round. The young lady whose mother sent me the email just missed the interview round as the judges had one person ahead of her that scored slightly higher by a percentage of a point. The other young lady, who served as acting captain the previous semester, wasn't even close according to the scores.

I emphasized that once in the interview round, I decide who will be on the team. Before the interview round, it is on the judges. They thanked me for taking the time to meet with them. I communicated that out of all the girls who ever tried out for Dancing Dolls, they were the first two actually to see their scores. I wanted to be as transparent as possible, even though I didn't give them the conclusion that they wanted. I had no idea if the two young ladies believed me or not, and I no longer cared as I could finally sleep well knowing that I did the right thing. The next step would be to pick the judges myself and possibly look for a new doll sponsor! Although I couldn't fault DT for pulling the trigger, I could fault her if the information provided to me to make the decision was misleading and biased!

Chapter 26

Our first football game of the 2017 season wasn't our typical type of first game. The season opener was nationally televised on ESPN due to the game being a competition between the two largest HBCU athletic conferences: the Southwestern Athletic Conference (SWAC) and the Mid-Eastern Athletic Conference (MEAC). Every year, one team is selected from each conference to play in the annual SWAC/MEAC Challenge, with each conference taking turns on who would be the home team and the visiting team. 2017 was the SWAC's turn as home team. The game took place at Southern since we were the home team, and our visitors were the South Carolina State University Bulldogs.

The game was aired live on national television with a start time of 1:00pm on the Sunday of Labor Day weekend. That timeframe is the hottest time of day with August/September being the hottest time of year. I took no chance by preparing the band for the heat. We performed in our dri-fit band shirts and mesh shorts. I also had over 1,000 bottles of water on ice ready as I mandated the students to drink a bottle after each quarter.

I made it home after the game and began resting by watching TV and relaxing. It was around 7:30pm when I remembered that I recorded the SWAC/MEAC Challenge game coverage on my DVR. I was just about to watch ESPN's coverage of our halftime performance when I received a strange text message from a gentleman who was a political appointee serving at the highest level in state government. The text message was straightforward.

"You looked very good today at the game!"

I wanted to give him the benefit of the doubt. The gentleman was much older than me, and sometimes older people aren't clear in the way they text. I assumed that he meant that the band looked very good at the game today.

Our performance was very strong! I created a performance playing only Bruno Mars tunes, and it was well-received. The band executed the drills perfectly, and the Dancing Dolls added the extra flare. Allowing the Dancing Dolls captain to come back for a fifth year to lead was a great decision as she led with grace, passion, and energy by giving the Dolls the extra swag that I wanted them to have! Overall, it was an entertaining and electrifying performance that represented the Human Jukebox's brand very well as they looked even better on national television!

I thought nothing of his text, so I responded with a pleasant "Thank you, kind sir!" I began to press "play" on my remote to watch the halftime performance when my phone went off again. It was the same gentleman with another text. This time I couldn't misinterpret his intentions.

"Yea … looking good. I got something that I want to slide in you (delete)!"

I was so upset from reading his text message that I wanted to throw my phone. Why would he send me this crap? Then, he added "delete" as an indication to delete the message. If you want someone to delete what you text, you probably shouldn't be texting them in the first place!

Seeing that message really put me into an instant depression. I thought about all of the things that I've been through: date rape, my inability to trust people, and the fact that I was already paranoid from what happened at the board meeting concerning the accusations during Brandon Dumas' termination hearing. Since the gentleman was a political appointee serving at the highest level in state government, I wanted to be careful in responding. Still, I knew that I had to say something. I couldn't believe that he would even come at me like that. The fact that he was so sloppy with it was even worse.

Juked

"I'm sorry, you must have the wrong person!"

"Is this the head band director at SU? If so, that message was definitely for you! (delete)"

Now, there was no plausible deniability. The man said everything other than my name as I responded for the last time.

"I'm sorry, sir. Apparently, you're into something that I am not. I do not share your sentiments. Please enjoy the rest of your evening."

"You will do what I say or else! (delete)"

I won't deny that his threat frightened me. It made me quite paranoid. I began to look out of my apartment window to see if anyone was watching me from the downtown streets and parking garage. I triple-checked to make sure I locked the door and to make sure I armed the security system. I did not entertain him any longer. I blocked him immediately. I couldn't believe that some people think that they can talk to others in any kind of way while asserting their power. I knew that he was a coward and a bully because only people who are ashamed of themselves while using scare tactics would text a person something so disgusting and inappropriate! I knew that coward would never disrespect me to that level in person! I couldn't sleep that entire night as I laid alone in my bed thinking of the many enemies who wanted to take me out, and I was afraid that somehow and some way this high-ranking official was going to set me up because I didn't give in to his advances.

Six days later, we played the University of Southern Mississippi. Prior to the game, the University of Southern Mississippi's Pride of Mississippi band director gave me a call. He wanted to know if it was possible for our bands to join in a performance together as a symbol of unity.

The month prior to the game, white nationalists marched in Charlottesville, Virginia and were televised saying anti-Semitic comments. At this time, the country was being led by Donald J.

Trump. Unfortunately, when the 45th President of the United States addressed the nation, his comments made the matter worse.

Due to his comments and the situation at hand, the band director's suggestion was something that the country needed. Plus, he expressed his desire to see and experience the Human Jukebox live. The performance would be after both bands gave their individual halftime presentations. The band director explained that he didn't know what we could possibly perform but getting me to agree to the performance was the most important matter. I immediately responded.

"Yes! I think it is a great idea. There are many things that divide us, such as race, class, politics, religion, and I can go on. But the two things that unite us as a culture are good food and good music! I can't think of a better way to show unity than a joint performance between a HBCU and a PWI. Don't worry about the music because I already have something, *America the Beautiful*!"

I explained to the band director that I did a transcription from Carmen Dragon's arrangement of *America the Beautiful*. I even sent him a link to the Human Jukebox performance of *America the Beautiful* at the 2015 Bayou Classic Battle of the Bands. He loved it, and we both agreed that it was the perfect song to send the perfect message.

On game day, we scheduled a rehearsal to get our placement on the field and work on *America the Beautiful* as a combined band. I knew the Pride of Mississippi could easily play through the music. My concern was about their interpretation of the piece as I prepared the Human Jukebox to deliver the piece with expression and emotion! To help them understand what I wanted without insulting their intelligence, I had the Human Jukebox perform *America the Beautiful* right after our warm-up. I laughed so hard at the band director's remarks.

"Oh wow, Professor Haymer! I see that I am going to have to use every bit of my doctorate in conducting to keep up with you!"

Juked

    I knew what he meant. I never conducted to keep the time signature of the music; that's elementary. I always conducted to paint a picture of what I want and demand. I conducted the band as a sound engineer, bringing in and phasing out parts of the music when necessary. I conducted for interpretation of the style and dynamic level of the music I wanted.

    After both bands put on a stellar halftime presentation displaying our unique and different styles as individual marching units, it was time to give the fans at the University of Southern Mississippi in Hattiesburg a treat. Both bands quickly moved on the field into their places and began to play *America the Beautiful*. The piece started softly, then the dynamic level grew to a climax at the part of the piece with the lyrics, "America, America, God shed His grace on thee." The sound was so powerful that the audience burst into applause. I don't think there was anyone in the place that did not feel the power of music that night as the Human Jukebox and the Pride of Mississippi Marching Bands came together in unity for the sake of a nation divided!

    After the stellar performance individually and collectively with the Pride of Mississippi, I had a private vendor to feed the band through a mobile unit when the game was over. In addition to their good food, I loved their convenient service. They could feed the band quickly, we could load the bus, and get home faster than going to a restaurant.

    The band eats in order of classification. The seniors eat first, then juniors and down to the freshman class. While the freshmen were eating, the upperclassmen who rode bus two began to horseplay with the upperclassmen on other buses. Due to lessons learned in 2008 as assistant director, I had a habit of watching the freshmen to protect them.

    Apparently, the upperclassmen were unsupervised, and their horseplay resulted in a student with a broken nose and another student who had ear damage. The worst part of the whole ordeal was that no one notified me. I learned of the incident from a parent that sent me an email on the Monday after the game concerning her son whose ear was bleeding. Later, I received another email from the other student's parent with a broken nose stating that he had to seek medical treatment. It was upsetting to me for several reasons, with the first being that no one on my staff told me anything. Both students who were injured and the students responsible for the injury had to be on one of the buses supervised by my staff. I had a flashback from 2008 and immediately went into crisis mode, and because I wrote the handbook nine years ago, at that time, I knew the policies and procedures like the back of my hand. If what the parents told me was true, then what their kids experienced was bullying, which is a form of hazing!

I called the two injured students into my office individually and interviewed them to verify what their parents reported to me was accurate. Next, I asked them to write a detailed statement revealing everything they remembered that occurred on the evening that they were injured. I told them to name everyone around them whether they knew if those individuals hit them or not. I knew that the students couldn't identify everyone because a group of people jumped them, but all I needed was one name. One name would open the investigation leading to more. Of course, I also knew that the students didn't want to tell me as well.

"You've been injured and had to seek medical treatment. Your parents are concerned, and why should they have to pay out of pocket for your treatment just for you to cover up the events that led to your injury? Think of your parents and think about what is best for your health!"

The students filled out a detailed report that named a few individuals that they thought were responsible for their injuries. I also had them sign the report, date it, and write their student ID number. After reading over their reports, I had all the students named as the aggressors individually come into my office and fill out a report following the same process. It allowed me to determine what happened.

I scanned all the handwritten incident reports and emailed them to the Dean of Students while saving the originals in my file. I sent the reports to the Dean of Students because I was about to suspend all of the students identified as the aggressors. I also didn't want the students to attempt to change their version of what took place.

After completing what was required of me as Director of Bands according to the policies and procedures outlined in the band's handbook, I suspended the aggressors pending further investigation by the Dean of Students. I told the two injured students to take as much time as they needed off so that their injuries could heal, and I emailed their parents, apologizing for what happened under my watch. I also notified them of the investigation by the Dean of Students.

I knew suspending a few students would allow the truth to come out. Later, I found out who was the main aggressor that caused the nose injury of one of the band members. I was very disturbed to discover that Kedric Taylor knew about the situation but covered it up. The student who caused the nose injury was from Mobile, Alabama, the hometown of Kedric Taylor. I don't know if he tried to protect his homeboy or not, but I immediately called him.

"Hey! I heard that the student from Mobile is responsible for causing the nose injury of a band member. The mother of the student threatened to sue because of the damages. What's even more disturbing is that I was told you knew all this time and never told me a thing! Here I am investigating and going through the process, and my Associate Director is hiding information that could have helped me earlier! Man, if this is true, then this implicates you in the crime because you attempted to cover it up!"

"I knew, but I was trying to protect you and the band!"

"Protect the band, how? By covering up a hazing incident? You have no clue of what I've been through in this position, and for you to be on my staff, which is an extension of me, and cover-up this incident implicates me as well!"

"Well, I didn't tell you because I didn't want to get a staff member in trouble. Lorenzo Hart told those kids to do what they did. He was the mastermind behind the students on bus two attacking students on other buses. It was an initiation process for the students to be able to ride bus two! Think about it Haymer, the students who actually attacked the others were sophomores listening to the juniors and seniors! The sophomores were new to bus two because this was our first away game of the season. When the sophomores were freshmen, they rode the freshman bus. Now that they are at the beginning of their upperclassmen status in the band, they had to prove that they were worthy of riding bus two by attacking innocent bystanders on other buses. As you supervised the freshmen while they were eating, the upperclassmen knew that it was the perfect time to begin the bullying event because they knew that you were occupied."

As I listened to Kedric Taylor, my mind went back to 1998. I was a sophomore student in the band and new to bus two. Although we didn't have to attack other band members to prove that we were worthy of riding bus two, there was an initiation process led by one of the assistant directors to ride the bus. The initiation process involved each new student running down the aisle to the back of the bus and running back to the front of the bus while getting struck with whatever the bus two aggressors had in their hands.

This was a tradition of bus two for decades. Due to a halftime brawl with Prairie View A&M University's band in 1998, the band was under the microscope by administrators. Because of that situation, we did not have to go down bus two as they've done the years before. To my knowledge, no class has gone down bus two since the 1997 sophomores, but I could be wrong.

I knew that the traditions of bus two were big problems. As a former student who rode that bus, I didn't need proof because I lived it as a sophomore. I also knew that I couldn't trust anything that Kedric Taylor told me. Although he had a valid point about the problems of bus two, he was only loyal to the agenda that served him. I told Kedric Taylor that I was disappointed in him because he still should have notified me.

"Covering up the situation, regardless of your intentions or its implications, makes the situation worse for everyone!"

I immediately left my home and went to the office to meet with the sophomore student from Mobile. I didn't notify any of my staff of what I was doing because I trusted no one! When the sophomore student made it to my office, I tore into him really hard!

"Son, I had an entire investigation, and you sat there quietly, willing to let other band members take the fall for your actions! That is the worst offense of them all! Now tell me the truth!"

The student told the truth. He admitted to striking the injured student in the nose because a few junior and senior band members told him to do so. I had the student follow the process by writing his statement down as I suspended him indefinitely from the band and forwarded his statement to the Dean of Students.

I talked to Lorenzo Hart the same day because he is the staff member that oversaw bus two. When he was a freshman, and I was a sophomore we marched in the band together. We knew the truth about the traditions of bus two from our days as students. I remember Lorenzo Hart was next to me the entire time on the evening of the incident. We both were supervising the freshmen while in conversation about a few stalkers trying to get to me.

I've always thought of Lorenzo Hart as a stand-up guy. I wanted to trust him. I hoped and prayed that when I talked to him on this day, he wouldn't give me a reason not to trust him any longer.

I informed him of all the allegations without telling him who told me. Lorenzo Hart looked shocked. He assured me that he had no clue what happened that night and would never instruct the students to behave in such a manner. Due to my long history with Lorenzo Hart, I believed him because I knew how he operated. Also, I had a few students that told me exactly how the incident went down, and that Kedric Taylor watched the whole thing. With this information, I knew that I had to immediately make a change in configuration of how we bussed students.

Historically, the band only traveled on four buses, except for one game. In 2014, I became the Director of Bands and promised a larger, more exciting band. Thus, the first year of my tenure, I introduced the addition of the 5th bus. Adding a 5th bus contributed to our financial struggle during my first three years at the helm.

To prevent anymore hazing incidents, I dismantled bus two. I assigned all seniors and a few juniors to bus one, which was my bus. Bus two would now consist of the junior class only. Bus three held only freshmen. Bus four housed all the girls in the band and the Dancing Dolls. Bus five would now contain the sophomore class.

In addition to restructuring the buses, I took the upperclassmen's privileges away from eating first at the restaurants. The freshman ate first for the next two away trips, followed by sophomores, then juniors, and finally seniors. I wanted to teach them a lesson that hazing, bullying, or any barbaric behavior wouldn't be tolerated. If I saw or even thought I saw any form of horseplaying, the students would be suspended indefinitely!

My final plan of action was to make a note of Kedric Taylor's willful neglect of duty. His justification wasn't good enough. I knew that I couldn't trust him, but that wasn't the problem. I knew that other issues would come soon, and I was no longer willing to sweep his toxicity under the rug. Although I did not officially reprimand him, I did write the incident down. As future problems arrived, I wanted to document his pattern of things that I considered unbecoming of a band director. I was now having to face the fact that I may have to fire Kedric Taylor due to his sneaky tactics. I didn't want to pull the trigger without a stack of official written evidence.

Chapter 27

The most significant offense and criminal act that I committed as Director of Bands was submitting false invoices to the SU Travel Office, the SU System Foundation, and the SU Alumni Federation. On trips for away games, I would often receive checks ranging from $15,000 up to $34,000 that were made payable to me. My responsibility was to cash the check, pay for the meals and other necessary expenses, and turn in the remaining cash minus the receipts. However, I began another practice that I didn't notify anyone about because I knew that it was wrong. I started paying for the media equipment and two extended staff members with funds left over after I paid the expenses for the band's meals while inflating invoices.

If the total of one meal was $2000, I would use my invoice software program to recreate the invoice and make the total $3000. I did it once in 2015. I repeated this practice a few more times in 2016. However, the inflation system process was operated regularly in 2017. I manipulated the system to work for me, and I also betrayed the University's trust. Subsequently, my submission of false invoices indicated a premeditated intent to defraud the system. Although I was only trying to help those who were vital to the organization's operations, it still was wrong.

Due to the media team needing new equipment, I needed money available to purchase their equipment through Amazon and many other vendors. In 2014, I paid for equipment out of my own pocket. I then began to fund the media team's needs through other sources. In addition to the equipment, I began to pay the director of the media team $2,000 per month starting during the summer of 2017.

Garrett, the director of the media team, was an employee of the University serving as the director of the freshman male dormitory. In 2017, he was no longer employed by the university. I felt obligated to pay him for the extraordinary job he performed for the band. Never did Garrett ask me to pay him, nor was he aware of how I paid him. He was just happy to get paid. I would pay him via Cash App or with cash, depending on which method was the most convenient for me at the time his payment was due.

Beddell was a dean of students for a charter school in New Orleans. As the band's announcer, he traveled to Baton Rouge from New Orleans and vice versa several times a month and he has been doing so consistently for all 21 years he has volunteered. Unfortunately, Beddell was laid off from his job during the fall of 2017 and faced the struggles of being unemployed. I felt obligated to do something as he has been loyal to the Human Jukebox for decades. So, I decided to pay him $1,000 a month in cash for his services as a token of my appreciation. Like Garrett, Beddell was unaware of how I paid him as well. I think he just appreciated the little assistance that I could give him.

The university took three years to finally own up to its responsibility to pay Kedric Taylor's salary but when it came to the media team, their equipment, and the band's announcer, I was on my own. I've tried paying them several times during my first year through the SU System Foundation and was denied by the acting chancellor at that time. So, I paid vendors and other expenses of the band using a third-party internet registration company that collected fees and deposited them into my bank account. Also, I submitted false invoices to the university to have money to pay individuals and expenses using the same bank account. I did what I had to do, and I'll live with that decision for the rest of my life.

My transformational leadership style was very bold and aggressive except for those on my staff. The unethical and criminal practices I committed played heavy on my conscience and made it difficult to confront the demons in my inner circle. How could I correct someone else's wrongs when I committed wrong acts myself?

From 2015-2018, I submitted false invoices to SU by means of the travel office, the foundation and the alumni federation. In a period of three years, I falsified invoices totaling approximately $33,400. In addition to paying for extended staff salaries and media equipment, I also began to pay band expenses using this method as well. I was literally robbing Peter to pay Paul! Nevertheless, I take full responsibility.

When I thought that things were getting tough, life showed me that things could get worse. I received a notification from the General Counsel to Dr. Belton that I, along with Brian Simmons, was under an investigation by the US Department of Education alleging discrimination against a student with a disability.

Jennifer was a transfer student from a university in Arkansas. She transferred there from another institution. SU was her third school. I talked to Jennifer's band director at her previous school, and he told me that she filed a complaint on him years ago.

Jennifer became really upset with me about a national band sorority. At the time, our chapter of the sorority was inactive and had been for 23 years. She wanted me to bring the chapter back and make it active again. I wouldn't allow the band's sorority to return.

On numerous occasions and at numerous times, I would constantly tell her NO. Eventually, I became frustrated with Jennifer and told her not to ask me again. It caused her to walk out of my office while slamming the door violently. I immediately went after Jennifer in the hall and lashed into her because she was playing with the wrong band director! It was the last conversation I had with Jennifer. She did not return after the spring 2017 semester. Apparently, she had a surprise waiting for me in the fall with her complaint with the US Department of Education and a transfer to yet another school.

The General Counsel explained the allegations. Among the allegations were my decision not to allow the student to march in the band, Brian Simmons allegedly cursing the student out, and some comments that I allegedly made regarding the student's attempt to represent the Human Jukebox at the 2017 Honda Battle of the Bands. I had to prepare a response. Fortunately, I was able to document part of my response. In 2016, a national network news channel produced a story on two students in the band who were also brothers. They both have autism. They, along with their mother, told a story on how music helped them cope with the challenges they faced. This news story aired the same year that I allowed Jennifer to join the band program.

If I didn't discriminate against the students with autism and the many other students who have disabilities in the band program, why would I discriminate against her? I remember Jennifer telling me that she couldn't wear the uniform because of her condition. I asked her about the condition, and she didn't go into detail. Out of respect for her privacy, I didn't push the issue. Instead, I informed her on what I was going to do and her duties which I told the General Counsel.

"If you cannot put on the uniform, then you cannot perform in the marching band. I will still give you a scholarship that will cover your out-of-state fees for the fall and the spring. In the fall, you will serve as the band's librarian organizing and filing music, and, in the spring, you will perform in the wind ensemble. Furthermore, it wasn't Jennifer's responsibility to tell me anything about her disability, but it was her responsibility to report to the University's Office for Disability Services. It is their job to contact me and let me know the accommodations, if any, that I would have to make for Jennifer."

The General Counsel seemed displeased that I knew the policies. I knew that she probably didn't have a clue about disability services. The General Counsel never notified me if the complaint went any further or if it ended. I knew that if the complaint had any merit, the General Counsel would have loved to call me back in. I suddenly noticed a pattern at Southern University. I would become the target of two more investigations that I would clear but was never officially notified of its resolution. Yes, the enemies of my past were coming after me, and the witch hunt would continue until they found something that would stick!

Another issue that plagued me was money. Since I had become the Director of Bands, I had secured north of 2 million dollars of revenue. Most recently, the first major sponsorship deal in the history of the Human Jukebox.

For the summer band and dance team camps of 2016 and 2017, we partnered with a Baton Rouge-based nationally franchised chicken finger restaurant. Now, that same company was sponsoring the band and even featuring us in their TV commercials. The deal was for 1 million dollars with the payout being $250,000 a year for the next four years. Even though this company contributed a one-time payment of $250,000 to both the University Academic Affairs Division and University Athletics, it was the first time the band received funding at a higher level than athletics.

More money definitely brought more problems! Zero percent of the money came from any effort of Dr. Belton or the SU System Board of Supervisors. Instead, they often dictated and set political tactics to keep me in check. Due to my fundraising efforts and the lack thereof to theirs, I became more arrogant with the administration, more confident in my abilities to lead the marketing and brand management arm of the band, and less tolerable of the current MBM team.

Claiming to be the reason behind the million-dollar sponsorship, I found myself laughing at the MBM team. They would waste no time getting their invoice into the SU System Foundation office for their cut from the deal if their claims were valid. Even though I gave them credit for the hits they had, they had way more misses I tracked. By my calculations, I was the one producing the marketing opportunities and bringing the money in for the band. It was finally time for me to take complete control of the Human Jukebox. I began freeing the organization from those who only attached themselves to us to take credit for the successes while pointing fingers at me for all the failures. We could no longer be in association with people that were divisive and always brought negative energy to even the best situations. I was finally developing the confidence that I could follow my instincts without fear of politics for retaliation. We were finally at a crossroads, as enough was enough!

In the fall of 2017, I was assigned my 5th supervisor. My new boss previously served as the Assistant Provost to my former supervisor. During her tenure as the Assistant Provost, she would help guide me and often sit in the meetings between the Executive Vice President-Provost and myself. I remember her attending a meeting in the spring semester of 2017. I recall that meeting since it was the one where I asked where the profits of the Bayou classic Battle of the Bands went after ticket reconciliation and splitting the profits with Grambling State University.

"Haymer, you raise a valid question, but I would advise you to think long and hard before stirring up that hornets' nest!"

The statement from the Executive Vice President-Provost obviously disturbed the Assistant Provost. I interpreted my supervisor's answer as a warning. I knew that the profits, which never made it to the band in decades, were secretly protected by the old guard of the University. I continued to ask the hard questions and demand answers. I was constantly told not to go there.

I dared to ask what they were hiding? Truth be told, I already knew! In 2009 when I was the assistant director, I did my research on the slavery of the Human Jukebox. It was at the time when the SU System Board ousted the President. Through the President's anger and frustrations, he secretly handed over information to the Director of Bands, Lawrence. He also cleared his account in the SU System Foundation and paid over $150,000 for new band uniforms before his termination. This is how we received the set of uniforms in 2009 that was finally replaced in 2017.

At some point during my research, the former President secretly delivered some documents. The documents revealed where the profits from the Bayou Classic Battle of the Bands went. The documents showed that the profits paid for hotel and game-day suites for administrators, the SU System Board of Supervisors, and other SU Elites, along with their families to include extended families and mistresses. The profits also paid for lavish meals and gatherings for the SU Elite. My predecessor, Lawrence, did nothing with the information, but I refused to sit idly by and allow the band to be used another year.

The Bayou Classic football game first took place in 1974. It was hosted at Tulane University in New Orleans. Isaac Greggs, SU's legendary band director, and Conrad Hutchinson, Jr., GSU's legendary band director, started the battle of the bands among themselves to raise funds for new band uniforms for both institutions. The bands battled at the New Orleans Riverwalk. The public could drop their spare change into a bucket to split between both bands. After a few years of this type of unregulated battle, the event became very popular and overcrowded! It raised so much money that the Bayou Classic organizers decided to oversee the event by making it an official regulated event for the weekend.

Now, this visionary event that was started to help the band was barely working for the band. The SU higher ups and elites were profiting and benefiting whereas the band staff would only receive a $5,000 bonus. Unlike the directors before me, I chose not to conform and obey. I searched for answers to solve the more pay needed for the band staff. The answer came in the form of the student referendum. Due to my efforts to get the student referendum passed, the band staff salary increased but I was forced to concede the $5,000 bonus.

Unfortunately for me, I did not follow the example of my predecessors or heed the warning of Dr. Brown as I kept pushing the issue. My new supervisor told me that I raised a valid concern upon learning that the Bayou Classic profits were managed by the SU System Foundation. This revelation led to more questions. The funds in the SU System Foundation are private funds. The funds in other University accounts are public. With private funds, it is possible to pay for the amenities that the SU Elite became accustomed to. The more I dived into the finances of the band, the more I began to understand why University officials would come after me so hard. By making the band camp funds public, it was under the administrators' control. Having the bands' revenue turn private in the foundation would have solved so much! Private funds would have allowed me to avoid the terrible practice of running funds through my bank account. It would have also made it impossible for university officials to use the money to pay their salaries and the salaries of their cronies.

My digging was not in vain. Around early September 2017, the CEO of the SU System Foundation approached me with some good news.

"Haymer, the profits from the Bayou classic Battle of the Bands will now go to the band!"

What terrific news, but I was very skeptical. It was too easy. It didn't make sense. They would allow hundreds of thousands of dollars to go to the band without a fight. I continued to hear the CEO out, express my thanks, and go into a wait and see approach! As the Bayou Classic got closer, I began calculating the cost of travel, food, and lodging while submitting the forms to the appropriate University officials. Approximately two months have passed since my initial conversation with the CEO. When I approached him again about getting a report on the profits, he performed a bait and switch tactic on me.

"Yes, we will use the Bayou Classic Battle of the Bands profit to pay for the band's travel, lodging, and food for the weekend."

"Wait a minute, that is not what we discussed earlier. You told me that the band would receive the profits from the Bayou Classic Battle of the Bands.

"Haymer, the profits are going to the band. That's how we're paying for your travel."

"OK! What you are really saying is that you're giving us $90,000 of hush money which is the cost of our travel, lodging, and meals to pay for our expenses for the Bayou classic weekend. Unless the profits are $90,000, which I am sure is way more, we aren't receiving the profits for our work! I will have my supervisor request a report from the ticket sales of the Bayou Classic BOTB!"

"That's fine!"

He wasn't worried. The CEO only reports to the SU Foundation's Board. The foundation is a separate entity from the University. Therefore, the CEO doesn't report to any SU Administrator or the SU System Board of Supervisors.

"Mr. CEO, here's my point. Let's say, I take your paycheck and pay all of your monthly expenses with it. Although I am paying your bills, are you receiving the profits from your work? You deserve 100 percent of what you worked for, not someone managing your check and not giving you what's left over after the bills are paid. In my case, using the same analogy, although you're offering to pay my bills, I have no clue on what the total amount of the check is before the bills are paid."

The CEO listened and told me that he would get back to me. The following week he told me that the band would receive the ticket profits from the Bayou Classic Battle of the Bands. I acted excited. I knew it was another "bait and switch" tactic, but I was tired of going back and forth.

After the Bayou Classic, I would find out that the band did receive ticket profits from the sales generated in the ticket office on the SU campus. It is safe to assume that less than 10 percent of the audience purchased a ticket in person at the ticket office on the campus of Southern University. On average, tickets are sold through Ticketmaster and can be purchased worldwide through any mobile device or computer. Why would they come on campus and pay for a ticket when it was not convenient? Furthermore, it is safe to assume that most of the attendees that supported the Human Jukebox weren't from Baton Rouge, so they couldn't come on campus to purchase a ticket physically, especially when the event is hosted in New Orleans!

Perhaps I should have heeded the warning about stirring the hornets' nest. Maybe I should have learned to accept the culture at SU! My constant meddling created more enemies. I was the band director with a reputation for being too arrogant and too smart for his own good! I never received a financial report from the Bayou Classic Battle of the Bands. In fact, my new supervisor no longer brought it up to me. She dropped the issue and no longer wanted to talk about it. Because of this, I finally realized that my days at Southern University were numbered. The SU Elite wanted me gone. I knew that it was only a matter of time before I would be ousted. My days were numbered. The only problem was the number of days was a lot less than I anticipated!

Chapter 28

It was the beginning of a new year and I had grown accustomed to the routine such as registration hiccups and preparation for parade season. Eager to change things up, I implemented my desire to emphasize the department's concert units, particularly the wind ensemble. To further expand the change, I appointed Kedric Taylor as the wind ensemble's conductor.

I had grown tired of Kedric Taylor's complaints. His main concern was the need to highlight the performances of the concert bands and the department doing more to encourage the high school band directors to offer what he called a comprehensive band program at their schools. Comprehensive band programs became a code for talking negatively about schools without a concert band. In reality, it means offering students a variety of styles such as marching band, jazz band, chamber ensembles and concert bands. I agreed with Kedric Taylor's concerns, but not his methods.

In an attempt to satisfy yet another one of the many problems he complained about, I placed him over organizing a pre-festival for concert bands. This new task entailed him getting adjudicators to listen to bands two to three weeks before their district concert band festival to tell the directors where they stood and what they needed to improve on before their big festival date.

"I want you to coordinate the pre-festival this year. You are in charge of getting the judges, trophies, food, etc. Just give me the cost of everything, and I will take care of it."

"Ok!"

Kedric Taylor was always complaining. I wanted him to have some "skin in the game" because I've grown tired of his ways. I was already making notes on whether I should keep him on the staff or not. I predicted that he would fumble while organizing the pre-festival, and I would have to come in at the last minute to fix it.

The first sign of Kedric Taylor's fumble came when a high school band director in Houston called me to ask about local trophy shops. It alarmed me because why would someone in Houston want to order trophies from Baton Rouge? As I gave the high school director the name of the local trophy shops, I began to inquire.

"Why do you need a trophy shop in Baton Rouge?"

"Oh! Kedric Taylor told me to help him with his project!"

I wasted no time calling Kedric Taylor. Here he was complaining about the band department not doing enough just to turn around and not do the job he created by complaining.

"Hey man, I got a call from the high school band director in Houston about trophy shops. I told you to let me know what you need. There's no need to get a third party involved."

He was shocked that I knew he attempted to outsource the job I assigned to him. I didn't even entertain his response. I gave him the name of a trophy shop and told him to call immediately. On the day of the pre-festival, I called Kedric Taylor early in the morning and asked how much we were paying the judges for their services along with what we are feeding them? Again, he stuttered.

"Uh ... Uh ... I haven't got to that part yet!"

"I told you to call me if you needed anything. Something was in my spirit telling me to call you, and I like that it landed!"

I told Kedric Taylor as he continued to make excuses for not calling me. I had the money available to pay the judges. I already had something prepared for the judges and the student workers. I ordered a seafood tray from a popular seafood and deli place for their lunch. I fed the student workers food from the popular chicken finger restaurant as well.

I knew that Kedric Taylor was in over his head. I've grown tired of doing things for Kedric Taylor. I purposely gave him this project to watch him fumble, yet I still came through as his safety net to catch him from falling to the ground. We averted the crisis because it was never a crisis in the first place. It was a lesson to teach Kedric Taylor to stop being divisive and messy, and the pre-festival went smoothly from there.

Communication between Kedric Taylor and the Director of Bands at Howard University was another issue. They made plans for the SU Wind Ensemble to perform in March at the HBCU Band Directors' Consortium in Atlanta, Georgia. While I had no problem with the idea of the performance, my problem was Kedric Taylor setting up a performance without notifying me. Eventually he had to tell me because he needed funding. The HBCU Consortium wasn't going to fund the trip, and neither was Howard's band director. By the time I got involved, the Director of Bands at Howard University was under the impression that I knew about the performance and approved it. I didn't explain anything to him because this matter of communication failure was an in-house issue.

I called Kedric Taylor into my office. I figured Kedric Taylor's consistent failure to come to me when he needed my assistance was because of the things that he said about me in the "streets." I don't know if Kedric Taylor suspected me of knowing that he was guilty or if his guilt chewed away at his conscience, but whatever it was, he definitely had a fear of coming to me as his supervisor.

"Why didn't you just tell me you wanted to schedule a performance? Call the Director of Bands at Howard University and tell him that the SU Wind Ensemble will perform. It means that the marching band must perform in more Mardi Gras parades this year because we don't have any money left in our travel budget. I will use the parade honorariums paid to me to fund the trip for the wind ensemble to Atlanta."

I took no chances in him fumbling this trip. I also told the entire staff that no one would receive parade honorariums this year as I planned to use the funds for the wind ensemble. I even let this staff see the quote for travel, meals, and lodging for the 60-member ensemble, which was a little bit more than $16,000. My willingness to come to the aid of a less than deserving staff member would come back to bite me pretty soon!

Kedric Taylor wasn't my only problem. Sharon came back like a new viral strain being more potent and deadly. She brought a new lawsuit which had more damning allegations than the previous one. The new lawsuit came with the addition of a detailed text message alleging that I asked for ten percent of the profit from a failed fundraiser. University auditors approached me about the alleged text message and the contract, which I did not sign, nor did I agree to.

"I did not ask Sharon for ten percent. I have no clue what ten percent would have looked like. Sharon failed to provide me with the required details, such as the expected profit and what percentage of the profit would go to the band and her company. How could I ask for ten percent of a number that Sharon didn't provide me with?"

The auditors took notes of my answers and verified that I did not approve the contract. I gave them a printout of emails that went back and forth between Sharon and me. I also told them everything about Sharon's infatuation with me, including the date rape incident. Eventually, the auditors cleared me of this investigation.

On the heels of the Sharon-ten-percent-gate-scandal investigation came another investigation. My leadership was under investigation. Due to the injury of two band members, the University paid $30,000 for a special counsel to investigate the band for hazing. I was under investigation as allegations surfaced that I fostered a secret society that allowed barbaric acts to exist.

Juked

While I would never say what a student will or won't do, I can say that my students knew my stance on hazing. They also knew that I had zero tolerance for it! I was more confident than ever that if the investigation uncovered any acts of hazing reported to me that I appropriately handled the situation as outlined by the band's policies and procedures in the handbook. I wasn't confident in whether something potentially was reported to my staff, and they covered it up.

I met with the Special Counsel, and we had a very positive interaction. I quickly answered all questions and provided all the information requested. The Special Counsel also notified me that she would interview a few band members individually as part of her investigation. I had no problems with this, and I didn't even warn the students that they would be potentially called in for an interview. I didn't want any appearance that I attempted to obstruct or tamper with the investigation. I can only assume that the investigation found zero evidence of hazing. Either there wasn't a conclusion of the investigation, or no one notified me if there were.

Finally, if dealing with Kedric Taylor's failures and investigations weren't enough, the university hired a new Executive Vice President-Provost. I now have a new boss; that's right, my sixth boss in four years! After adjusting to the leadership styles of four other supervisors and adapting to their individual, specific requirements caused confusion, frustration, and severe concerns. I felt like I was in a game of "hot potato," with me being the potato thrown around from individual to individual. How was I ever going to move forward with the band's business by constantly dealing with an administrator who didn't understand me and the unique problems of the organization? I wanted to throw my hands up and just continue to do my own thing. Besides, they never cared about us unless they needed us to perform somewhere to make them shine. The lack of structure and oversight forced me to operate the Human Jukebox as my own enterprise.

My sixth supervisor was also troubling due to his past job as he was the President of Florida A&M University. The fallout of the

2011 hazing incident that led to the death of one of the band's drum majors led to his termination. While I didn't know what role my new supervisor played in that particular situation, I did expect that he had a low tolerance for bands.

I met with him once, and I thought it was a positive meeting. He began to talk about the vital role that HBCU Bands play in the school's overall culture. I was happy to hear his stance on bands, finances, and overall support.

"I look forward to working with you. I am in my 4th year as Director of Bands, and I've dealt with many supervisors."

Unfortunately, our tenure together was short-lived. Approximately three weeks later, he called me to another meeting where he wasn't present. I met with the Dean of the College of Humanities and Interdisciplinary Studies. She had a memo from him stating that she was now my supervisor. So now, I've been assigned my 7th supervisor within four years, with THREE supervisors in the 2017-2018 academic year alone.

While I mean no disrespect to the Dean, the persecution, problems, pressure, and politics of the band department and our needs are way beyond her scope of duties. Deans specialize in overseeing budgets from an academic perspective as they are not equipped for the politics and public relations aspect that the band demands and commands. The budget of the band's equipment alone is more than the equipment budget of all of the departments combined that fell under her supervision. The Dean had no clue how to advise me on anything. It was my job to help her help me since she was new to her post.

The first issue I immediately brought to my 7th supervisor was my issue with Kedric Taylor, the Associate Director of Bands. Being in over her head, Dean advised me to see her supervisor, Dr. Ammons (Executive Vice-President-Provost). Dr. Ammons directed me to see the General Counsel to Dr. Belton. I knew that this was a mistake due to my history with the General Counsel. However, I followed his advice because I wanted to see if

Juked

the General Counsel was who I suspected her of being, a gossiping snake!

After revealing to the General Counsel my thoughts on whether to terminate Kedric Taylor or not, she was too eager to tell me how to go about doing so. Yet, she could not quote one university policy or procedure to help me with this process. Listening to my novice supervisor's advice along with Dr. Ammons would be another issue that would come back to haunt me soon. I knew that trouble was on the way. The SU Elite made it evident that they wanted to water my power and influence down. If or when they strike, I have no place to report that's high enough on the chain of command!

CHAPTER 29

It was January 2018, and I was pushing my vision even more. The pressure to highlight the entire band department not only pushed my vision but also forced additional performances and fundraising. The commitments were grand and sure to let the world know that Southern University's Department of Bands was the "Greatest of All Time"!

The first commitment was accepting an invitation to perform at the 2020 Tournament of Roses Parade, the Rose Bowl Parade, in Pasadena, California. A professor from the SU Law Center called to see if we would be interested in performing. I jumped at the opportunity to be a part of the historic event. Admittedly, I initially wasn't excited about the possibility of performing. Although I had this great desire to expand the Human Jukebox's portfolio, I liked to be unique. Events like the "Floyd Mayweather's Grand Arrival" taught me never to sell myself short. We were the only band, and the organizers paid all expenses. The band performed in The Tournament of Roses Parade in 1982, so going back in 2020 wouldn't be a first for the organization.

Another reason for my apprehension was the official invitation. To qualify, the parade organizers must send you an official invitation. But once the invitation arrives, I would have to plan an enormous fund-raising engine. For a band of our caliber, it would cost more than $100,000 to participate. While I was confident that we could raise the money, I didn't think it was wise to spend that type of money for a one-time event when the band had more pressing needs. In order to provide an experience for the students to participate in yet another historic event, I knew that we would have to start another fundraiser in the fall.

Juked

The professor contacted me in 2018 because she realized that it would take at least 18 months to successfully fund-raise for the event. Even though I had apprehensions, I didn't want to pass up a golden opportunity. I told the law center professor that I was on board as she began to reach out to her connections in high places on The Tournament of Roses committee.

Also in January, Kedric Taylor was preparing the wind ensemble to perform at the HBCU Band Directors' Consortium in late March. The consortium is an organization for HBCU band directors to network and address the issues that are unique to HBCU bands. Every year, bands perform at the consortium, such as various honor bands and other ensembles to include a featured performance by an invited HBCU concert band and 2018 was Southern University's turn.

Due to the commitment I made to fund the wind ensemble's travel to Atlanta, Georgia, we were looking at a particularly long parade season this year. We started the year similar to the previous year, in Shreveport, Louisiana, for the Shreveport Martin Luther King, Jr. Day parade. We had our usual parade lineup for Mardi Gras, but we were adding the Zulu parade. I never liked performing for that parade because of how early we would have to leave Baton Rouge to prepare for the parade. This year we had to report to the band hall at 4:30am to arrive on time. Also, I didn't particularly appreciate how SOME Human Jukebox alumni band members, affiliated with the Krewe of Zulu, approached me in a "shady" way about performing in that parade.

The Zulu parade is one that I wish I would have never agreed to participate in. Throughout the many Mardi Gras seasons of my career, I have always received an honorarium for most Mardi Gras parades. I handle the details of the parades either in person or over the phone, but I would always follow up with an email for the sake of clarity and transparency. I didn't use personal email. I've always used the email account provided to me through my employer. It was the same approach that I took with the officials of the Zulu parade, which was an approach that would come back to bite me later. I am not blaming the Krewe of Zulu officials for anything involving this situation. I had no evidence that they tipped off the Louisiana Board of Ethics to my practices. I am only mentioning them due to the "shady" representatives of their krewe who contacted me concerning the parade. Shady representatives who were also past members of the Human Jukebox.

Band directors receiving honorariums isn't anything new. If a band director who participates in Mardi Gras parades, especially in Louisiana, tells you that they've never heard of this practice, it is probably because they don't want you in their business. Parade honorariums did not start, nor did they end with my situation. The fact that I used my employer-issued email either reveals that I was transparent in operating what I considered normal band business, or it proves that I am the biggest fool on the planet! I am sure some would rather the latter to be true than the former. Still, if I had any unethical/criminal intent, I definitely wouldn't use my personal email yet along with my employer-issued email. Also, I would have at least requested cash and not a check that authorities could easily trace.

My commitment to fund the wind ensemble's travel had me feeling obligated to deal with people I otherwise wouldn't. If it wasn't evident already, Zulu was not my favorite parade. My favorite parade was the Krewe of Bacchus. Moreso, I loved the annual battle before the parade, better known as "Bloody Sunday."

During the fall of 2017, I began to observe the Director of Bands at Miles College, an HBCU in Alabama, calling out a particular band director in a subliminal manner during his social media interviews. Although he never said a name, I knew that the Miles "Purple Marching Machine (PMM)" director referred to me. I never entertained him, but I did notice his band making some "noise" in the HBCU band world. Even though they were in the process of making a more prominent name for themselves, I always knew that they would be no match for the Human Jukebox.

"Perhaps the PMM will battle the other lightweights."

Juked

I prepared the Human Jukebox for battle mode. Although I didn't anticipate battling anyone this particular year, I was no fool. I knew it was better to prepare for battle than to not prepare at all. I began to receive more subliminal warnings on social media from Miles' director.

Maybe the Miles' director took my going back and forth with Dr. Bonds, Talladega College's band director, in the past as a sign that I was easy to bait. I held my cool. It served no purpose to trash talk Miles as nothing good would come out of it for us. However, my staff kept me current with the latest trash talk for Bloody Sunday.

"Nope! We are not entertaining that this year! I am not responding because not only don't I want to battle, but Miles College also isn't a worthy opponent. Still, I won't allow them to disrespect us. If they come up to us, they will be dealt with accordingly!"

We made it at our usual time the day of the Krewe of Bacchus Parade. As soon as I got off the bus, instigators were already telling me that Miles College was there and what their director "supposedly" said. We moved to our usual spot and began to warm up by playing a few school-spirit tunes. While conducting the band, in my left peripheral view I could see a crowd of people running towards us. It wasn't the type of running where bandheads were attempting to get a better view of us. It was a violent type of running as if they were ready to fight. I immediately looked to my left and saw Miles running towards us. The director must've thought that they were in a place called Somewhere, Alabama, because clearly, he had no clue what a real street battle in New Orleans entailed. He was about to learn today!

The Bacchus parade official asked us to shake hands like two boxers before a fight. I had only said one thing, "Welcome to Louisiana!" I turned towards Brian Simmons and said, "Hey man! It's on you. Handle this lightweight!"

I chilled out for the rest of the battle. Miles College started the battle with a mishap. Apparently, they were too excited and started their tune off beat as the crowd began to "Boo!" It was now time for the Human Jukebox to answer what I considered a "high school band on steroids." Brian Simmons called the tune "Both Sides" by NAV & Metro Boomin featuring 21 Savage and the rest was history!

We could have ended the battle with one song. We destroyed Miles' pride! Basically, the look from the director expressed that he didn't expect that type of monstrous sound to slap him in the face! The staff wanted to continue to punish them, so I just let them have fun. The director ran up to me in one part of the battle. From the looks of it on YouTube, it appears that he trash-talked me, but he didn't. "I love your band!" I responded with, "I know that you do!" Brian Simmons and the director went back and forth. I stayed back laughing. Bloody Sunday 2018 went down in history as the most "lopsided" battle of the Bloody Sunday series!

Mardi Gras was in February and by Valentine's Day it was over. February was also the last time that I experienced a season of true happiness. Towards the latter part of the month, my twin and I turned 40 years old. Friends and family made a big deal of it. It was an eventful day from sun-up to sun-down.

I knew that my birthday would be my last "hoorah" for a little while as I already had a surgical procedure scheduled for the following week. I was finally getting rid of a problem that I had suffered with since I was 8 years old, tonsillitis. From the age of 8 to 39, I had to deal with my tonsils swelling at least four times a year. I finally had enough of it, and I scheduled surgery to have my tonsils removed as a 40th birthday gift to myself. The procedure caused me to be down for two weeks.

I returned to work two weeks later, around noon. It was a beautiful sunny day, not a cloud in the sky. For some reason, Marissa, Human Jukebox Alumni Association President, was in town. I remember walking to the student union with her and talking

Juked

to a couple of students. It is something that I have never done. I wanted to be outside and around the students for some reason. Marissa and I made it back to my office and we began to talk.

"It is a really beautiful day. I've been cramped up inside for two weeks recovering from having my tonsils removed. Let's go outside and talk!"

We proceeded to the front doors of the building and walked outside. As Marissa and I engaged in conversation, I noticed a news vehicle parked next to my truck. As I looked at the news vehicle, two individuals ran towards me as if they were on a "sneak attack" and their camera was on.

I received a warning about a week before that an infamous local investigative reporter sought information on me concerning something about Dancing Doll fees. I wasn't clear why a reporter would want to know about that, but it alarmed me. What disturbed me was the reporter's trashy tactics, which include coming to an individual's house while knocking on their door with a live camera ready to record. Although I can understand why the reporter's tactics may be entertaining to some, this practice is very misleading.

In the situation concerning me, the reporter and the cameraman (who was also a former SU band member from Kedric Taylor's hometown) rushed towards me while I conversed with Marissa. Because I was familiar with the reporter's tactics, I knew I had two choices: to walk away while being recorded or stand still and hold my ground. I knew that either way, whatever the reporter wanted from me would be on the local news, and I didn't want to be on television with the appearance of running away from him. I've seen that same reporter do it too many times to other prominent African American figures in the city. I decided I would stand my ground. As I did, the reporter began to ask me about an arrest from 13 years ago in Lake Charles, Louisiana involving missing band money.

It was March 2005, and I was the band director at Washington Marion-Magnet High School. Seniors at the school were the only ones to wear letterman jackets. The process for the band seniors begins the second semester of their junior year. The band department paid for the jackets. The students were responsible for the patches and designs to customize their letterman jacket.

That month I collected money from the junior class for their senior jackets. I collected approximately $1,200 one day. The school's bookkeeper was out so I decided to lock the money in my desk drawer while leaving for my thirty-minute lunch break. When I returned to the office, the cash was gone. I reported the missing funds to the principal, and she immediately called the central office and notified the school district's auditing department.

After the interview, I was informed that the auditors conducted a full audit on the band from 2001-2005. The auditors suspected that some of the band boosters were taking advantage of the system that was in place for concession stands and band fees. All receipt books in my possession were quickly turned over to the auditors. Focus moved to everyone who signed the receipts indicating they received payments for fundraisers, band trips, band fees, etc. In all, there were three people that signed the receipt book, two-band boosters and me. The auditors decided to get detectives from the local sheriff's office involved. Instantly, things took a turn for the worse.

Sometime during the formal audit, a janitor confessed that he had taken the money out of my desk drawer when I was out of the office. He was arrested, and the school district terminated him from his position. Even though the person that took the $1,200 had been discovered, the results of the audit stated that $40,000 was missing. How they arrived at the magic number of $40,000 missing was unknown to me.

As the reporter asked me about the situation, it puzzled me. In that case, I was never charged and was cleared by the District Attorney. I went through an extensive criminal background check

Juked

upon my hire at SU in 2006. I knew that I had no criminal record. I stood there unbothered. I answered the questions about my past as the reporter attempted to draw a connection between it and the lawsuit filed by Sharon. I also knew that the reporter would continue digging because his poorly viewed news station needed whatever ratings they could get.

Once the reporter left, I called my twin brother. He just so happened to be leaving the courthouse in Lake Charles, Louisiana. He went to the DA's office to forward proof to the reporter that the questions asked about my past were a dead issue. When the story aired on the 6 o'clock news, the reporter showed the DA's document which stated no charges were filed. Still, as he displayed the document for the viewers to see, the news reporter made some very misleading comments. "Haymer's twin brother 'just so happened' to have a copy of the document handy." The comment was an attempt to make the viewers doubt the validity of the document. What was also disappointing was SU's attempt to keep me quiet while refusing to make a public comment in my defense. I suspected that "The SU Elite" wanted me trashed through the news as I've become too popular and too influential for them to manage. I was at the height of my career, and the news coverage of the new lawsuit filed by Sharon along with the trashy TV reporter's investigation was just enough to begin swaying the public's opinion that caused me to lose support slowly. It was only the beginning of the heat being turned up, ready for the boil!

Coming off my two-week recovery to face the reporter was a challenge. However, it was now March, and I was ready to go to Atlanta for the HBCU Band Directors' Consortium. We managed to do a fantastic job promoting the Human Jukebox through our various ventures over the years, but we didn't emphasize the same energy in our concert ensembles. I've made my opinion of Kedric Taylor well known at this point. Although I may have left out a few adjectives to describe him, I never denied the fact that he's a good teacher when focused.

Even though I questioned Kedric Taylor's motives for his desire to perform, I knew that it was best to get behind this trip because I understood that the moment was bigger than any ego. In fact, the moment was bigger than any of us. I saw it necessary to display to our peers "the secret side of SU." I wanted to introduce the excellent musicianship that the Southern University Department of Bands offers to the other HBCU band directors because they have never seen it!

The consortium was held at the Ray Charles Theater of Performing Arts on the campus of Morehouse College. The architecture and sheer beauty of the place represented the type of auditorium where awards shows like the Academy Awards would take place. Morehouse's concert band warming-up on stage gave me a sense of the auditorium's acoustics. After hearing them, I knew the wind ensemble would really shine.

The wind ensemble went to the warm-up room. I noticed that Kedric Taylor was quite fidgety and nervous. I told him to calm down. He appeared to be under pressure, but everything was going as planned. I assume that his pressure was having to make sure that we represented the department at one hundred percent or the fact he now had to produce. Either way, I knew he would succeed as I sat calmly with my conductor's baton ready to conduct *Slava* by Leonard Bernstein.

As we began the performance, Kedric Taylor went from being nervous to becoming a little more comfortable. By the time it was my turn to conduct, the wind ensemble had already performed about four selections as they were warmed up and tuned up. I approached the stage like a maestro, then I took a bow and turned around to face the wind ensemble and gave the downbeat. It was an effortless performance for me, and my conducting helped bring more life into the music. Little did I know that would be the last time that I would ever conduct any ensemble of the SU Band again, and it was a great way to "drop the baton!" After the selection that I conducted was over, Kedric Taylor kept the performance going with three more pieces. I closed my eyes and exhaled while listening to the beautiful sounds of the SU Wind Ensemble. He did a phenomenal job preparing the wind ensemble to perform at the HBCU Band Directors' Consortium.

We left Morehouse College feeling good about our performance, and it was what I expected it to be. That performance made a statement! We made it perfectly clear that Southern University has the premier band department and that there wasn't a genre of music that we couldn't master. The Southern University Wind Ensemble represented the University at a high level of excellence and integrity! I was really proud of Kedric Taylor and the students. They looked like a million-dollar band on stage in the nicely architecture auditorium in their elegant formal wear and their new top-of-the line concert band instruments.

After we made it back to the hotel, Lorenzo Hart and I drove the rental van to the closest pizza place. I wanted to make sure that the students ate well so I paid for 70 large pizzas and sodas. Like typical college students, they were overjoyed with having pizza for dinner. I was thrilled and excited about our superior performance. However, I knew that the euphoria would only last a few days before Kedric Taylor would return to what he does best, dividing and hating!

It didn't take long for him to get back to his old tricks. I always looked forward to being on the road recruiting with the staff, but this year was a bit different, thanks to Kedric Taylor and Jabari. Due to the wind ensemble's trip to Atlanta, Georgia, we broke this year's recruiting trip into two parts. The first half of the trip had us going west. We went to our usual stops in Texas and as far east as Mississippi. Although this trip showcased a high interest of high school seniors wanting to join the Human Jukebox, it also sealed the deal of wanting to terminate Kedric Taylor and Jabari.

While on this trip, I grew tired of playing games with Kedric Taylor. Jabari knew my every move thanks to Kedric Taylor telling him, as he would often call during the most "convenient" times while we were on the road. I caught on to their games. I noticed every time I ignored Jabari's call, he would call Kedric Taylor shortly after.

Not only did I notice but, Brian Simmons noticed as well. In fact, he confronted Kedric Taylor. When the confrontation happened, I laughed so hard because he told him the truth. Kedric Taylor sat there looking like a deer caught in headlights. I also noticed Kedric Taylor being on his phone during my most vulnerable times, such as when I was in fellowship with the alumni, social drinking, and when I was distracted. I knew that he was reporting to someone my every move. My final straw was the celebration in Dallas.

While in Dallas, we celebrated with some of the Southern University Alumni Federation-Dallas Chapter members. We took a celebratory tequila shot to commemorate our success in recruiting more students from their area. In addition, the Dallas chapter looked forward to the Human Jukebox and the SU football team coming to their town for the first time since the 1980s for a football game scheduled for fall 2018. Everyone celebrated except for one person, Kedric Taylor. He was busy "reporting the news" to his sources through text messaging. Brian Simmons caught on to Kedric Taylor's tactics as well. He and I went to the bar to get a shot to drink. I spoke with Brian Simmons.

"Man, I can't deal with this anymore. I don't trust Kedric Taylor, and I don't want him anywhere around me!"

I've seen Kedric Taylor drink with us on many occasions, but he wouldn't partake on this day. It was as if he tried to stay away to let whomever he reported know that we were the bad guys! Brian Simmons was fed up too. He took a shot glass full of gin and slammed it on the table in front of Kedric Taylor.

"You are sitting over here all standoffish, drink!"

Kedric Taylor continued to look like a deer caught in headlights. He refused the drink. I was tired of playing the game, and soon he and I would have to have a serious conversation. I

Juked

finally had to let him know everything that I knew, which was very disturbing details that I've been sitting on for years and never mentioned. I was finally ready to talk about it, but I knew once I started that conversation there would be no way that he could lie his way out of it. I also knew that once I let the "cat out of the bag," serious consequences and repercussions would follow! The confrontation had to hold until after the performance in Atlanta and the concert scheduled for late April on campus.

The major performance at Morehouse College was over and it was time for the scheduled second half of the recruiting trip with the band staff. I had one exception, I told Kedric Taylor to stay home. I didn't bother to explain as I was simply tired of his catty ways! I told him through his favorite form of communication, text message.

"I need you to hold everything down at work. The rest of the staff and I are going on the road to recruit."

"What am I supposed to do at work while everyone is gone?"

"Do what you normally do!"

I thought that was a rather stupid question, but that was the end of the conversation. I was preparing to "sweep the house and take out the trash," which simply means I was on the move, with the first on the chopping block being the MBM team.

Approximately two weeks before our second recruiting trip, I had a meeting with Attorney Castille, General Counsel to the SU System Foundation. He was the same gentleman I met four years earlier when I was trying to push the contract through for the MBM team. It was a very difficult meeting for me. Although Attorney Castille didn't say it, his expression and tone of voice gave me "I told you so vibes!" I remember his initial concerns about my decision to go into business with Jabari due to his very questionable and shady background!

I wanted to make sure that it was okay to no longer conduct business with the MBM team. I wanted to be extra careful. Due to the media circus that was already present from a lawsuit from Sharon, I didn't want to cause any more problems for the university.

"The contract actually expired with the MBM team in September of 2016. They added a clause that automatically renewed the contract for an additional year if you chose not to end the contract in September of 2015. That has expired as well."

"Well, when I notify them that I will move in another direction, can I direct them to you if they have any further questions? I am not going to go back and forth with Jabari!"

"Sure thing, Nathan!"

My next step was to confront Sonja. I needed to let her know that I fulfilled my promise by waiting an additional year to think about the conclusion that I'd already come to a year prior.

"It's now almost April of 2018. I told you last March that I did not want to renew the MBM team's contract! Because I didn't listen to you regarding Sharon, I wanted to make sure I wasn't making an emotional decision concerning the MBM team. A year later, I still feel the same way!"

"OK, Haymer. You did what I asked, so do what you feel is necessary but prepare yourself for the backlash!"

"I've been receiving backlash along with backstabbing from the MBM team since day one!"

We had a very relaxed time on the road as everyone could finally be authentic. We always got along well as staff but the tension from the fakeness was always so thick that you could cut it with a knife. On this trip nothing felt fake or forced. I didn't even get the usual annoying 20 to 30 calls a day from Jabari, but he wasn't done with his petty tactics yet.

Juked

I'd made my mind up a year ago, so any decisions I made at this point were truly made with zero emotions involved. Since I planned on notifying the MBM team of my intent to move in another direction as soon as the staff and I return from the second recruiting trip, I purposely ignored one or two emails from Jabari while on this trip. He kept sending me the same emails that I ignored. However, he kept adding in the subject line "2nd notice, 3rd notice, 4th notice." I checked my email while leaving Memphis, Tennessee and screamed.

"I am sick of him bothering me! It's like Jabari sensed when I was at peace so that he could purposely disturb me!"

Lorenzo Hart and Brian Simmons just looked at me with concern. They didn't know where I was coming from, nor did I share my intentions of moving on without the MBM team. My annoyance would not allow me to wait until the trip was over. I immediately replied to Jabari's pestering emails:

I regret to inform you that I am immediately moving in another direction without the MBM team. Please see the Southern University System Foundation's General Counsel if you have any further questions or comments, as your services are no longer needed!

After sending the email to Jabari, I no longer received any communication from him again. I was so happy that "the pest" was finally out of my life and out of my business. I knew that he wouldn't go out without attempting to strike back.

The following day while still on the road recruiting, I got a call from the Chief of the SUPD. Chief and I regularly talked, so for her to call me wasn't an alarming situation.

"Hey, Chief! What's going on?"

"Mr. Haymer, Jabari is on campus with an 18-wheeler trailer that has the Human Jukebox logo on it. There is nowhere on campus to park it, so I told him to leave it at the police lot for now. They had some kind of ceremony on campus, and Jabari had Kedric Taylor to speak!"

I was so annoyed. He didn't have my approval to bring a trailer on campus. I remember us talking about getting a trailer in 2014. The trailer would follow the buses while the band traveled to away games, but I thought it was a bit too much because we had enough storage space underneath our buses. The nerve of Jabari! I told him via email that I was going in a different direction, and I know he got the message. I also know he and Kedric Taylor were on campus "cooking up a plan!" I thanked her for the news, and we ended the conversation.

Kedric Taylor should have known not to speak on behalf of the band without contacting me. I knew that he was in his feelings because I left him at home. Actually, Jabari and Kedric Taylor were both in their feelings. I knew that I needed to continue moving forward and terminate Kedric Taylor! The only problem was I didn't want to "pull the trigger" until the end of the semester. We still had a band concert featuring the performances of the symphonic band and the wind ensemble. Plus, we had the band banquet coming up and the spring graduation performance.

Due to my frustrations of waiting, I let my intentions of terminating Kedric Taylor out. In all, five people knew that I wanted to terminate Kedric Taylor. Brian Simmons; Mr. Carter, the trusted high school band director who would give me information; Dr. Bryant (the Dean), my 7th and current supervisor; Dr. Ammons, the Executive Vice President-Provost; and Attorney Woods, the General counsel to the President-Chancellor all knew and had to keep the secret. For five people to keep this secret, all FIVE of them would have to be dead. Take a guess – they're all alive and the news of my decision on terminating Kedric Taylor leaked!

Chapter 30

If my life was a ticking time bomb, then April 2018 was the detonator! It was as if my life had turned into a landmine and from April 1st to April 30th, each day saw another bomb explode. The month began with a call from my 7th supervisor, Dr. Bryant, Dean.

"Mr. Haymer, they want us to come to the President-Chancellor's office for a meeting tomorrow."

"OK. Do you know what the meeting is about?"

"I don't know much, just something about some emails that you sent that were not above board."

I knew what the term "above board" meant. I did a Google search on the word anyway because I knew it couldn't have meant what I thought. According to Google, above board meant "legitimate, honest, and open." I've never sent an email that I would consider not above board.

I waited in anticipation for the next day. Due to the series of investigations I've gone through thus far in the 2017-18 academic year alone, I knew that it was nothing good. I called Sonja to notify her of yet another potential investigation. I told her that I would keep her posted because I knew that I had no allies in the office of the President-Chancellor.

The following day, I went to the meeting prepared to expect more allegations and another "witch hunt." I brought my briefcase with my second cell phone inside. I already had the voice recorder app running to record the entire meeting.

The individuals present at the meeting were Attorney Woods, General Counsel to the President-Chancellor, Janene Tate, Director of Media Relations, Dr. Bryant, and me. Attorney Woods started the meeting. She mentioned the reporter who used trashy tactics in the news story dealing with my past issue as a high school band director. Although the news story intended to shame me publicly, it never went anywhere. Whoever was the mastermind behind the plot to destroy me kept feeding the trashy reporter more information. I learned in the meeting that he submitted a public records request for my emails. Because of this, university officials discovered that I conducted some "unethical practices" by receiving parade honorariums in 2018.

Dr. Bryant was flabbergasted at the fact that I received a little over $14,000 in parade honorariums. She was just not equipped or experienced enough to understand the complex business of the band. Attorney Woods seemed shocked. I guess that she anticipated a "gotcha" moment. I assume she expected I would deny everything because she had a printout of my emails in a folder ready to prove that I was guilty. Before we even got that far, I blew her mind and the "gotcha" moment that she anticipated never materialized.

"Yes, I received $14,000 in honorariums this year. That's normal practice. I've been receiving honorariums every year!"

"How long have you been receiving parade honorariums?"

"I've been receiving parade honorariums since the first year I became a band director, 2001!" At this point, Attorney Woods opened her folder that contained my emails. Also, in the "folder of evidence" was data on something else.

"Mr. Haymer, you're supposed to take a mandatory online training every year on the state's ethics laws. According to your data in Human Resources, you haven't completed the training in three years!"

"For me not to take a mandatory training in three years tells me two things. First, I obviously didn't know I had to take the training because no one ever communicated the information to me. Second

Juked

and most importantly, it lets me know that there isn't any accountability at SU!"

"No accountability! What do you mean, Mr. Haymer?" Attorney Woods asked. I could tell that my statement puzzled her. She also had a look of pleasure on her face as I interpreted it as "I finally got you!"

"You just stated that I haven't taken the 'mandatory training' in three years. How 'mandatory' is it? I never received any write-ups or warnings. The fact that you know that I didn't do what I was supposed to do for three years tells me that there is a system of checks and balances in place. The fact that no one notified me about the violation also tells me that there is a bigger problem at this university: no accountability! If my staff didn't do something that I told them was 'mandatory' in three days, let alone three years, there would be a serious discussion. My three years of not doing something 'mandatory' would have been four years or more if this situation hadn't come up!

"Perhaps the fact that you didn't take the mandatory ethics training may be a good defense for you. The President-Chancellor isn't here, but I'll speak to him on your behalf!"

Attorney Woods's statement brought me no comfort. I knew she was never for me years ago. Janene Tate responded.

"Mr. Haymer, you have nothing to worry about. I know how annoying that news reporter can be, and I will be your 'Olivia Pope.' Just let me handle this. I don't want you to make any comments to the media!"

Ms. Tate's statement drew reference to the ABC television series called *Scandal*. She was likening herself to the main character named "Olivia Pope." I had no faith in her. She was definitely an "Olivia NOPE." The only thing she would say on the news in my defense was "no comment!"

Due to the public records request, Southern had to release my emails. The tabloid reporter continued his negative coverage on the "SU Band Director." Simultaneously, the news put the most damaging parts of my emails on the air. They piecemealed my emails. Never did the media state the standard practice of band directors regularly operating with honorariums. They also never showed my complete emails or referenced the context of the emails.

The most disappointing part was not the media but the lack of public support from my fellow band directors. When Niles (attorney and twin brother) raised the point that college band directors received parade honorariums regularly, not one band director came to my defense. Publicly, they all kept silent but privately they would send me support through social media DMs. The lack of support and denial of honorarium knowledge was extremely hurtful, and their "private support" meant nothing to me! Two years after the fact, the FBI verified the honorarium practice, especially in the city of New Orleans. Although the media smeared me with their misleading facts, it's great to go on record to clearly and unequivocally state that all school level bands that march in a Louisiana Mardi Gras parade are paid for the band's performance and the directors receive payments as well!

When the 2016 Baton Rouge flood occurred, my house was uninhabitable. However, I would go to my house once a week. These weekly visits consisted of me checking on the house, mowing the lawn, and checking the mail. One of the routine checks delivered a notice from the Louisiana Board of Ethics. Here was my official notification of being under investigation due to my receipt of Mardi Gras parade honorariums. The notification also included a copy of the complaint letter. With tons of grammatical errors, the letter was so poorly written which made it impossible to figure out who wrote it. However, after reading the letter, my mind went straight to the MBM team.

Eric, the other half of the MBM Team, may have been the more "Christian" partner but really, he was more passive aggressive and thus more dangerous. At times, he would tell me about his

Juked

connection with a lady that worked at the Louisiana Board of Ethics while giving me all types of subliminal warnings about receiving honorariums. Jabari and Kedric Taylor were bad, but Eric was the undercover, secret weapon.

I remember being on the phone with Eric and Jabari after the first Crankfest when Eric told me that he knew for a fact that I received an honorarium for the event. He was adamant that I lied to them about receiving an honorarium and shared that someone on my staff told him. Eventually, he revealed that his source was Lorenzo Hart. I knew he was lying. I was already aware that Kedric Taylor told a lot of people in his circle, including Eric, about the honorarium.

Kedric Taylor was upset because he wasn't satisfied with "his cut" of the money and thought I held out on him. His thought process was ironic especially since I didn't make one dime but instead split the honorarium equally amongst my three staff members. Unfortunately, I had to respond to their accusation and remind the MBM Team that they were the employees.

. "I didn't receive one dime from Crankfest. Furthermore, you are not my board of directors. I don't report to the MBM team, y'all report to me!"

While taking in the news of the investigation, I continued to reflect on previous conversations with the MBM team. Then I recalled a recent conversation with Kedric Taylor and his attempt to confirm the rumor of him about to be fired.

The first half of April 2018 the wind ensemble was about to begin rehearsal when Kedric Taylor knocked on my door. Although it was upsetting and I was not happy to see him, I gave him a nod to come in. He approached me with a screenshot on his phone. The screenshot was from a gentleman I didn't know, although I was familiar with his name.

The screenshot had Kedric Taylor very nervous. His hand was trembling when he passed me his phone. On the phone was someone he knew very well but denied knowing when asked. The screenshot read, "Haymer is going crazy. He fired his marketing and brand management team, and next, he will fire Kedric Taylor!" I gave him his phone back.

"Go rehearse your band, man!"

Through tears forming in his eyes, he responded. "Man, I hope this isn't true. We are a good team. We are like the Chicago Bulls of the 1990s!"

"Who is that in the screenshot?"

"I don't know. Somebody sent it to my phone!" Kedric Taylor answered.

When Kedric Taylor answered my question, I wanted to shoot him right there on the spot because I knew that he was lying to my face. However, I played along because I knew now wasn't the time to tell him what I knew and how I knew of the gentleman in the screenshot. If I had revealed what I knew at that moment, I would have had to fire him on the spot, and I wasn't ready to "pull that trigger" due to the unfinished business of the semester. He had no clue what I knew. The guy in the screenshot is a name that I've been hearing about for five years.

"Now isn't the time to discuss this matter. Besides, you don't know the guy in the screenshot, so why are you so worked up about what he stated?"

I knew for a fact that the guy in the screenshot was somebody in Kedric Taylor's circle which is why he was nervous. If he was going to play dumb, I was going to help him. Besides, he already looked dumb by bringing me his phone. Also, he didn't want to let the conversation go, but I insisted that he return to his rehearsal as now wasn't the time!

I admit I was disturbed by the screenshot. It angered me. It further confirmed everything that I knew all along. It was now personal. I knew things before I even hired Kedric Taylor, but ignored them. It was foolish to let two known snakes in the front door. However, I quickly realized that I wasn't dealing with just two snakes. With the investigation staring me in the face, I could admit that Kedric Taylor and Jabari were not snakes but part of a bigger group!

I began to suspect that my recent dismissal of Eric and Jabari coupled with Kedric Taylor finding out that he may be next on the chopping block, sparked them to work together to bring me down! I knew that the MBM team would strike back after I fired them. Even more confusing was Kedric Taylor working with Eric and Jabari after years of speaking out against them. Yet, the MBM Team denied having any part in the scandal, but I knew better.

A local tabloid investigative reporter made a public records request for my emails. An anonymous letter sent to the Louisiana Board of Ethics dated shortly after the dismissal of the MBM team. A coincidence maybe, but not in this case when it comes to me. There was no coincidence!!!

"Christian" Eric already told on himself a couple of years before this incident by revealing to me his source on the Board of Ethics. Jabari's sister, a former employee in Southern University Auditor's office, had the connections and knew the buzzwords to get the Louisiana Board of Ethics and the tabloid journalist's attention. Kedric Taylor knew precisely what I received in the honorariums that were being investigated because I used that money to fund the trip for the SU Wind Ensemble. Not only was it the group that he conducted, but the honorariums were also for a trip that he accepted without my authority!

I was frustrated by the investigation. It was a waste of time and taxpayers' resources. The evidence was in my public emails. I already admitted receiving the money as it was a mode of normal operations. If it was unethical, I didn't know, and I've been doing it my whole career. I realized that ignorance of the law is no excuse. I was willing to be held accountable. Don't cherry-pick who to enforce the law with when damn near everyone in my profession who performed in a New Orleans Mardi Gras parade were and still are doing the same thing.

Further reflection of the investigation highlighted a point that Kedric Taylor would often tell me. "We would never get ahead with the use of the MBM team because they are going about it the wrong way. They are making everything about them, and that's not of God. God won't bless that!"

I found it mighty "rich" for Kedric Taylor to profess what is "of God." The hypocrisy of Kedric Taylor and "Christian" Eric amazed me. At this moment in my life, I could plainly see that they discovered a new biblical verse, "The enemy of thine enemy is thine friend." I could now see it. Jabari, "Christian" Eric, Kedric Taylor, Brandon Dumas, Attorney Woods, and Sharon were a pack of wolves. Individually, they were harmless. However, once united, they were powerful and dangerous. Together, they united in a "bible-thumping" plot to take me down!

Chapter 31

Thursday, April 26, 2018, was the day of the band's annual banquet. Although it was banquet day, it was so much more.

Another year, another banquet and some last-minute things to do to prepare for the event. I had to go to my office to unload my truck of all the awards. I had to get my haircut and stop by the mall to get a new dress shirt. Headed to my apartment, I received a disturbing phone call from Dr. Bryant, my 7th supervisor.

"Mr. Haymer! Where have you been?"

"I've been running around taking care of last-minute business for the band banquet tonight."

"We had a one o'clock meeting! Did you forget?".

"Meeting! What meeting?"

"Mr. Haymer, you should've come to the meeting."

"The band banquet is one of the most important events of the year. I hope that you can understand why it slipped my mind."

I realized I had accepted a meeting for 1:00pm. I apologized. I didn't understand what the big deal was. I'd never missed a meeting before, nor was I aware of the nature of the meeting.

"I need you to pull over because it sounds like you are driving."

"Yes, I am driving, but I am on the Interstate. I can't just pull over, but you can go ahead and tell me what you need to tell me."

"Mr. Haymer as your direct supervisor, it gives me no pleasure to say this, but I am following an order to tell you that either you resign, or you will be terminated!"

"WHAT THE HELL DO YOU MEAN! AHH ...UGHH!"

I screamed at the top of my lungs. I screamed out of concern for my safety. I screamed for sanity.

"Please pull over and calm down!"

"Don't tell me to calm down. You called to tell me I'm fired? OH, HELL NO! WHY?"

"Mr. Haymer, I am only the messenger. I wish that you would have come to the meeting. 'They' wanted to reassign you as a professor in the music department, but when you didn't show up, 'they' took your absence as an insult and arrogance. Wait a minute, let me call you back! Since I have you on the phone now, I am going to see if the offer for you to reassign is still on the table!"

Driving along Interstate-10, I found myself near the campus of Louisiana State University. I was in heavy traffic. I screamed and wanted to drive my truck over the barrier on the busy corridor.

The Southern University Administration, mainly the President-Chancellor, fired me without meeting with me once throughout the whole media slander campaign. Even the offer to "reassign" me was a slap in my face. I'd done a lot and I put my neck on the line for the progression of the band program. It was good that the meeting slipped my mind because I wouldn't have reacted too kindly to being reassigned, and I wasn't going to resign either. "They" can go ahead and fire me!

Despite the conversation with Dr. Bryant, I still drove towards home to get ready for the banquet. I told myself I would go on campus and give the students their trophies. I decided not to mention anything about the situation. Tonight, was all about them. My phone rang again. Dr. Bryant was calling me back.

"Mr. Haymer! I am sorry. 'They' told me that the opportunity for you to be reassigned to the music department is no longer on the table. It's now either resign or be terminated!"

"Yeah, whatever!"

I was so disgusted that I hung up the phone in Dr. Bryant's face. I realize that it wasn't Dr. Bryant's fault. As my 7th supervisor in four years, she was just a pawn! She couldn't defend me. She hadn't worked with me long enough to do so, nor did she have the respect and political fortitude to assert her opinion to the higher-ups. Furthermore, Dr. Bryant was in over her head. I could easily tell that she was more emotionally torn than I was, and I was the one getting fired!

Once I made it home, I decided that I wasn't going on campus. I called my twin brother to tell him the news. It was news that he didn't take too kindly. He called the General Counsel to the SU System Board of Supervisors to find out what was going on.

"Nathan, the board's attorney doesn't know anything about this. So, your termination isn't official. Maybe the President-Chancellor is trying to get you to resign!"

I don't know what it was. All I knew was that I wasn't in the emotional shape to face the students. I called Lorenzo Hart and Brian Simmons to tell them the news. I also told Brian Simmons to come by my apartment to get my office key so that he could get the trophies for the banquet. Walking down the street to the corner market to get a bottle of liquor, I told Brian Simmons, "Y'all are going to have to do this without me!

When I made it back to my apartment, I put the liquor bottle on the counter. I was about to pour a glass when I heard a knock at the door. Brian Simmons had arrived. He walked into my apartment, and I burst into tears.

"They finally got me, man! All of the shit I've been through to advance the program, and now they want me to resign!? FUCK THEM! FIRE ME, DAMMIT! I will not run!"

"Have you been drinking? I see the bottle!"

"No, you just caught me. I was just about to start."

Grabbing my office key, Brian Simmons told me that he would call me once they set up the banquet. While exiting the door, he spoke. "You should really consider coming to the banquet. The students need to see you, and it's better for them to hear the news from you than in the streets or social media!"

I turned around to pour me a glass of liquor and the bottle was gone. Apparently, Brian Simmons distracted me and walked off with the bottle. He was aware of my recent struggle and depression being magnified by alcohol abuse. I immediately laid in the middle of the floor, collecting my thoughts until I fell asleep.

My phone rang and awakened me. I looked at the time and approximately 30 minutes had passed. As the phone kept ringing, I wondered why I was on the floor. I hurried and answered the phone. It was Brian Simmons.

"Hello."

"Haymer! Lorenzo Hart and I couldn't get into your office. The key isn't working!"

I thought his comment to be odd. That key was the key I used to get into my office, and it was also the master key that unlocked every door in the building.

"Try to open the instrument room or any other room because my key is the master key to every room in the building."

"OK. Hold on!" I could hear him putting the key in a couple of doors. "Haymer, the key works with every door other than your office!"

"Those bastards changed my lock so I couldn't get into my office without even telling me that I was terminated! Furthermore, the most valuable things in the department were not my office, so if I wanted to do something bad, I still had access. I guess I'll be late because I now have to come up there to tell the kids why they don't have any trophies. They picked the wrong night to mess with me, and by changing my office locks, they messed over the entire program!"

"Do you want me to see if I can call someone who may have a key?"

"No! Don't call anyone. Leave it locked. I'll be up there shortly. Just tell the students that I am on the way and do not tell Kedric Taylor what's going on!"

"OK! I will hold it down until you get here."

I was very hurt and emotionally unstable. I knew I had to get off the floor, shower, and get myself together to tell the band what was going on. Besides, I would very much rather the students hear the news from me and not the lying and ineffective President-Chancellor, who is a puppet but the board's politics.

As I made it to campus, I called Brian Simmons to meet me in the band hall to unlock the door one last time. As he came into the band hall, he told me that all band members were waiting for me to start the program. He also told me that Ms. Byrd, the band's administrative assistant, and a few other guests were there. I looked at him and said, "Twelve years of blood, sweat, and tears led to this day! I am just going to go in and say what comes out naturally."

As we made our way into the student union's ballroom, the students clapped. I don't think they realized something was wrong. Lorenzo Hart had the senior jackets ready for me to present. "It's a good thing that those jackets were in your office and not mine!" I told Lorenzo Hart and laughed to indicate to him that I was doing just fine. I didn't even look at or acknowledge Kedric Taylor because once I told the band the news of what transpired earlier that day, I was more than sure that he would be thrilled!

I approached the podium and mic to address the students. It was very easy for me to tell the truth. The University left me no option since the band's awards and trophies were locked in my office. The President-Chancellor had to give the authorization for my office locks to be changed. Although I don't think it was his idea, he had no clue that they picked the worst day of the semester to mess with me. I had the attention of the entire band, dancing dolls, and their guests/dates for the banquet. I was willing to let this pressing matter go by not showing up for the banquet, but when they changed my office locks, it showed a lack of empathy for the students. As a result, it encouraged me to walk on campus with my head held high and speak out!

Students, I want you to know that I've never been prouder to be your director, and I want you to know that no matter what, serving as your band director has been the honor of my life!

I had to pause right there as I became very emotional. Although the students were still trying to figure out where I was going in my address to them, I could see the looks of concern on their faces. They had never seen this side of their band director.

On behalf of the University, I would like to apologize that your awards and trophies aren't here tonight. Someone in the administration thought it was necessary to change the lock to my office with your awards and trophies locked in! I'd rather you hear this from me than in the streets.

I had to pause again to collect myself as the tears began to fall down my face.

I got a call from my supervisor, who basically said the matter was out of her hands. Someone told my supervisor to tell me that either I resign immediately as your director, or I would be fired!

I could hear a massive gasp. The noise in the crowded room of more than 350 people grew out of control as I began to lose control of my emotions. Seeing the tears and hurt on my students' faces caused me to hurt even deeper. My staff came to comfort me immediately, including the band's administrative assistant, who's been there for decades. Everyone on my staff was with me except for Kedric Taylor. He walked into the hallway. I tried to get myself together and began to comfort the students. Brian Simmons was upset.

"I'll be right back! I am going to see what Kedric Taylor is out there doing. I know his sneaky ass is up to something!"

While Brian Simmons was checking on Kedric Taylor, I got on the mic in an attempt to have some normal resemblance of a band banquet. I asked Lorenzo Hart to get the jackets ready to present the senior class! Eventually, I managed to calm the room down for the jacket presentation. Before I could present the jackets, Brian Simmons came to me.

"Hey, I saw Kedric Taylor out there texting. I asked him why he wasn't in the room with us. He claims he was trying to contact someone to open your office door!"

"Fuck him! We both know that is a lie. I'll deal with him later, but right now, let's just get through the banquet for the sake of our students!"

While presenting the seniors with their jackets, Kedric Taylor slipped in and made it on stage. After the jacket presentation, the news that I released began to circulate through the campus community. The new Vice-Chancellor for Student Affairs came into the room to tell me to present the students with their awards and trophies. It was my first time meeting her as she had only been on campus for maybe two weeks. She tried to convince me to see things her way.

"I can't present awards and trophies that I don't have. I've been through hell the past month, and it is time for the students to know and understand that the President-Chancellor and his administration doesn't give a damn about them! Lady, no disrespect but you're new here. Talk to me after you've seen and experienced 'the real SU!' Until then, we have nothing else to discuss!"

The new VCSA was wiser than I. She didn't last on that campus for two years. When she learned "the ways of Southern University," she packed her bags and left!

Dr. Bryant told the senior-level administrators that I had a band banquet that night. It was evident that "they" didn't care! As I continued to console the students, I looked up and saw that my "Guardian Angel" was there. As a member of the Southern University System Board of Supervisors, she had a surprised look on her face. She wasn't even aware of the President-Chancellor's decision to fire me. I went up to the board member and gave her a big hug and thanked her for the opportunity. "Serving as the director has been the honor of my life!" I told the board member as she continued to look stunned and was really at a loss of words at the moment.

It was a sad way to close a successful year as the vision I boldly stated four years ago came to pass. I realized achieving the bold vision came at a huge cost...my career! Every time the administrators told me "No," I found a way to turn it into a "Yes!" Every time I was told "there are no funds available" or "be patient and learn how to do things on their time," I found a way to blaze my own path!

In four short years, I managed to solve all the problems that plagued the band. Although some of my methods were unorthodox, the Human Jukebox as we know it today wouldn't have been in existence had I given up on the vision I promised to the students. The media team would not have been as progressive and would have been more of the same. The summer band and dance team camps wouldn't have been as successful. The recruiting efforts wouldn't have been plentiful without my creative strategies, such as the Midnight Madness and Crankfest BOTBs, the mastering of social media, and the bold innovations sparked by my leadership.

In fact, the 2014-2018 era of the Human Jukebox, affectionately known as the Haymer-Time era, sparked all HBCU bands and media teams to "step their game up!" The "Haymer effect" was the communication to the band world that the same old stale way of doing things had to stop as business as usual was no longer. I had a lot to be proud of, and if this was indeed the end, I was ready to

Juked

walk away with my head held high! I just wanted the President-Chancellor to tell me why he decided to terminate me.

That night at the banquet, I hugged and talked to over 200 students individually. In the process of consoling them, I noticed that my hand was swollen. I kept doing what I was doing and ignored the pain. After talking to a lot of students, particularly those who I was the hardest on, I went home to get some rest.

It shouldn't be hard to realize that my rest was burdensome and weary. I had a nightmare that my dreams were slipping away from me as my job was in jeopardy. As I awoke to a call from the band's administrative assistant, I realized that the nightmare was my new reality!

"Hey! The guys just left out of here saying that they change your locks back. You might want to come and see if your key works!"

I continued listening to Ms. Byrd. As she spoke, I looked down at the palm of my right hand and it was very swollen. There was a big lump in the middle of my hand, and it was concerning. "I need to go to urgent care to check on my hand; then I'll be up there," I said to Ms. Byrd as she was familiar with my hand swelling the night before.

I arrived at urgent care and told the doctor what was going on. He was familiar yet fascinated by the swelling. He numbed my hand, cut the huge lump with his scalpel, then squeezed greenish-yellow pus out of it. He must have called in every nurse and doctor in the building as they began to look at my hand like it was some type of science experiment. Yet, he began to explain what was going on with my hand.

"Oh my! I've heard of this in medical school, but I have never seen it before today! What do you do for a living?" His question made me even more tense as the doctor could see it in my facial expression, and he apologized.

"No, it is OK. I am a teacher. Well, I used to be. I am probably going to give my profession up!"

"Well, I am sorry to hear that. The world needs more great teachers! So, where do you teach?"

He must have seen the look of disappointment on my face. "I apologize. You don't have to answer that question if you don't want to. I asked because a stressful situation triggered the swelling in the palm of your hand. Usually, something traumatic and unforeseen causes the body's immune system to go into overdrive, producing more white blood cells than normal. I believe this is what caused your hand to swell. If you are no longer in the situation that caused you to stress, whether it is work or your personal life, then I'll say that's a good thing!"

"Thank you for letting me know. I probably won't have to worry about the stresses of the job anymore as I did all that I could do, and it's time to move on."

The doctor stitched my hand and wrapped it with a bandage. He gave me a prescription for antibiotics along with instructions on how to care for my hand as it heals. Before I left the urgent care center, the doctor stated, "You look familiar, and I've seen you somewhere before!"

Laughing and still moving, I told the doctor, "Yes, you probably saw me on the Evening News!"

I left urgent care center, got into my vehicle, and called Brian Simmons.

"Hey, man! I am on the way to the office. I got a call earlier this morning that they changed the lock back to the original lock!"

"Well, maybe that's a good sign. You never know."

"I don't know, man. It just doesn't seem right to me. To go through all of the drama of changing my locks and ruining the band banquet just to change them back in less than 24 hours. I'll see when I get to the office. Anyway, what are you doing this weekend?"

"Nothing! What's up?"

"I already told the Southern University Alumni Federation-Houston Chapter's President that I would make an appearance at the alumni crawfish boil this weekend! I don't feel like going, but I am going to go ahead and honor this commitment. I think I'll just show my face and leave this year. Do you want to come?"

"Cool. I'm down!"

I instructed Brian Simmons to be ready to leave later in the evening. As I parked in my reserved parking spot and walked into the band hall, I received many stares from the university employees. I assumed the word of the banquet and my termination was widely known but I really didn't know. Honestly, I've been getting stares on and off campus all month due to the non-stop damaging news coverage of my "investigations!" I made it to Ms. Byrd's office and thanked her for having my back over the years. We didn't always see eye to eye, but I knew that Ms. Byrd always wanted what was best for the department.

"Nate, what's for you will be for you. I don't care what any of those devils back there have to say, walk with your head up and be proud. I've been here for a long time, and you don't last this long without knowing who does what around here!"

"I think that maybe I know too much, and they're discrediting me in advance just in case I go public with how they've been stealing from the band for decades. It is easier to get rid of me than to fix the problem! The situation with honorariums can easily be fixed by putting me on a payroll deduction."

"Say no more, Nate! I've been knowing this, but you had to see for yourself."

"Well, I now see the light! OK, let me see if my key works for my office door, so I can start packing my stuff up!"

I put my key into the lock and unlocked my door. The lights were still on in the office, and I was nearly blinded by the glare of the lights on the gold trophies. They were still there looking beautiful. Immediately I had a bright idea and texted the staff in our group text.

"I am back in the office. They changed my lock back! I will send a message to all students that we will have a trophy presentation on Tuesday evening, May 1, 2018, at 6:30pm. We will dress casually and close the semester the right way!"

Although I addressed the entire staff in the text message, my true agenda was to provide information to Kedric Taylor. He left the banquet under the guise of "trying to find someone to unlock my office." I believe that he actually was texting Jabari and "Christian" Eric an update that whatever they planned was working. Now, I wanted him to know that I was back in my office.

I sat down at my desk, gave a deep sigh, and began to cry again. I knew in my heart that it was the end. I thought about my first day as Director of Bands and the massive weight and pressure that I felt. Now that we have achieved everything that I set in the benchmarks, the weight turned into sorrow! I was ready to go, but I didn't want to leave in the way it appeared that my tenure would end. April 2018 taught me a lot. I learned that no job, regardless of the power, prestige, position, and popularity, was worth my health. Although I knew it was time to leave, my pride wouldn't allow me just to walk out and let the enemy win. I wanted to be terminated as resigning and walking away was the cowardly thing to do, in my opinion. I turned on my computer, answered several emails, and then emailed my supervisor.

Good afternoon, I am back in my office, and I was pleased to learn that my lock has been changed back. What does this mean? I just want to make sure I comply, as the last time we talked, I was given the option to resign or be terminated. I will be leaving out of town for the weekend, but I want to know if I should return to work Monday or not?

Juked

My email didn't state it, but I wanted it to be clear that I would not resign before I clicked the "send" button. I read over the email a couple of times to ensure that I had the right words along with the right tone then I sent it to my supervisor.

I stayed in the office for an additional 20 minutes. I sent a notice to all the students using the app that I made mandatory for everyone to download. I let them know of the trophy presentation scheduled for Tuesday, May 1, 2018, at 6:30pm in the band hall. I also apologized to them for having a less than desirable banquet the night before. I prepared to leave the office and checked my email one more time. I noticed that Dr. Bryant replied to my email.

"Good afternoon Mr. Haymer, I checked with the appropriate administrators, and I was told that it was OK for you to report to work on Monday and resume normal operations!"

Excited that I checked my email before leaving for the day, I needed some positive news. However, my twin brother's voice immediately popped up in my head. "Nathan, don't trust them!"

I had time to plan an exit strategy, but who was I fooling? I knew that leaving Southern University was the best option for my health, but I had what I would consider "battered woman's syndrome." I loved an institution that could never love me in return. The love I had for it required transparency but the only love that the institution could give me required me to shut up and listen! I am not wired that way. Perhaps if I were, I could have easily ascended up the ranks to be the President-Chancellor one day. Board members constantly told me to "follow the script." I would rather take the road of an uncertain future than to be anyone's pawn or puppet-like the current President-Chancellor!

As I prepared to leave the office for the weekend, I hugged Ms. Byrd. I gave her the news from my supervisor and told her that I would see her on Monday. Once I got into my truck, I called Brian Simmons and told him what time to be ready to leave for Houston. I also told him the news about returning to work on Monday. He saw it as a positive sign, but I knew better. For the sake of not "beating a dead horse," I agreed, although I couldn't trust anything from my supervisor or any other administrator on campus. I also couldn't trust Kedric Taylor. While on the phone with Brian Simmons, he attempted to call me twice. Both times I hit "ignore!" Whatever he wanted would have to wait for Monday. I informed Brian Simmons, "I am going to tell Kedric Taylor everything that I know on Monday, and if I am still employed, he is fired!"

The drive to Houston was good. The company on the trip was great!. The decision to go to the SUAF-Houston Chapter alumni crawfish boil was insane. I know I committed to the Houston Chapter President, and I wanted to honor my commitment, but I don't know what I was thinking. I should have canceled.

I was greeted with cold stares from many alumni in attendance. People that used to "break their necks" to speak to me and shake my hand looked at me as if I had a disease on my face. It appeared that the month's extended damaging news coverage was working in the court of public opinion. Although a few alumni welcomed me and treated me the same, I knew that it was best to leave as soon as possible.

Brian Simmons was by my side. He wasn't as "politically polished" as I was, but he was there with me through this ordeal. Upon seeing the cold stares, he truly spoke unfiltered. "Man, fuck them people! They don't do anything for you anyway!"

"Hey, man. Let me just go over here and play the game right quick, and then we can get the hell out of here!"

On the way out I waved at a few people. I walked as fast as I could to get to my truck to get the hell away from there! While in the truck, I looked at Brian Simmons. My encounter at the crawfish boil hurt but allowed me to speak truth to my travel buddy.

Juked

"I needed to see and feel that. The unwelcoming spirit is an indication of how the Jaguar Nation feels about their band director. It's time to give it up, man!"

"You can't make a general statement like that based on them old ass people. What do they know?"

We both laughed but I knew what I felt inside was the truth. I dropped him off at Marissa's house. My next stop would be the hotel.

"Man, be careful and don't go get nothing to drink tonight!"

"I'm good, man! I'm just going to go to bed. I'll call you in the morning to let you know what time we are leaving to go back to Baton Rouge!"

I drove off and asked the Lord to forgive me. I just lied in Brian Simmons's face. I stopped at the liquor store, got myself a small batch of 1792 Kentucky bourbon, and had a good night in my hotel room with just me and my 1792!

On the way back to Baton Rouge, I had a great revelation! Brian Simmons has always been a good friend. When times are at their most challenging and you feel that you've hit rock bottom, life has a way of revealing who is a real friend versus who is a fair-weather friend. Sunday, April 29, 2018, I perceived Brian Simmons to be more than a friend. He was the younger brother I never had! He stayed in my corner, whether right or wrong, and even though he had no clue of some of the "wrong things" that I've done. Later when he found out my crimes, he still supported me. He never enabled me. Even when he would tell me when I was wrong, his love and support for me never wavered. He and I could turn the darkest situation into a funny moment. I appreciated that about him, as laughter is truly the best medicine. In the middle of our "laugh sessions," my phone rang. TJ was calling me.

"Hey, man! I heard the news. What can I do to help?"

I explained to him how I had the option to resign or be fired. I also went into detail about changing the locks on both doors to my office. Finally, I explained how everything affected the banquet.

"When will you be back in town?"

"I should be back in Baton Rouge around 3:00pm."

"OK, cool. Do you mind if I set up a meeting with Cleo Fields?"

Cleo Fields is the same guy who ran the Louisiana Leadership Institute. He and I had a very positive relationship. I was still the director of performing arts for the institute's All-Star Band. I didn't know if he could help, but I thought meeting with him surely couldn't hurt. I gave TJ the nod to set the meeting up.

"I just want to see what type of insight Senator Fields can provide on your situation. I think that the whole situation is messed up. Man, you put the band on a trajectory of success that I've never seen, and I want you to know that I support you 100 percent. This ain't about Crankfest or making money. I support what you have done for the program!"

"Thank you, my brother! See if Senator Fields wants to meet around 5:30pm. If so, I'll be there. I want to bring Brian Simmons with me, is that OK?"

"Absolutely, I don't see a problem with Brian Simmons attending the meeting. I'll text you once Senator Fields confirms the time!"

I was so happy to hear the genuine support from TJ. His confidence in me renewed my energy. I told Brian Simmons that I appreciated the genuine support of TJ. I also let him know that I trusted Senator Fields. I knew if he could help, he would, and if he couldn't, he would be honest to tell me that as well.

The remainder of the trip consisted of Brian Simmons and I's continual laughter. We proceeded to turn the dark and depressing situations of the semester into humor. Eventually, I received a text

Juked

from TJ confirming the 5:30pm meeting and the okay to bring Brian Simmons with me.

Pulling into Senator Fields' house, I noticed that TJ was already there waiting on us. I was grateful for this meeting because it gave me better insight into the plot against me. I learned that the President-Chancellor was forced to fire me through some "outside influencers" who wanted me out of power. It was no longer about what was best for the band. The outside influences wanted me gone because they deemed me as too popular and influential through outlets they couldn't control. The "outside influencers" accused me of thinking that the university's band was my band. In addition, due to the public shaming of Brandon Dumas and termination a year ago, the outside influencers forced the President-Chancellor's hand the entire year to find something on me. Therefore, they were behind the unprecedented number of investigations. Finally, they found something on me. They uncovered the $14,000 I received in parade honorariums during the 2018 parade season.

Finally, the most shocking takeaway was learning that "they" contacted Lawrence Jackson, my predecessor, about taking over the band on an interim basis. I thought it was odd that he wouldn't notify me about something of this magnitude. I also thought it was odd to be blasted all over the news for a month, and he did not attempt to contact me one single time. I was in complete disbelief. Lawrence Jackson is like my second father. I needed to believe that it was just a misunderstanding.

"After this meeting, I am going to call Lawrence Jackson to see what he knows because if he is involved in any way, shape, or form, the 'father-figure' I know and admire would've contacted me. I am very loyal to Lawrence Jackson, and I know for a fact that he is just as loyal to me! If Lawrence Jackson knows anything, I am sure there's a valid reason why he didn't tell me, and I am sure that he would speak up on my behalf to whomever he's in contact with!"

We continued to discuss the President-Chancellor during our meeting. It was revealed that he fired me on the day of the band banquet but quickly reversed his decision the next day once he learned the details of what happened. His "puppet masters" were very displeased with his reversing the decision to fire me. "They" told him either he gets rid of me, or "they" would get rid of both of us! I couldn't believe the level that some people would stoop to when playing politics. There I was, at the fate of the "puppet masters" whose hands were dirtier than mine could have ever been!

I learned what I've been suspecting for quite some time. All of my known enemies had a small part to play in my demise. The plot to have me removed started and ended with the ties associated with Brandon Dumas. Since I've never personally dealt with them, I didn't know why those "bible thumpers" hatred for me ran so deep. I could only think that it was my name that they hated. The "Haymer" name is something that they were familiar with long before I was born. Still, I thought it was a chance to save my job as I now knew I needed to reach out to Lawrence Jackson.

I also shared with Senator Fields my desire to fire Kedric Taylor, and he strongly advised against it. Basically, he said things were too hot at the moment, and getting rid of someone, no matter how much of a traitor they may be, would be the wrong move. I wouldn't say I liked hearing that one bit, but I knew that he was right. I thanked him for his valuable insight and left the meeting with one last thing to do.... I had to call Lawrence Jackson to come through for me!

"Hey, how are you?"

"Oh, I'm good, Nate."

Immediately, I knew something was wrong. Based on his response, I knew something was up. Lawrence Jackson doesn't greet me in a regular kind of way. He's always been animated. Typically, he be like... "NATE! What's going on, man? I haven't talked to you since Pecky was a puppy!" But when he speaks "regular," I knew it was a sign that something was wrong.

"I am in a situation, and I need your help. I was told that the SU Administration reached out to you concerning terminating me. Would you please speak up on my behalf? They may not listen, but I just need your support!"

"Nate, I know something about that. It's just a bad situation, man. I... I don't know."

At this point, I was devastated. Here is a man that I held in such high regard, and he let me down. I saw him as a second father. Although he doesn't owe me anything, I thought the loyalty that I gave him for eight years would be returned by a simple phone call. A phone call to warn me what was about to take place as he knew well in advance and never attempted to reach out to me one time.

"I let some snakes in the house, and that was my mistake. I just need for you to speak to the administration on my behalf, please!"

"Yes, Nate, you did let some snakes in. I'll talk to them and see what I can do. Oh, something just came up, Nate. I have to go. I'll call you back!"

No matter what, I still wanted to think the best of a man I had so much faith in. I knew beyond a shadow of doubt that he would call me back. I knew Lawrence Jackson to be an honest man, a man of integrity! If he could help me or not, his "yay" would be yay, and his "nay" would be nay; I knew that he would tell me straight up! As I waited on his call back, I let Brian Simmons in on my thoughts.

"If what I learned in the meeting is true and Lawrence Jackson is the key to my future at SU, then I should be good."

Brian Simmons agreed with my thoughts. However, a couple of minutes turned into an hour. An hour turned into three hours. Finally, I realized that Lawrence Jackson was not going to call me back. I had time to think about the situation and realized that maybe he was in on it too! I went from calm to extremely angry. Then I went back to calm as I made excuses for him not calling me back. It was time to get ready for bed because I had to go to work in the morning and I looked forward to seeing what the first day of the week would bring.

The last three days had been hell! First, I was terminated and then not terminated. I don't want to forget the cold shoulders at the crawfish boil, the messed-up band banquet, and the shocking revelation of Lawrence Jackson. These last three days were traumatic and had caused me to become very paranoid and insecure. Since Friday, I have been through the wringer. Now it's 5:00am Monday morning and time for me to get ready for work, but I didn't want to go in. I lounged around for a while. I drank some coffee, watched the news, and just tried to get in the right headspace. Finally, around 8:00am I decided to get ready for work. Eventually, I made it in around 9:30am.

The office was oddly quiet. The trophies still sat around the office ready for Tuesday's presentation to the students. I longed to see the students. Hell, I needed to see them. I needed some form of normalcy unlocked and they were the key. We were at the end of the semester and the students were taking final exams, so we didn't have band class anymore.

Without the students around, I dove into the paperwork side of my job. I stayed in the office emailing recruits and offering scholarships. I had about 14 manila folders full of band applications, with most of the students who had already auditioned and accepted to the University. I was further ahead with getting students processed than I had ever been in the past years. With our increased scholarship budget and new "tier" system, I quickly separated the applications, awarding students according to the recommendations by the band staff on their audition sheets. As I spent a couple of hours dealing with the business of the incoming freshmen, I noticed that it was a little after 1:00pm. I told Ms. Byrd, administrative assistant, that I was leaving for lunch and would be back shortly.

Juked

I walked out of my office and proceeded down the hall to the front door when I saw a black Chevy pickup truck blocking the doorway. It was Kedric Taylor's truck. He was sitting in his vehicle and appeared to be in the middle of a phone conversation. Sunday's conversation with Senator Field played in my head. His advice to let things cool down, wave, and keep things moving was on loop within my thoughts. But as I walked out the door, I could no longer play the game. I couldn't just "wave and keep it moving!" Before I knew it, I had stopped the loop in my head and was knocking on Kedric Taylor's driver-side window. As he let the window down, I saw that he was indeed in the middle of a phone conversation, but I no longer cared. I became furious instantly as all of the anger, rage, and resentment that I bottled up inside for years came out.

"Hey, man! Who in the hell is Marcus Mason (false name)?" He looked at me with a stunned look on his face. I knew he couldn't believe that I came at him like that, but enough was enough! As he continued to give me a deer caught in headlights look, I repeated myself. "I am going to ask you again, who is Marcus Mason?"

He quietly whispered in his phone, "Hey, let me call you back" and looked at me with that familiar "deer caught in headlights look!" "I don't know who you are talking about I ... I ... don't know who ... who that is!" I've been around Kedric Taylor long enough to know when he's lying because his body language, along with his stuttering, always gave it away.

"So, you're going to sit there and lie in my face? You are telling me that you don't know Marcus Mason?"

I was boiling hot. I laughed in his face. It wasn't a humorous laugh. It was a laugh to let him know that I was pissed off! Kedric Taylor hurried and got out of his truck and looked around to ensure that no one was watching.

"Hey, can we go inside and talk?"

"Yes, we can talk inside as soon as I find out who Marcus Mason is!"

We walked inside the performance hall adjacent to the band building. Once in the building, we went inside the reception room and sat at the table. There is where we continued this conversation.

"If you cannot tell me who Marcus Mason is, then there's no need for us to continue this conversation!"

"I don't know him. Well, I used to talk to date sister."

"Which one is it? You know him or not? If you don't know Marcus Mason, how did you know that you dated his sister? I'll tell you exactly who Marcus Mason is! Remember around two weeks ago when you brought me your phone with the screenshot? The screenshot read, 'Haymer fired the MBM team, and he was going to fire Kedric Taylor next?' The person who made the comment in the screenshot was Marcus Mason. I'm sure you already know that, considering that you brought his name to me!"

Stunned, Kedric Taylor finally admitted to knowing Marcus Mason.

"I haven't talked to Marcus in a while. He was somebody that I was cool with a while back."

"Oh, so you do know Marcus Mason?"

I was very sarcastic. I was already aware that Kedric Taylor knew him. I also insisted on referring to "his friend" and "future frat brother" by his first and last name. As I continued Kedric Taylor constantly gave me that deer caught in headlights look. It was obvious that he was puzzled and curious to see where I was going with my statements.

"Marcus Mason surely thinks highly of you! Marcus Mason works at the governor's office, doesn't he?"

Kedric Taylor's body language revealed discomfort because he didn't know how I knew the information.

"Look, I just know him through his sister. When I stopped talking to her, I lost contact with him."

"You are lying, man! Marcus Mason played in the SU band in the early 1990s. He now works at the governor's office, where you've been the topic of conversation for a while. Marcus Mason often repeats the things that you 'claim to happen' around here. He talks to a particular young lady that works with him, telling her that 'Kedric Taylor does all the work while Haymer doesn't know what he's doing!' Marcus Mason...."

"Man! That's not true, Haymer! I ..."

"Wait a minute. I am not finished yet! Marcus Mason likes a young lady that he works with. Apparently, his game is so weak that his only way of making conversation with her is through what 'Kedric Taylor says about me!' Marcus Mason told the young lady, who happens to be my source, that you told him that I am gay, and my wife left me because she caught me in the bed with a man!"

Kedric Taylor became even more nervous. His eyes turned red and watered up. I don't know if it was tears of guilt or tears that I was finally on to him. As he tried to explain, I cut him off to finish my statement.

"I am not finished. I heard this rumor before I even hired you, man! Knowing this, I still hired you and found a way to fund your salary among everything else that I sacrificed for you. I am the fool. I've been knowing this, but I'll get to 'the turtle and snake story' later. Let me continue with Marcus Mason. So, Marcus Mason told the young lady everything you supposedly told him about why my wife left me. Finally, the young lady had enough of Marcus Mason's shit. Besides, what does my relationship with my ex-wife have to do with Marcus Mason trying to hook up with that young lady?"

Kedric Taylor was very uncomfortable. I wouldn't let him say a word! I continued with my remarks.

"As Marcus Mason kept giving the young lady a daily report of what Kedric Taylor told him, she finally had enough. The young lady pulled her driver's license out and slammed it on the desk for Marcus Mason to read, and when he saw the name on the license, he froze up. The young lady told Marcus, *'Yes, that's right! The last name on my license is HAYMER, and I am Nathan's ex-wife!* My ex-wife went by her maiden name at work and never changed her license after we divorced. She then asked Marcus Mason, *'Now who did I catch Nathan in the bed with? I have to call Nathan to let him know how evil Kedric Taylor is. I've never met Kedric Taylor, and I don't know why he would lie on my ex-husband like that.'* Marcus Mason later apologized to my ex-wife, while blaming you!"

Kedric Taylor was in tears but still tried to deny it. I looked him square in the eyes and told him, "I don't believe a damn word that you say!"

By now, I had had enough. I was agitated and wanted to fire Kedric Taylor. I knew that my days were coming to a close. I knew that I was just a fading figurehead who most likely could no longer sign for the band's mail, let alone fire anyone! Even though I was still in the seat, the power attached to it was already gone. I got up from my chair and walked out. Kedric Taylor followed me as I went to my office.

With my arrival back from lunch so quickly, Ms. Byrd knew something was wrong. She also saw the look on my face as Kedric Taylor followed me, trying to explain his side of the story. Finally, enough was enough and I had had enough!

"Say what you got to say, man!"

"I am not like that! I've had your back since day one. Brian Simmons is the person that you need to watch. He has single handedly tried to destroy this department!"

At that very moment, I became calm. Immediately, I realized that Kedric Taylor would not take responsibility for the wrongs that he's done, and the conversation wasn't going to go anywhere. I also knew that I had bigger things to worry about. I felt that this would be my last week on the job.

"If what you are telling me about Brian Simmons is true, then I'll deal with him at the appropriate time, but right now it's 'The Kedric Taylor's show.' It's all about you right now, not him! I don't even want to talk any further. I just wanted you to know that I knew what you've been saying about me for years. Yet, I still hired you when the university refused. You have no clue what I had to do to make sure that the money was there to pay you. I also gave you a raise and a promotion. I did all of this while knowing the garbage that you were spewing to Marcus Mason!"

Kedric Taylor kept denying everything as he asked me to pray with him. If looks could kill, Kedric Taylor would have been shot dead on the spot in my office when he made that remark.

"Look, man. Let me briefly tell you the story about the snake and a turtle. The snake wanted to cross the river but couldn't swim and asked the turtle if he could ride on his back. The turtle told the snake that he would take him to the other side of the river if the snake promised not to bite him. The snake assured the turtle that he wouldn't bite him, but as soon as the turtle dropped the snake off on the other side of the river, the snake bit the turtle. The turtle screamed, *'You promised that you wouldn't bite me.'* To which the snake responded, *'Man, you knew I was a snake all the time!'* That is a good analogy for our relationship. You rode my back, and as soon as I got you to the Promised Land, you bit me! I knew you were a snake all along, so I am not disappointed in you because I never believed in you. I am disappointed in myself!"

Kedric Taylor continued to cry, but I didn't care. I continued with my predictions for the future. "I will probably be fired in the next day or so; it seems that you're going to have your way! Just take care of my band when I am gone!"

"Don't talk like that, man! You're going to be alright!"

Suddenly, Ms. Byrd walked into the office. Her presence was due to her becoming alarmed. Apparently, we were loud enough for her to overhear our discussion.

"Nate, I told you from day one that you were sitting in a powerful seat! There are many people after you because of the attention and respect that seat demands and commands!"

Ms. Byrd gave me a side-eye! Although she and I never talked about Kedric Taylor, I had a feeling that she knew that he couldn't be trusted. Throughout the conversation, Kedric Taylor had asked me to pray with him and I declined. I've grown tired of people at SU with their convenient "Christian values' ' that they put on and take off as if it was a pair of underwear. I did not want Kedric Taylor to pray for me as he's been PREYING for me for years!

However, I respected Ms. Byrd. She is what I call a "prayer warrior." She asked us all to stand up and pray and I saw no harm in a prayer with her. Besides, I've said all that I cared to say to Kedric Taylor.

As we stood to pray with Ms. Byrd, I appreciated that she came into the room with a calming spirit. Actually, I thank God for her at that moment. Her presence brought a much-needed sense of peace in the office, especially since I had nothing else to lose. There's no telling what would have transpired had I kept listening to Kedric Taylor's lies. He did so many disrespectful and underhanded things that I would have been there for days telling him everything that I knew. Besides, it was pointless as Kedric Taylor would only keep denying it using his famous line, "Man, you know my heart!"

After we prayed, I left the office for the day. Telling Kedric Taylor some of the things I had bottled inside helped to relieve me. Still, I was upset. I sat on that information for so long. I had every reason to fire him years ago without the appearance of it being so personal. Forget that, I should have fought harder for the assistant I initially wanted instead of hiring Kedric Taylor. Although I had very personal reasons for wanting to fire Kedric Taylor, my decision was really because of the divide and negative energy he brought to the staff. Either way, firing him was no longer an option as my fate as Director of Bands was left hanging in the balance.

I woke up on the morning of Tuesday, May 1, 2018, in a bad mood. I called Ms. Byrd around 9:00am to let her know that I wouldn't come in on this day. She understood and shared a Bible scripture with me. I prepared for what I thought would be a relaxed day. I went to the barbershop to get a haircut. Next, I went to my house to check the mail and other routine things that I did at my home every week. Around 11:00am, I received a phone call from my twin brother. I immediately went into a state of panic because he never calls me in the middle of the day unless it was something important. As I answered the phone, my brother began to speak.

"Nathan.... (sigh).... The General Counsel for the SU Board of Supervisors just called me. He stated that the university is giving you until 1:00pm to resign or they will fire you!"

"There they go with the games again. Tell them to fire me now! I am not resigning!"

"Are you sure you don't want to resign?"

"What difference does it make? Fire or resign... it is a matter of semantics. I told the kids that I would give them a trophy presentation today and those bastards are robbing me of the opportunity again! So yes, tell them to fire me!"

I had no more tears left to give. I had already cried a river. Now, was the time to take action. I called Brian Simmons to provide him with the news and instructed him to come to get my keys. Once again, I needed him to get into my office so he could get the trophies for the students.

"I will no longer be the Director of Bands as of 1:00pm today, so I can't come tonight. I don't want anything to happen or cause any accusations of inciting violence by riling up the students!" Brian

Simmons was sad to hear the news but assured me that he would carry on with the program.

I immediately called Sonja. She was upset about my unofficial termination last week. I told her that the President-Chancellor rescinded my termination. Still, I would let her know if/when it became official. Neither one of us trusted the puppet President-Chancellor and his puppet masters. I also promised her that I would tell her before anything hit the media.

Like clockwork, SU was ready. The news alert went out at 1:00pm sharp. Plastered from all the local news stations, the headlines read *Haymer Terminated as SU's Director of Bands!* Shortly after, the announcement was all over social media, along with various memes from being in a pair of "red bottoms" to my face placed on the $100 bill. Surprisingly, I became numb to the insensitive jokes as people laughed and partied to the news of my termination.

Through all the craziness, I stood my ground. I refused to deactivate my social media. Why should I? Social media has a way of revealing who people really are. I began to see the same people who "slid in my DMs" saying they were praying for me, posting and laughing at memes. I needed to see and experience all of this to understand never to take the few genuine people in this world for granted.

I received a call from campus human resources notifying me that I needed to be there at 2:00pm to sign a document. I told them I would be there, but purposely didn't show up until 4:30pm. I signed a document then I received an envelope that contained my 30-day no-fault termination notice. My termination would be effective immediately, but my last paycheck would be May 31, 2018.

Upon leaving human resources, I called the chief of the SUPD. She was distraught by the news. We spoke for about 20 minutes or so. Sometime during the conversation, I told the chief that I would be back in my office Friday, May 4, 2018, to get my personal belongings.

Juked

I arrived back at my apartment. At 40 years old, I was officially unemployed for the first time in my adult life. I didn't know what I was going to do or how I would provide for myself, but I knew that no matter what, I would be fine. I began to think of getting out of Baton Rouge. Due to the public scrutiny and the attempt at public embarrassment through the local media, I knew that a future in Baton Rouge was no longer possible. Besides, I'd outgrown that city anyway. Nothing against my hometown of Baton Rouge or my home state of Louisiana. It is an excellent place for tradition, music, food, and culture. However, the city and state have so few resources that everyone is fighting each other to be at the top of every industry's "food chain." Also, to be successful as an African American in Baton Rouge requires you to go through "the gatekeepers" regardless of the industry. I wanted to go somewhere else, where the resources are plentiful, the opportunities are limitless, and the politics aren't as personal.

As I thought of "life after Southern University," I became excited. Since my days as a high school band director, I always wanted to leave Louisiana, but I was sucked into my "dream job." Although Baton Rouge held my dream, it has been nothing but a nightmare since day one! As I turned on the TV, there I was at the top of the news cycle. I refused to watch the coverage about my situation during the whole month of April. I just couldn't let the media coverage of my situation affect and effect me. I was officially terminated, so I didn't give a damn anymore. I began to listen to what the media said about my termination, and I became upset again. I learned that Lawrence Jackson would be taking over the band's leadership!

How is this possible? Now I realized why he didn't call me back the other night. Lawrence Jackson sold me out! How is it possible to allow him to take over the band's leadership when he taught me? The more time I had, the more I could think about it. Lawrence Jackson's "abrupt retirement" never sat well with me. I began to think long and hard on the successful journey over the past four years and how Lawrence Jackson never wanted to come around. When I called him with bad news, he would be there to listen. We would talk a long time about everyone and everything. When I called him about the successes, he would hurry and get off the phone.

I also thought about the passing of Isaac Greggs in April 2014. Many people approached me to congratulate me on taking over the band after the passing of Isaac Greggs. I had to explain to them that Isaac Greggs retired eight years before he passed away and that Lawrence Jackson took over the band after him. As I thought about that situation, I couldn't help but wonder. Maybe Lawrence Jackson was very distant with me because he was upset that the people had forgotten about him. As I tried to think of every scenario of why he sold me out and never spoke up for me, I stopped making excuses for his actions. I learned to accept him for who he really is, A FAKE… A PHONY… A REAL CON ARTIST who hides behind the Bible!

Lawrence Jackson had me so fooled and so blinded by the "bling-bling" that I couldn't see the evil and manipulative things that he did. Whether right or wrong, I had his back throughout his entire tenure, and he couldn't have my back one time. The man I knew and respected was not real. The last "superhero" in my mind was no longer. I thought of the many times I put his needs and wants before my ex-wife and family. I thought about the late nights I spent in the office my first couple of years on the job typing, creating documents, and doing tons of paperwork for him because he didn't know how to type. I thought about how I covered up the 2008 hazing scandal to protect him. I thought about how I let him manipulate me into changing the handbook to get rid of a few Dancing Dolls. It was an honor to do these things for him as I thought it was my duty to have Lawrence Jackson's back!

Perhaps the most insulting thing was learning about the conversation between him, the President-Chancellor and his puppet masters. When they called to talk to Lawrence Jackson, not only did he not tell the truth about parade honorariums, but he also pushed Kedric Taylor to be my replacement. The SU

Administration wanted Lawrence Jackson to serve as interim director of bands. He declined. However, he would "have his cake and eat it too" by being paid as the band's consultant. His new job was to train the new band director and serve as a liaison between the director and the administration. It is pretty ironic that the SU Administration now wanted "training" for the director when none was provided for me. In fact, I set the blueprint by which administrators could measure any future band director by creating my own benchmarks, as none were provided for me.

I hope that Lawrence Jackson's semester's pay was worth selling out someone he used to refer to as his "son." Besides, I knew it would only be a matter of time before Kedric Taylor showed Lawrence Jackson who he really was. Both are backstabbing, double-talking-Bible thumping hypocrites. As I suspected, Lawrence Jackson ended his "semester consulting job" being backstabbed by the very man he pushed to be the next director, Kedric Taylor.

Chapter 32

On Friday, May 4, 2018, I went to my former office for the first time since my termination. I was there to collect my personal belongings. Two SUPD officers were there to escort me in and out of the building. I grabbed everything I wanted and left behind the personal items I didn't want, but I forgot to clear the bottom left drawer of my desk. Huge mistake!

In that drawer were the receipts for all the band's expenses that I paid using the band camp profits. I'm talking about bank receipts from cash withdrawals used to pay the director of the media team, band announcer, and receipts from paying the band staff their summer band camp honorariums. Also in that drawer were receipts from camera equipment for the media team and other equipment/uniforms for the Dancing Dolls. It was a terrible mistake. Even worse was that I wouldn't think about its contents until a month later. By that time, it was too late!

The director's office was vacant for about a month. A reliable source told me that nothing was in the drawer when the backstabbing new director, Kedric Taylor, moved into the office. Although I've become very bothered by what was to be discovered after my termination, I kept quiet. I didn't tell anyone, not even my closest allies, who were defending my actions.

Before my termination, we were in the process of collecting band camp fees. At the time of my termination, we collected approximately $30,000 in band camp fees. I called Lorenzo Hart and gave him a cashier's check made payable to Southern University for half the amount and instructed him to take it to the university's cashier's office for deposit. The other half of the money collected wasn't in my account yet. The registration company who collected the band camp fees on my behalf only deposited funds twice a month. I would have to wait until the date of the second deposit to turn in the rest of the money owed to the university. I was very nervous and hoped that the other half of the camp funds were available before anyone noticed.

As I waited for the money to come in, I decided to just walk away from my alma mater and the Director of Bands Job. I knew I was a great leader and band director, so getting a new job would be easy. Then I learned of Lawrence Jackson's betrayal and how it benefited a guy who was never a team player or loyal. If he was going to support Kedric Taylor, then I was going to fight for my job!

I knew forgetting the contents of my desk drawer was damaging but I had my bank statements. I could prove where the money went from the Mardi Gras parade honorariums that I received. I received a little over $14,000 in honorariums, yet I spent a little over $16,000 on the wind ensemble's trip to Atlanta, Georgia. I knew that I had a case. I was confident that if I filed an appeal through the Southern University System Board of Supervisors, most of the board members would see things my way. I only needed 9 of the 16 board members to overturn Dr Belton's, the puppet president-chancellor, decision to terminate me. Although this was an uphill battle, it was possible to win. I hired an attorney specializing in state ethical and labor laws, and I was confident that we had a winning strategy to get my job back.

Why did I begin to fight for my job? It was a nightmare since day one. In my heart I wanted to be away from Southern University, Baton Rouge, and the state of Louisiana but I needed to clear my name and fight back those I felt wronged me. Finally, I needed to fight for my students. As I was clearing my office, many of my students went to the board meeting and spoke on my behalf. I was proud and honored. I taught them to stand up for what they believed in and to fight. As their teacher, I couldn't go against what I instilled in my students. I was speechless and humbled to watch them at the board meeting via live stream on YouTube. Although my termination was not an item on the board's agenda, the board's chair allowed my students to speak out. Later, the students' support started to dwindle. Kedric Taylor threatened some while getting in the heads of others, he was able to convince them not to speak up for me.

I called Brian Simmons so he could relay instructions for me. I wanted to make sure Lorenzo Hart knew how to go about verifying that the band and dance team camp funds were posted in the appropriate account in the comptroller's office. Apparently, Lawrence Jackson was right next to Brian Simmons as he interrupted our conversation by getting on the phone.

"Nate! How are you doing man?"

"I am doing just fine."

I was short in my response. I didn't want to talk to him. I was still upset at how he sold me out. It took every ounce of discipline for me not to curse out the man who I once viewed as a father figure.

"Nate, you're going to be just fine! You were a good band director. By the way, South Carolina State needs a band director. You should consider applying …"

"I WAS a good band director! Yea. Ok! I'll talk to you later!"

I became even more upset. I was at the beginning stage of filing an appeal to get my job back, but Lawrence Jackson already counted me out. In fact, it hadn't even been a week since I was terminated. He refused to come around just to give advice when I was the director, but he was already on campus running things and collecting his "SELL OUT PAY!" At this point, I had endured a lot, but this moment was the most hurtful.

The reality of my termination began to set in. I canceled the band's website, linked it to my credit card and contacted various vendors to cancel orders that I placed for the future. Brian Simmons came by to tell me that Kedric Taylor had no clue how to run the high school band and dance team camp or the location of the funds collected. At this moment, I knew there would be a major problem.

Even Brian Simmons didn't know how I ran band camp funds through my account or the actions that led me to begin this terrible practice. I knew if I handed over my access to the camp's registration company, it wouldn't be good for me. I began to stall and think of a way to make sure that the camp could operate without revealing my practices. Besides, the money I collected was already in the University's custody. I just didn't want anyone to know what I did in the past. Although my intentions and reasons for doing so were pure, I knew that running funds through my account was an indefensible practice and would be very hard to explain once the public found out. I told Brian Simmons that the funds were in the band account in the university's comptroller's office and to talk to Lorenzo Hart. I ended that conversation and attempted to buy more time to get out of a sticky situation!

Towards the end of May 2018, the local newspaper had a detailed auditor's report concerning my situation. The news was encouraging. It recommended that I pay restitution for the $14,000 received in parade honorariums to the university. It did not recommend termination. It was further proof that the "puppet masters" forced their puppet, Dr. Belton. to "jump the gun" and fire me.

I knew they were searching for anything they could find on me due to the non-stop investigations during the 2017-18 academic year. I also knew that it was wise of the university to issue me a "no-fault termination" as they knew that my receipt of honorariums wasn't something that could stick. However, by being an at-will employee, I could technically be fired for no reason at all. I know that if I had to pay restitution for $14,000, the University would essentially owe me a little over $2,000. I had verifiable receipts in my possession of where the funds went, and ZERO percent went to my personal benefit.

I also received a letter from the Southern University System Board of Supervisors approving the request to appeal my termination. The hearing would take place during the latter part of July 2018. It was now a race against the clock. Although none of my supporters or haters knew about my practice of running funds through my bank account, my goal was to keep the narrative on the initial reason for my termination. If I could keep the focus on parade honorariums, I had a good chance of overturning Dr. Belton's decision.

The most disappointing thing about the "internal auditing process" was Kedric Taylor denying having received honorariums from me throughout his four-year tenure as Assistant/Associate Director of Bands. I found it quite strange that Brian Simmons and Lorenzo Hart told the truth about receiving honorariums throughout my four-year tenure as Director of Bands. It is a fact that I paid my staff honorariums various times, with everyone receiving an envelope of cash each time during the same meeting. I paid everyone together because I did not want one to think that the other received more money than them. I would tell my staff to open their envelopes and count their cash in front of each other. I wanted to eliminate any potential problems or jealousy, especially from Kedric Taylor.

It's the end of May 2018, and I began to prepare for my termination hearing with the Southern University Board of Supervisors. Up to this point, I've received calls, texts, and social media messages from numerous supporters encouraging me to continue to "fight the good fight." I met with my attorney regularly, who advised me that I had a good case against the University. Two months away from my termination hearing and things took a turn for the worse!

Brian Simmons came by my apartment to let me know that Kedric Taylor wanted access to the camp registration company that I used to collect fees. Although the band staff had access, it was limited. They did not have access to the dollar amount collected. They could only verify registration information such as names, addresses, phone numbers, etc.

My only concern in turning over access was not only the dollar amount collected for the current year's camp, but the dollar amount of fees collected for four years from the high school band and dance team camp, University band fees, and Dancing Doll tryout fees. The total was a little more than $297,000 collected in four years. The funds went to purchase the items for which I collected the fees. I knew that once the auditors saw the big number of $297,000, it would mean big trouble. I had no justification in which the University or the public would understand that $297,000 was the revenue over four years. Although it may seem like a lot of money to most, the "big number" that the registration company revealed only gave the headline and not the story.

The revenue collected over four years was $297,000, but that was not the profit. The profit is what is left after paying all expenses and I had a lot of expenses. We hosted a band camp, paid food costs, and paid the registration company services, etc. The university students paid approximately $130 a year in fees, and in return, they received five band shirts, athletic shorts, name brand warm-up suits, and gloves. Finally, out of that enormous amount of $297,000 for four years was Kedric Taylor's salary, which was $180,000. It is easy to determine that there wasn't much profit left considering all of the expenses. The problem was the perception of having access to close to $300,000.

The university and public would only focus on $297,000 and not consider where the money went. I completely understood as I should not have had access to the funds in the first place. Wiring money to my bank account was the worst thing I could have done as I lost the confidence of most of my supporters. The dollar amount dominated the headlines, and there was no room for an explanation of revenue versus profit. The public only ran with the fact that a large sum of money passed through my hands. I knew learning this news would make Dr. Belton and his puppet masters happy. They now had a valid reason to terminate me. I knew my quest to get the Southern University System Board of Supervisors to overturn Dr. Belton's decision just got 297,000 times harder.

The public's opinion and convincing the board to overturn the decision was hard. The hardest conversation I had in justifying my actions was with Sonja Norwood! She was very upset with me and understandably so. She had been my most prominent advocate and source of support for four years. For her to find out that I ran funds through my account, especially in the way she found out, deeply offended her.

University auditors and administrators contacted the registration company to gain first-hand access to the information that was only accessible to me. A member of the "SU Elite" approached Sonja to inform her of my activity. They also told her that the University would go public with the matter in a further attempt to shame me. Finding out in this manner was "egg on her face." Before this damning discovery, Sonja had her *5th Quarter* social media group on fire and lined up to support me. The discovery caused her to take a step back from me. As a matter of fact, it would be close to a month before I talked to her again. Losing the support of my most prominent advocate caused me once again to become depressed. I began to repeat the past by coping with my depression with alcohol abuse.

When the news story about the camp registration company broke, I avoided talking to my attorney, family, and friends. The news was one-sided. The media never attempted to contact my attorney or me to release a statement in my defense. I don't think that any statement that I could have made at the time would have been justifiable. For the first time throughout this whole ordeal, I'd become embarrassed and just wanted to take my own life! I drank so much that I would wake up on some nights in the middle of the bathroom floor covered with vomit. My life no longer had a purpose and I no longer wanted to live. Luckily, Brian Simmons had the access code to get into my apartment or I probably would have been successful in my attempt to take my own life.

It was a very dark time in my life. In fact, it was the darkest time of my life as my memory from a day-to-day basis is still not clear. Brian Simmons often reminds me of how he visited me daily, ready for any and everything. "On some days, you were good, but on other days I will go to your apartment, and you would be passed out or rambling saying crazy stuff!"

He has seen me at my best and my worst. Had he not video recorded me at my worst one day, I wouldn't have believed that I behaved the way I did. Seeing myself on video during one of my "weakest moments" was the wake-up call that I needed to get myself together. It made me realize that my life is much more valuable than some job or someone's opinion of me based on a misleading headline.

I began to contact my attorney again. We formulated another strategy to win the appeal to get my job back. My family and closest friends were very disappointed in me, not for what I did, but because I felt that I couldn't share "my secret" of wiring money to my bank account with them. Although "my secret" was indeed bad and hard to defend, those who genuinely loved Nathan B. Haymer eventually came around to support me and my mental health. They were no longer concerned about my return to Southern University but about Nathan B. Haymer, the man and not the band director.

My mother was an employee of the University from 1975-1986. It was nothing new to her as she began to share the scandals of her era with me. My mother was disappointed that I had to go to such extreme measures to protect the band's money, but she definitely understood. My second mother, Sonja, eventually came around as well. She let me know that I never lost her support. She had to exercise "tough love" to get me to understand that I had to be 100-percent transparent with her.

I began to gain weight because of my depression, and I needed "Chef Nate." In 2017, during one of my most challenging times, my character "Chef Nate" was created. "Chef Nate" was more than a character who cooks with fun and excitement. "Chef Nate" was therapy that helped me cope with stress even during the biggest storm of my life. Because of past experiences, I couldn't get close to anyone or trust anyone to ask for help. Since I knew I needed help and couldn't trust anyone enough to help me, I needed "Chef Nate" to come to the rescue again.

"Chef Nate" was in full therapy mode. I discovered several things about me and my life. I've been loved, and I loved. I've been hated, and I hated. I've been lied to, and I've lied to others. To move forward with my life, I had to focus on myself and the wrongs that I've done; even if my wrongs were trusting and surrounding myself with people that I should have never dealt with. I saw the signs with everyone who has ever wronged me in my role as Director of Bands. Even though I saw the signs in all the wrongdoers, I ignored them. I knew if I were ever to be happy and become whole again that I couldn't achieve that at a place like Southern University or in the state of Louisiana. I began to understand that I no longer wanted the position as Director of Bands. I was now fighting for my legacy while focusing on the long list of accomplishments during my tenure. I am afraid ever to love again because everyone and everything that I love eventually leaves me!

However, "Chef Nate" was also in full healing mode. Even though I was no longer the Director of Bands, I kept my commitment to attend the Southern University Alumni Federation - Dallas Chapter Bayou Bash in Dallas, Texas, along with the SUAF National Alumni Convention in Baton Rouge. I wouldn't let my termination and the negative connotations associated with me, such as being labeled a thief, deter me from supporting key individuals. Besides, I was more than a SU employee. I am an alumnus as well. Ms. L. Thomas, SUAF-First Vice President, who was very instrumental in securing brand new uniforms, was towards the end of her campaign for President. I thought it was necessary to attend the Bayou Bash and national alumni convention to support her. Also, my twin brother was recognized and honored at SUAF's inaugural Forty Under 40 event. Although we were 40 years old at the time of my twin brother's induction, he became an honoree a couple of months before our 40th birthday.

Going into full "Chef Nate" mode, I hosted a dinner party in my downtown apartment. I cooked for my twin brother and other SU Forty Under 40 honorees, such as the media director for the Human Jukebox, Marissa, and a few other honorees who also marched in the band in the past. We had a great time as my apartment became one of the hangout spots of the SUAF Alumni Convention since it also took place in downtown Baton Rouge. It was truly uplifting. I had a good time because it was no longer about Nathan B. Haymer, the terminated band director. It was about Nathan B. Haymer, the brother; the friend; the alumnus of SU; and the all-around charismatic person I genuinely am. "Chef Nate" showed up and showed out. It would be the last of the "good times" in Baton Rouge. The Southern University System Board of Supervisors meeting was approximately two weeks away.

I knew convincing the board to overturn Dr. Belton's decision would be an uphill battle. Still, I did gain many supporters, struggled to pay massive legal fees, and wanted to protect my legacy. My fight became more about those who opposed me than those who were on my team. I wanted it to be that way because the opposition is what motivated me. Perhaps I was too afraid to let my supporters know that I really didn't want to go back. I just wanted to clear my name because I never had peace as Director of Bands at SU. I knew that if I were lucky enough to get the majority of the board's vote, my return would be even more disastrous than before my termination.

I know the "SU Elite" would've taken me out. I've been told that "they" didn't support me because I never accepted their invitation to the many private gatherings of the "SU Gentlemen's Club." I came across as arrogant when I didn't want to hang in the social circles of those who could have helped me "cover up" any wrong I had done. Just as "they" covered up the wrongs of others in the past accused of misappropriating university funds or worse and covering up the crimes of those who were sexual harassers and/or sexual assaulters. If it weren't for Sonja's *5th Quarter* social media group, the University's board would have gone through with a ceremony naming the gymnasium on one of the system's campuses after a known sexual harasser. In fact, the "known sexual harasser" actions caused the University to settle a lawsuit for an amount that is far greater than anything that I would be accused of hiding from the institution. Yet, the "known sexual harasser" only received a transfer from one system campus to another. I could go on about those in the "SU Gentlemen's Club" who did worse than what I was accused of, but why bother? Besides, I now understood that I just didn't fit in the culture, so "they" had to excommunicate me.

I'd been waiting almost three months for the Southern University System Board of Supervisors meeting, and we were finally at the day. This particular board meeting was at the system's community college campus in Shreveport, Louisiana. My family and I drove close to four hours for a termination hearing that I was not excited about, nor was I any longer interested in winning. I knew if I managed to do the "impossible" by having Dr. Belton's decision overturned, the "witch hunt" would continue. More importantly, I knew it was time to move on by relocating as I would never find happiness at Southern University or in Baton Rouge again.

Between my termination and the termination hearing with the SU System Board of Supervisors, I received an offer for a band director position at Allen University, a small HBCU in Columbia, South Carolina. I was flattered by the offer. They were starting up a new program. They haven't had a marching band since the 1960s, and the president of Allen University wanted to give me an opportunity. I appreciated the Allen University President for being willing to accept me despite what he may have heard and despite the constant negative news coverage that I received. Still, I declined the offer. I had to see my termination hearing through at SU. The Allen University President warned me that anytime an employee tried to take on the state, the employee would more than likely lose. I appreciated his honesty as I understood my chances of winning were slim to none, but it was no longer about winning versus losing to me. As I previously stated, I really did not want to go back to that "hell hole." It was about my legacy and my name. Besides, looking back on the situation, I was not in the correct mental space to take on a new director's position at anybody's University. 2018 was not when I wanted to "get back on the horse" and start a new band. I knew I at least needed the 2018-2019 academic year off.

The Southern University System Board meeting lasted over four hours. My situation was the last item on the board's agenda. My family waited in the meeting as I stayed in my truck while praying, listening to talk radio, listening to music, and praying some more. I mainly prayed for peace and God's favor to have my heart's desires. My heart no longer desired Southern University. My heart desired me to live carefree. I no longer wanted to look over my shoulder or watch my back for those who wanted to harm me. I wanted to be a "regular person." I wanted to go back to being someone who could walk down the street, and no one paid attention to; someone who had a regular job and came home at a decent time to spend the day with family and friends. As simple as that sound, I've never had a chance to enjoy this due to constantly feeling like I was a prisoner of my own success since day one and year one in my profession.

I finally got the call to come into the meeting. My attorney and I went over the game plan one last time before we entered the hearing. I requested a closed hearing, so it was not open to the public. Once the board resumed the meeting in executive session, the board chair began to read the rules of the hearing. I sat quietly. I was ready to get the meeting over with and apparently some of the board members must have felt the same way because I began to notice that they were disengaged. I particularly noticed the gentleman who approached me twice in the past. I knew that I didn't have his support as he played on his cell phone the entire time. Through the admission from several sources in high levels of state and federal government, I would later learn that he was responsible for my future FBI investigation and prosecution.

Although disengaged, at least that particular board member wasn't asleep like others that I noticed.

My attorney began to plead my case. He distributed the ledger sheets to the board members explaining how I used the funds. I paid close attention to those who were engaged versus those who were not, and out of all board members present, maybe half of them were present in body only as their minds were somewhere else.

When one of the board members heard my attorney speak on my behalf, revealing the large sums of cash that I carried in my briefcase to away games, it angered him. The angry board member tore into Dr. Belton as the University received a warning from the legislative auditors in 2005, to discontinue this practice. We were now in 2018, and no changes were made. Another board member from Shreveport made a rude remark as he interrupted my attorney to address me. "I am sorry that you have to sit through this long process, Mr. Haymer, but I hope you didn't pay a lot of money for this attorney as he is doing you a terrible disservice!" Another board member immediately apologized on his behalf.

It was now time for Dr. Belton to speak. I've always known him to be very "delayed" in his speech, often pausing in the middle of his statements with "uh …uh …uh." On this day, Dr. Belton did his homework because I didn't hear a single "uh …uh …uh" throughout his whole address to me in front of the board. Dr. Belton's puppet masters trained him well. I found his prepared remarks to be quite insulting.

"I used to be a Nathan Haymer fan, not only just a fan of the band. As I observed your mistakes and your criminal ways, I began to understand that perhaps you shouldn't have been the director in the first place. You're obviously not equipped for the job!"

I was taken aback by Dr. Belton's statement because it seemed quite personal. I wanted to respond by interrupting him because I already knew the outcome of the hearing. I decided to wait and listen a little more.

"I found out that you turned all the money in that was in your bank account collected in band camp fees to the university. You get no kudos for that because you never should have had the money in the first place! I don't care what caused you to begin the process of wiring money to your account. It is the university's money, and we could pay whoever I see fit with band money or any other money!"

Immediately I blurted out. "Well, it's a good thing I am fired because you have the right band director now. Band money is for the band, period! Also, if I am not fit to be the band director, you are not fit to be the president!" My brother and attorney side-eyed me to shut up!

Dr. Belton was shaken by my "clap back" as he forgot his "prepared remarks." The nerve of him telling me that he could spend the band's money how he wanted when my labor and efforts brought in the funds. It was not some state budget or allocation for the band; it was funding that we secured on our own through our branding efforts along with performances by the Human Jukebox. My "clap back" took him off his game as he started speaking with his usual "uh …uh …uh."

"You were arrogant and never asked for … uh …uh… help. The interim band director asks for help and tells us what he needs! He doesn't take matters into his own hands."

It was hard for me to sit and listen to Dr. Belton lie any further. I did more than ask for help! In 2014, I made a YouTube video asking for help which landed me in trouble with the acting chancellor and vice chancellor. In 2015, I was reassigned to a new supervisor because my previous supervisor wasn't equipped to help me. In 2016, we had a failed financial meeting in Dr. Belton's office, who was currently feeding the board members lies. In 2017, I had to get the student body to vote for a referendum to fund the band and get the vice president of the SUAF to lead a fundraising campaign for new band uniforms. So, I am not clear; how wasn't all of that not a cry for help?

"I gave you and your staff a raise even when I was advised not to do so!"

Again, more lies! Although approved by Dr. Belton, our raises came from my efforts with the funds secured by the student referendum of 2017. He had nothing to do with that. If he were the student government association president, then his point would've been valid. He is a liar and the worst leader that I have ever seen. In fact, I wanted nothing more at that moment than not to be reinstated as director of the SU Band because I refused to submit myself to the authority of incompetent leadership ever again.

I wouldn't submit to just Dr. Belton, but the board members as well. I looked around the room and saw several key board members still disengaged and playing on their smartphones. At that moment, it became obvious who the "puppet masters" that were pulling Dr. Belton's puppet strings. The head "puppet master" was the person who arrogantly approached me about spelling the governor's initials for the 2015 Bayou Classic performance. As the meeting continued, we were asked to leave so that the board members and Dr. Belton could talk in private.

My attorney was very optimistic that I would be given another chance, or at least the issue would be delayed pending further information that I had to provide. My twin brother was realistic, and we had the same thoughts. We knew it was over! I didn't want my attorney to be right as I came to the meeting with the intention of not being reinstated. Besides, why would I want to go back to work under Dr. Belton who just attacked me on a personal level or for a board of supervisors that uses their power to intimidate others to get what they want while willfully neglecting their responsibilities and duties when it goes against their politics? It was apparent where some of the board stood by their disinterest during the entire hearing. At least the board member from Shreveport who insulted my attorney was engaged the whole time. Whether he voted to reinstate me or uphold my termination, I respected him just because he did his job, unlike 50 percent of his colleagues.

Juked

While the board and Dr. Belton were meeting privately during the recess, I noticed quite a few board members leaving the meeting and walking towards the parking lot to their vehicles. Some of the board members leaving were the same ones who were disengaged the entire time. I didn't know what to think of that, but I knew something wasn't right about it. I began to talk to my mother, stepfather, and twin brother about moving on and the whole draining experience of the moment. Shortly after, everyone went back into the building as the board went from an "executive session" to an open or public meeting.

It was now time for the moment that we'd been waiting for — the up or down vote concerning my fate as Director of Bands. I think my family was more nervous than I was, as I already conceded. Before the roll call vote transpired, one board member motioned to table the vote to have more time to look over the documents that my attorney submitted to them and also have the time to request further documents if needed. Thank God that that motion failed as I could no longer wait to be released from my obligations in seeing the appeals process through. It was time to move on. Three months was enough, and I didn't want to extend the nightmare.

As the roll call vote concluded, six votes favored my reinstatement and five votes for upholding my termination. I won the majority of the board members that were present. Still, I needed a majority of the board's body for a motion to pass or overturn Dr. Belton's decision. The board is a 16-member body, so a majority is nine or more members. I counted approximately four members that left early and went to the parking lot. They did not vote at all, neglecting their duties as a member of the board. Because I did not have the majority of the body, Dr. Belton's decision to terminate me was upheld.

I was happy and sad at the same time. I was happy that I could finally move on but was sad that the enemy won! I also knew that there would be more to come after my termination. During his comments, Dr. Belton hinted a warning to the board that if they overruled his decision, it would make the university a laughingstock when other things concerning this situation "came down the pipe!" It was a threat that meant that somebody somewhere sought further actions against me to teach me a lesson! Although I was never really worried about his threat, I would never forget it as it was a clear warning that "they" were not happy by the public humiliation and loss of my career and employment. "They" wanted me to suffer and wasn't going to stop until I was "underneath the jail!"

In the meantime, my depression turned into excitement. I knew where I wanted to go to escape Louisiana. I wanted to leave the state but still be close enough to come back when I needed to. A place where I often visited as a "quick getaway" during my time in Lake Charles and Baton Rouge. The place was Houston, Texas. I saw Houston as being the most diverse city in the nation and an opportunity to blend in with millions of people without anyone knowing me or caring about anything I did. Houston could give me "Louisiana" along with other cultures of this great country all wrapped up into one city. I did not have a job or a solid plan, but I knew staying in Louisiana was no longer an option. To prepare for Houston, I had to wait for the money from my annual leave and sick days that I never used over my 18-year career in Louisiana to post to my account. I also had to wait for my retirement benefits to post. Since I was officially unemployed, I could no longer afford my nice apartment or the mortgage on my flood-damaged home that I haven't lived in since 2016. I moved out of my apartment to an "extended stay" type of motel for $800 for August, and I planned to move to Houston by September.

Chapter 33

My termination from Southern University was final and it was time to transition to Houston to start my new life. I found a rental property online and went to the city for a weekend to check it out. The house was absolutely gorgeous! It looked just as pictured online. There was just one problem...the neighborhood!

I wished that the landlord would have used a 360-degree camera because all around the house was a dump! But I was desperate. I wanted to move from Baton Rouge as soon as possible. In my haste to relocate, I signed a nine-month lease paying the landlord the total amount of the lease before I moved in. I took a huge gamble in finding employment within nine months of moving to Houston.

I called the movers so I could move forward with my new life in Houston. I was taking a leap of faith by moving to a city with no family, no plan, and hope that things would work out. I knew that I could depend on my character, "Chef Nate," to get me through. Who knows, I may start my own meal prep and catering business.

During my first three months in Houston, I became very comfortable with my new setup. I managed to network with a couple of SU alumni in the Houston area who didn't change on me. It was through them that I gained opportunities to provide meal prep and catering services for pay. Chef Nate became very popular so quickly that I couldn't keep up with the demand. Although I loved cooking, I hated cooking under pressure. My cooking was my outlet. I realized very soon that I did not want to cook to provide a living for myself. Due to my unemployment, I had to do what I had to do for the moment. Still, I knew that I would eventually teach at one of the local community colleges because I applied for every job opening other than music positions. I wanted nothing else to do with music anymore!

My family came to visit me for my first Thanksgiving in Houston. Everyone loved the house, but they were very skeptical of the neighborhood. I assured them that despite the area being rundown, it was safe. Wouldn't you know… the night after Thanksgiving, we heard gunshots right behind my house! The sound was very explosive, and my mother ran to protect my niece and nephews. I couldn't believe it! The whole time I'm telling my family that I was safe, we were in the middle of a war zone.

Sometime later, I learned that the shots were fired at the house facing the next street directly behind mine. Thankfully, no one in my house was injured. I was embarrassed to have my family witness dangerous violence. I also found out that it was a drug-related shooting at a targeted place. Learning that made me feel a little better because at least I knew it wasn't a random act of violence. My neighbor told me he lived in the neighborhood for over 40 years, and things like this would happen once every five years or so. I would never find out if my neighbors were correct because that would be the first- and last-time hearing gunshots my entire time there.

In February 2019, I went to Allen University to conduct a high school honor band. They treated me like royalty. They also gave me another offer to come on board and work with the new band. The band director is a much older and experienced gentleman that I deeply respect. His resume was top notched. He ran two excellent programs at Morris Brown College and South Carolina State University. Now, he was at Allen University, and he wanted to pass the baton to me. I admit I wanted to take his offer and expressed to him that I was very interested. However, I had a feeling that my past was not over. I never forgot SU's puppet President-Chancellor's, Dr. Belton, threat about "things coming down the pipe for me!"

Although everything was quiet, my past experiences taught me the signs for the "calm before the storm." I knew now wasn't the time to uproot again. It was best to stay put in Houston, Texas just in case I needed to be able to get to Louisiana quickly. Some people in Baton Rouge were still plotting to come after me because I posted positively on my social media platforms, turning my pain into purpose, and I guess they didn't like that. Plus, I would receive phone calls from my attorney for payment in reference to the work he was doing on the ongoing Louisiana Board of Ethics' investigation against me.

My visit at Allen University sparked a renewed energy for the band. I loved standing in front of that honor band. Coming off the second offer at Allen University, I decided to apply for the Director of Bands positions at Grambling State University and Mississippi Valley State University. I was a finalist for both jobs, but ultimately didn't get the job. I knew that I was tainted, and no one wanted to touch me. I didn't let it discourage me from going after what I thought I could achieve. Even though I knew it was an uphill battle, I knew that no candidate could match my vision, wisdom, and experience. I had a track record of achieving and putting words and vision into action!

Besides tainting my employment opportunities, my past also wrecked me! I understood that the public perception of me was negative because the Baton Rouge media market followed by HBCU news publications and social media users performing fantastic smear tactics. After being denied the Director of Bands positions, I realized that I couldn't discredit or hide from my past any longer. I had to face myself every day in the mirror, and it forced me to own my past and walk in my truth, regardless of how the naysayers wanted to paint me. Eventually, I no longer was concerned about how people felt about me. I thank God for intervening in my life. I fell in love with everything about myself again. Suddenly, I began to view my "unique" career path as a blessing to teach a lesson to others who aspire to one day serve in a leadership role.

God's intervention and my revelation came at the time when the ethics investigation was heating up. May 2019, I met with representatives from the Louisiana Board of Ethics in New Orleans at my attorney's office for a deposition. I was grilled about parade honorariums, cash advances for away games given to me by the university, the high school band and dance team camp, and all my financial dealings with the SU band.

The deposition reminded me of everything that I went through. It was very emotional, depressing, and overwhelming. I wanted to just "throw in the towel" and get charged with whatever crime that I was guilty of. The entire situation was no longer worth a moment of my life and required more money than I had. I was so financially strapped that my mother and stepfather had to dig into their savings to shell out a large sum of cash to cover my legal expenses. My legal fees exceeded $50,000, and I felt like a huge burden to my family. I was tired of the ongoing investigation. I had no issue with going to prison if it meant that I didn't have to depend on someone else to pay for my mistakes.

The summer of 2019 I knew I had a problem when the state officials discovered the false invoices. I was so focused on running camp funds through my bank account that I forgot about the actual crime I committed by submitting false invoices to the SU System Foundation, the SU Alumni Federation, and the SU travel office. The "SU Elite" left no stone unturned. They kept digging to assure that I would face prosecution. The false invoices were a game-changer because that was a clear display of a premeditated motive to defraud the university of approximately $33,000.

Not only did the summer of 2019 place me further under the investigation microscope, but it made me face my pride. By now, I had been unemployed for over a year and my lease ran out. I couldn't afford the rent. I had no idea what I was going to do and no desire to move back to Baton Rouge. Moving back there would be a death sentence. Returning to the same people, places, and things could trigger another depression. My mind was made up. I would rather be homeless than return to Baton Rouge.

Juked

My mother wanted me to move back to Gulfport, Mississippi, with her and my stepfather. Albeit moving there was a better option than Baton Rouge, I didn't want to go there either. While making plans to move home with my mom, a friend called me to intervene. He insisted that I live with him until I got on my feet. It was tough for me to accept his offer because I am a private and prideful person. Also, I don't like living with anyone or feeling like I was a burden, but I had a choice to make. I could swallow my pride and live with someone temporarily or be miserable in Mississippi or Baton Rouge.

I chose to swallow my pride. Because I did so, not only did I become a housemate, but I also gained a big brother and mentor. A gentleman 15 years my senior, he was more seasoned, experienced, very professional, and an alumnus of Southern University! He began to give me pointers and encouragement on finding my purpose, trusting God, and believing in myself. Living with him made me realize that although I was a mentor who invested knowledge and encouragement in others over the years, mentors need mentors as well!

Surprisingly, the situation wasn't what I thought it would be. His house was huge. Huge enough to house two adult men comfortably, but also huge enough that at times I found myself lonely. We may have shared a space, but we had separate lives. He traveled a lot which found me at the house alone. I refused to just sit in someone's house doing nothing, so I began an aggressive search for employment.

While on my aggressive search for employment, I received a call from the Director of the Texas Southern University's "Ocean of Soul" Marching Band. I was very familiar with the band director. He called and asked me to consider joining his team as a contracted employee. My responsibilities would consist of arranging music, rehearsing the band on a part-time basis, and creating halftime show concepts. It was a no-brainer for me. I was living with someone and was desperate for any type of income. I accepted his offer.

He also had connections with an elementary school principal searching for a general music teacher for pre-kindergarten through 5th grade. Although I never worked with kids that young, I was excited about the opportunity. I loved that my work would be from 7:30am to 2:50pm, but the salary is what elevated my excitement and took this opportunity over the top. The position paid $70,000 a year. This is probably the most I've ever made, considering the number of hours I will have to work versus my past!

My excitement was off the charts. I finally secured a job, and it had benefits. I wanted to teach elementary school because the job was low profile. It was the opposite of everything I experienced thus far in my career. Plus, working with the Ocean of Soul Marching band on a part-time basis was me "having my cake and eating it too!" Here was a beautiful opportunity to supplement my salary from the elementary school.

My Louisiana teaching certificate expired in 2011, so I had to hurry and apply for a Texas teaching certificate through the Texas Education Agency. It took about four weeks for them to grant my temporary teaching certificate. I eventually took the necessary certification exams and easily passed them. Thus, changing my temporary certificate to a permanent certification in music for grades early childhood through 12th grade.

I was so thankful for this accomplishment, and it was now time to teach and lead again! The first item on my list of duties was to meet the freshman band class of 2019 and be ready to rehearse them whenever the band director needed me to step in. Unfortunately, my stint with the Ocean of Soul Marching Band would only be for a few days.

My first day at Texas Southern was when the freshmen had their first meeting. On purpose, I sat quietly and humbly in the back of the band hall. I wanted everyone to know that I was "the help," and I didn't come to run anything! Unfortunately, some of the band's alumni took pictures of me sitting in the band hall without my knowledge. They posted it on social media along with texting my photos in their private text groups. Also, I posed for a picture taken by the official photographer/videographer of the Ocean of Soul, and that picture was posted on social media as well.

The following day, I came to rehearse for only one hour. I rehearsed my arrangement of, *I Feel Good All Over* by Stephanie Mills. It was hard to work due to the distractions of alumni and others recording but we managed to make it through the arrangement. Although it needed more work, I was satisfied with the day's progress. I thanked everyone that allowed me to work one hour and left. I felt very uncomfortable by all the attention and very unwelcomed by the assistant directors. I could tell that they didn't want me there!

On my walk home, I listened to my cell phone recording of the freshman band playing my arrangement with the intent to take notes on what to fix for the next rehearsal. Listening to the introduction of the song, I began to cry. All the pain and embarrassment of the past came rushing forward. I thought I was over everything. I believed I had nothing left. Upon hearing the recording of my arrangement, I became very emotional. Being real with myself, I had to admit that music still lived within me.

I was on cloud nine when the director spoke with me. He told me that the media in Baton Rouge found out that I was working there and asked the upper-level administrators some questions. From my past experiences, I knew that the director was being truthful, but I also suspected the assistant directors of sabotage. Although I was hurt, I knew that it was best to move on, especially since my presence was a distraction for everyone.

Nevertheless, I was thankful. My time with the TSU band may have been short lived, but it was a catalyst in finding full-time employment at the elementary school. The first day of school was drawing near and the excitement was mounting. I had a job that paid bi-weekly. I marked the paydays on my calendar and began to make financial plans. My truck note was three months behind, and I would be able to start making payments. I also made plans to regain my independence by living on my own again. Things were finally working out!

Chapter 34

During my first semester as an elementary music teacher, the investigation expanded beyond the Louisiana Board of Ethics and the Federal Bureau of Investigation entered the picture. I received a call to meet. So, I drove to Baton Rouge and met with the FBI. The meeting wasn't long. I knew that anything that the FBI asked me, they more than likely already knew the answer. I told the truth when asked about the band camp revenue, false invoices, and honorariums.

The FBI dropped the honorarium issue. They were able to verify that band directors receiving parade honorariums was standard practice in Louisiana. I was 98 HOT! The honorarium was the issue that led to my termination. But, I also had numerous band directors privately tell me how messed up my situation was while NONE came running to my defense.

Just like running band camp funds through my bank account, I told no one about my unorthodox method of writing false invoices that I submitted. The band announcer did me a solid and sent me an email to prove that I paid him. However, the media director, Garrett Edgerson, denied getting paid altogether. It was stupid for me to jeopardize everything for those who couldn't even acknowledge that they got paid.

The FBI was able to verify that I paid the staff from the false invoices and band camp revenue and informed me that running funds through my account could potentially cause a bigger issue. Even though I had my reasons and could explain them, it still doesn't justify the criminal act I committed. I take full responsibility for committing fraud, but I was relieved to have evidence that there was no personal gain. In the end, I was satisfied with the FBI agents' professionalism. While I was relieved that they verified some of my claims, the FBI did not let me off the hook. Submitting false invoices is fraud and illegal, no matter how noble the cause. For the first time throughout this whole ordeal, I knew that I was in big trouble!

When the nature of my situation went from a civil matter to a criminal, I had to get a second attorney. Having already admitted that I submitted false invoices along with the reasons, the US Attorney in charge of prosecuting my case offered me a plea deal and my attorneys thought it would be in my best interest to take it. At this point, it had been two years. I'd grown tired and wanted the matter behind me. Plus, I was strapped for cash. I could no longer afford to pay my attorney to prepare for a trial that could take another year or two. Waiting another year for a trial would be a waste of money that I didn't have but more importantly, it would be a waste of time! Already in a two-year limbo, a trial wouldn't guarantee a favorable sentence if convicted. The plea deal indicated that I misappropriated approximately $33,300; the amount derived from the false invoices I submitted to the university. So, I took the deal!

June 2020, I pleaded guilty through a virtual federal hearing with a judge and was charged with a federal felony. Instantly, I felt the weight and gravity of the moment. All my life I worked to make my family and community proud and in a blink of an eye, I felt like I let them down. I was now a convicted felon. It was a surreal experience.

The next step was waiting for my sentencing hearing and hoping that the judge would give me mercy. In preparation on my part, I reached out to 40 people that were either former students, colleagues, or people I considered a friend. Out of 40 people, I received 24-character reference letters of support. Once again, people I thought supported me showed me exactly who they were. I was now playing "the waiting game." I didn't know the exact date of my sentencing hearing, but I did know that I wasn't going to spend another day worrying about things that I couldn't control!

Juked

December 2020, I got a call from my attorney telling me to check my email. Apparently, the US Attorney who was the prosecutor in my case went back on his word. Someone pressured the US Attorney to add an additional $45,500 of charges to the case. Since I had already taken the plea deal, there was nothing that I could do as signing the deal waive my rights to appeal. I had to have faith that my attorney could successfully argue the deceit during the sentencing hearing. It was a game-changer in relation to sentencing. With $33,300, there was the possibility of probation while paying restitution. However, the addition of $45,500 brought the total amount of charges to a little more than $78,800. According to sentencing guidelines, the addition of $45,500 would make it nearly impossible for me to avoid prison time.

Due to the signed plea deal, my attorney explained that our hands were tied, but he still had hope and advised me to do the same. We were to hope that the judge would be merciful. The entire plea deal situation was depressing but once my attorney shared which judge would be presiding over my sentencing hearing, I lost all hope.

It was obvious "The SU Elite" was in the background calling the shots. I was aware that several members were upset by my initial plea deal. But now I knew they were playing dirty. They were able to manipulate the situation to fit their narrative by having me agree and sign one set of facts and then force the prosecution to change the facts. But the selection of the presiding judge screamed "bought and paid for" by "The SU Elite!"

My attorney told me that my sentencing hearing would probably take place by the end of January 2021. I began to prepare myself for the worst outcome. I was not optimistic on December 31, 2020. When the clock struck midnight, it was January 1, 2021, and I entered my third year of limbo. I waited patiently during the latter part of January, and I still didn't have a date for the sentencing hearing. Finally, my attorney called to tell me that the judge rescheduled the sentencing hearing for a later date, and he didn't know when it would be.

At that precise moment I knew I had to go out and live. I had wasted three years of my life on waiting and I was ready to stop waiting. I went to a car dealership and financed a new vehicle on February 3, 2021. Due to my car being repossessed while attending church one Sunday, I was driving a car that my mother owned but hadn't driven in almost ten years. Over the year and five months of driving her old Toyota Avalon, I had multiple car problems. I had to change the transmission, change the ignition, pay for maintenance for everyday wear and tear such as brakes and tires, and I even had a major repair since someone ran a red light and hit my car. If I was going to start living then my new lease on life would start with a new vehicle.

Around the middle of March, I finally got the call that my sentencing hearing was set. I left Houston early on the morning of March 29, 2021. I wanted to avoid traffic and arrive in Baton Rouge in time to relax, eat a good meal, and rest well in preparation for my sentencing hearing the following day.

I was a ball of emotions. I cried every tear. I said every prayer. I talked about my situation with every loved one that I care to share it with. I never lost hope, but I knew I had to be prepared to be sentenced to prison. I am a firm believer in preparing for the worst while hoping for the best.

I awoke at 5:00am on the morning of March 30, 2021. I had to be ready by 8:15am to be at the federal courthouse in downtown Baton Rouge for 9:00am. I knew that no matter what the judge threw at me, I would accept it and walk forward knowing that I was at the end of the three year "limbo phase" of my life. A sentence to prison or hopefully probation would officially end my years of limbo. I would finally know my fate and could start planning for life after.

I walked into the courthouse to meet with my lawyers for the last time before the hearing. I looked at the monitor on the wall and it read "The United States of America versus Nathan B. Haymer, 10:00am." The weight and gravity of the moment sat in. I couldn't believe that Southern University, being a state institution and my alma mater, would escalate matters to the level of reading my name as a defendant against my country. I knew in my heart that the possibility of probation was slim to none, nevertheless, I was willing to accept my fate as I knew that I had to end the three years of limbo!

My lawyers seemed optimistic, but I did not. I sat there in silence having difficulty erasing the December 2020 phone call and email from my mind. They finished going over minor details dealing with court procedures when I asked about the $45,000 taxed onto my case. I wasn't sure where that amount came from, but I had an idea.

Mid-2020, I had a conversation with a person on the inside of "The SU Elite" circle. During that conversation, it was explained how some individuals of "The SU Elite" were upset with my plea deal and admission of guilt to the $33,000. They were stating that I would get off free and wanted to teach me a lesson. After taking the plea deal and waiving my rights to a trial, surprisingly the additional $45,000" appears. Just the right amount to guarantee prison time!

Since I knew all this information, there was nothing my lawyers could say that would convince me that they could pull a "rabbit out of the hat." I was confident "The SU Elite" would have their way with a judge who, in my mind, was a member of "The SU Elite" as well. Still, I wanted to give the judge the benefit of the doubt that he would be fair and impartial, but I wasn't hopeful as I checked out his Southern University ties.

It was time for the hearing to begin. I was ready to get it started and over. I was ready to accept my fate.

Well, that was it. It was over! The decision had been made and I now knew my fate. While preparing to leave the courtroom, I hugged my family, apologized for putting them through such a tragic situation, and thanked them for their support on that day and through the years. We all were sad about the outcome but happy that the battle was over.

It was March 30, 2021. The judge told me to voluntarily surrender myself to prison on May 3, 2021. This gave me a timeline of a month and two days to continue living my best life. It was time to get back to Houston.

Once back home, I immediately resigned from my teaching position at the elementary school. I had to pack up my belongings to put them in a storage facility. Also, I needed to prepare for the visitation of my family. They really wanted to come and spend a week or two with me during April.

While waiting to receive a letter informing me which federal correctional institution to report to, I began to imagine how the next 13 to 14 months of my life would look. I would have never guessed in a hundred years that I would go to prison. Still, one thing that I knew, I was going to leave prison a better man than when I entered.

My family made it to Houston during the latter part of April and the month flew by. As I prepared for my time out from the real world, I knew it was essential to develop a plan for life after. I am a very creative person, and I began to look at prison as the government doing me a favor. The government was giving me 13 months to plan my next phase of life. I was so much more than just a band director. I was adamant that this period in my life would be a blessing and not a curse.

Time drew closer to May 3, 2021, and I still hadn't received notification of where I would have to report to serve my time. I never got anything in the mail. Thankfully, in June 2020, I had a probation officer assigned to me after my virtual court hearing when I officially took the plea deal. I notified my probation officer about my situation. She told me that she would inform me as soon as she got the information. I became optimistic that I would be on home confinement instead of prison because the reporting date was a week away.

Later that week, I met Marissa at a restaurant. We laughed and talked about moving forward from this situation. Then, I received a text message from my probation officer. I knew it would be something that I did not want to read but I opened it anyway. The text read that I had to report to Three Rivers Federal Correctional Institution in Three Rivers, Texas, on Monday, May 3, 2021, by 2:00pm. That message was the last reality check I needed. It began to sink in that I actually would go to prison. I immediately looked up Three Rivers, Texas, and discovered it was about a three-hour drive southwest of Houston in the middle of nowhere!

Marissa could tell that I was no longer in the mood for fun and games. I called my family and gave them the news. The movers came the next day, I was ready to go. I went to Baton Rouge to see my family one more time on May 1st and 2nd. Then my brother and I would leave Baton Rouge around 4:00am on the morning of May 3rd to take the dreadful long drive to Three Rivers, Texas. Spending the last moments with family before I left for prison was surreal. Everything became an out-of-body experience. It felt as if I was watching myself from another point of view as I told my family goodbye. I was optimistic. I knew I would see them again, but not knowing where I had to go and what to expect consumed my mind. I knew that there wasn't anything anyone could say or do that would ease the tension.

On the morning of May 3, 2021, my brother and I had a long quiet drive to Three Rivers, Texas. I drove the entire way and made it to the small town with a population of 1,800 by noon. I didn't expect to make it so early. The prison site was 8 miles away from the town's major road. I mentioned to Niles that we should "just drive to the prison site to see where I would have to report!" Upon seeing the prison, my heart dropped. The sight of all the fencing and razor wires was my new home. We drove back to town and stopped at the gas station. I made my final calls to loved ones and then I called my cell phone provider to discontinue the service. The absence of my phone's service was the last "nail in the coffin. "Let's go! I am ready!"

We made it back to the prison, and the correctional officers took me into custody. My eyes full of tears hindered me from turning around and telling my brother goodbye. It was nearly 20 years to the day that I received my bachelor's degree in music education from Southern University. Everything I've accomplished in my life no longer mattered. I was now "one of them!"

The guards quickly let me know that life would be different for the next 13 months by the last thing they told my brother. "He won't be able to call you or the rest of your family members for 20 days. Inmate 03184-509 will be placed in a quarantine cell before we place him in the general population!" It was at that moment that I knew that I would need God more than ever before!

Afterword

My Southern University and Agricultural and Mechanical College story is a journey with many detours, roadblocks, and destinations. As an alumnus, I have deep pride and unwavering love. I try to always present the positive attributes and represent the best the school has to offer. As an employee, it was my job to instruct the students' music class, manage the band department, and showcase the talent of the Human Jukebox and concert ensembles. As a leader, I was supposed to safeguard the band's interests and ensure the fair distribution of our hard-earned funds.

My intentions were noble. There were many factors that brought me to the challenging crossroads. The isolation I experienced while grappling with the complexities of the department, coupled with inadequate guidance and support left me adrift. The revolving door of supervisors hindered my ability to establish a consistent rhythm causing further challenges in adhering to policies and procedures. I was unexpectedly thrust into roles beyond my scope such as handling leaky roofs and attending to the smallest details on the floor. My unwavering sense of responsibility extended to caring for staff and extended team members which filled a duty I embraced as the person ultimately in charge. Due to all these things and more, I carry the weight of accountability for my actions.

Within the whirlwind, I made decisions that I now acknowledge as ill-advised. My biggest decision that should have been reconsidered was submitting false invoices and routing band camp funds through my personal bank account. While I possessed evidence of university officials misusing "band funds" for personal gain, I was handcuffed by my position with recognizing the university's prerogative to allocate funds as they saw fit. This reality, though uncomfortable, cannot excuse my actions. A wise friend once told me that if I were to expose others' secrets, I must also reveal my own, for in truth lies liberation. My silence during that "limbo period" was a disservice to myself and those who cared for me, leading to a painful betrayal of their loyalty.

Unfortunately, my termination stemmed from accepting parade honorariums and a barrage of negative media attention which casted a shadow on my beloved alma mater, Southern University. My departure set off a series of events that laid bare my missteps and mismanagement, revealing the cracks I had concealed. My lack of political connections or ties to the "SU Elite" rendered me vulnerable and made it distressingly simple for the President-Chancellor to sever my ties. This abrupt change thrust me into a whirlwind of torment and trauma. Unexpectedly, this painful termination acted as a hidden blessing, pushing me to confront the stressful and unorthodox methods I had adopted in managing the band's finances. The adversity, although painful, ultimately spared me from the depths of a hole I had unwittingly dug. Ironically, the turmoil within the SU community played a significant role in this challenging chapter and unexpectedly paved the way for self-discovery and healing.

Amidst the turmoil, I've come to believe that life unfolds with a purpose, often beyond our immediate comprehension. My quest for transformational leadership exposed me to a spectrum of emotions – love, distrust, truth, deceit – serving as mirrors that revealed profound truths about my character. I sought guidance externally, only to realize that the answers I sought were nestled within me all along. My transformational journey also unveiled a subtle reluctance to confront conflicts head-on, often appeasing others to maintain a facade of goodwill. Yet, beneath this veneer lay the desire for people, especially my team, to see the best in me. My instinctive discernment alerted me to potential troublemakers, individuals driven by their motives rather than genuine concern. My failure to heed these instincts proved costly, as I grappled with the consequences of welcoming those who betrayed my trust.

Amidst the genuine connections, I encountered fair-weather friends who vanished when adversity arose. Many, newcomers to my journey, exhibited fleeting loyalty, only to abandon me when the storm clouds gathered. This fickleness, though disheartening, taught me the impossible nature of pleasing everyone. In the wise words of Martin Luther King, Jr., "In the end, we will remember not the words of our enemies, but the silence of our friends." Regrettably, I succumbed to the pressure of appeasing others, often extending financial help to so-called friends who manipulated my kindness. These actions came at a great cost – not just financial, but also mental exhaustion brought on by entitlement and ingratitude. Amidst these challenges, a small circle of true friends emerged, individuals who remained steadfast through the trials. To them, I offer my gratitude, acknowledging their unwavering support.

In the world of leadership, my story weaves together unique components while also delving into the shared challenges that leaders encounter across various industries. I refer to it as **The Seven Ps of Leadership**. Throughout this tale of leaderships' intricate dance, we've witnessed the interplay of these seven-Ps: Power, Prestige, Position, Persecution, Problems, Pressure, and Politics. Each thread is woven into the fabric of leadership's tapestry, a testament to its complexity and the enduring qualities that leaders, from all walks of life, share. As the tides of time usher in new leaders and changing dynamics, these seven-Ps remain a guidepost in the ever-evolving journey of leadership.

Power: At the heart of leadership lies the power to catalyze positive change. However, this power can also be a double-edged sword, capable of being wielded by those who are arrogant, manipulative, or narcissistic. It's a reminder that influence must be wielded responsibly.

Prestige: Ascending the leadership ranks brings with it a certain prestige—a perch atop the proverbial food chain. The perks of this position grant access to influential circles, coveted destinations, and material luxuries that come with the territory.

Position: Leaders not only occupy positions but set the very climate and tone of their domains. The atmosphere they cultivate trickles down, shaping the attitudes of their subordinates. Their influence can either create a positive or negative workspace, thus underscoring the power of their position.

Persecution: In the realm of leadership, the spotlight often falls under the leader, casting both blame and praise upon their shoulders. Whether justified or not, the leader becomes the Crucible for success and failures. This unrelenting scrutiny accompanies them through victories and defeats, a compass guiding the ship through every twist and turn. Change, an unceasing companion, brings with it both joy and pain. As leaders instigate change, they frequently encounter resistance rather than embrace. Every choice made is met with a chorus of criticism and alternate proposals. Any and everything about your past will be highly criticized and scrutinized; especially if it is something that could be discovered through a quick Google search. Here, transparency becomes the lodestar, as leaders navigate the delicate balance between addressing concerns and cultivating unwavering morale during times of transformation.

Problems: Effective leadership hinges on adept problem-solving. The challenges faced by subordinates inevitably rise to the leader's desk. These issues become the leader's own, demanding swift resolution, further illustrating the weight of leadership.

Pressure: The mantle of leadership is laden with high stakes and higher pressures. The drive to achieve organizational goals by the clock's ticking hands fuels anxiety. As the organization's pulse races towards its targets, leaders are the heartbeats that keep it in rhythm.

Politics: Navigating the complicated corridors of leadership involves more than operational competence. Entertaining connections with influential figures, though detached from day-to-day operations, becomes necessary. Yet, discernment becomes the leader's compass, determining which paths to tread among ever-shifting political landscapes.

Perhaps the most crucial lesson learned from my ordeal is the value of trusting my instincts. These instincts, a divine gift, offer guidance that I regrettably ignored at times. I recognized the wisdom in being obedient to the signs provided by a higher power, understanding that obedience is the true path to enlightenment. My failure to heed these instincts led to my own downfall, as I appeased others against my better judgment.

Through my journey, I have found solace in forgiveness – not just towards those who wronged me, but most challenging of all, towards myself. From 2001 to 2018, my career as a band director was marked by encounters with manipulative actors that my instincts had forewarned me about. Had I listened, my path may have been different, yet the captivating and unique narrative of the Nathan B. Haymer Story may not have unfolded. I've lived through three years of uncertainty, where the media and the university system dictated the narrative. Today, by sharing my truth, I embark on a new chapter, liberated from the shackles of appeasing or offending others. My truth is my path to peace.

From transforming marketing and branding strategies to revolutionizing performance models in the age of social media, I paved the way for the evolution of the band program. I ensured that the department received new instruments, expanded the profile of the Director of Bands, and fought for respectable salaries and increased budgets. As the Human Jukebox takes the stage, it stands as a living testament to "Haymer's Vision." As I bid farewell to the past and embrace the future, I stand firm in my commitment to honesty and authenticity. While my trust will not be easily given, my dedication to helping others remains unshaken. My motto now echoes, "It is better to be an honest enemy than a deceitful friend." I left behind a band program that is stronger than when I inherited it, a testament to my enduring commitment along with the Power, Prestige, Position, Persecution, Problems, Pressure, Politics and PROSECUTION, that was inevitable in achieving the enormous goals and benchmarks that I set for myself.

In closing, I extend my gratitude for Southern University and A&M College, a place teeming with rich history, traditions, and a strong sense of community. My journey, marked by both triumphs and regrets, is a testament to the enduring spirit of the institution. Through sharing my story, I embark on a journey of healing, liberated from the burden of past mistakes. As I embrace my truth, I usher in a new Nathan B. Haymer, open-hearted and honest, driven by purpose and a steadfast commitment to never give up on people. May my story inspire others to listen to their instincts and embrace their path with unwavering courage.

With deep gratitude and newfound peace,

Nathan B. Haymer - "Haymer-Time"

Appendix A

The chart below illustrates the effect of the passage of the referendum of 2017:

Before the Referendum of 2017	After the Referendum of 2017
Scholarships $90,000/Year	Scholarships $270,000/Year
	(I added 180k, which tripled our original amount)
Salaries (Paid through SU):	Salaries (Increases from the Referendum):
$76,500-Director of Bands	$33,500-Director of Bands
	$15,000-Assoc. Dir. of Bands
$41,500-Asst. Dir. of Bands	$18,500-Asst. Dir of Bands
$37,500-Admin. Assistant	$12,500-Admin. Assistant
$25,000-Percussion Instructor	$25,000-Percussion Instructor
Total for salaries plus fringe benefits (33.3 percent):	$240,606.00
Note: Da Beast's Salary of $45,000 isn't in the equation because it was funded through Band camp revenue	
Band Travel $60,000	Band Travel $120,000
	New Instruments $150,000/year for five years
Total for salaries plus fringe benefits (33.3 percent):	139,298.00
Note: In the 6th and 7th year, $150,000 would pay for New Band Uniforms and accessories. In the 10th year, 150,000 would pay to replace 50-percent of the band's instrument inventory.	

About the Author

"Music doesn't lie. If there is something to be changed in this world, then it can only happen through music." — **Jimi Hendrix**

If this quote by the late, great Jimi Hendrix proves correct, then Nathan Haymer is the truth. He has always had music in his blood. Born in Baton Rouge, La., Haymer moved to Gulfport, Ms. at 8 years old and later graduated from Gulfport High School. It was at GHS his musical talents flourished and he became a model band member. He was recognized as an all-State French horn player and the high school's first black drum major. But it was during his undergraduate years at Southern that Haymer was able to hone his musical acumen and allow music to change his world.

Under the tutelage of the late, great Southern University Band Director Dr. Isaac Greggs, Haymer thrived in the ensemble's brass section and excelled as a trombonist, an instrument he taught himself to play. He became Trombone Section Leader of the marching and symphonic bands. All of his efforts climaxed during his senior year when he was awarded the coveted Bandsman of the Year Award.

Though Haymer's musical talents thrived as an undergraduate, it was his maturation after finishing at Southern with a Bachelor in Instrumental Music Education that secured the groundwork to become a helmsman of bands. He was immediately selected as the band director at Washington-Marion Magnet High School (Lake Charles, La.). During his five-year tenure at WMHS, he developed a band program that has now become a comprehensive model for other prep directors to follow. Under his direction, the band received numerous accolades throughout Texas, Louisiana and Tennessee and garnered over $20,000 in prizes. He created WMHS's first concert band, which performed at the 2001-02 District Festival of the

Louisiana Music Educators Association. The Concert Band, along with his esteemed Wind Ensemble received many Superior and Excellent ratings throughout the 2001-05 academic years.

Haymer's leadership perspicacity grew while at WMHS, along with his goals to grow as an administrator. He later received a Master's in Leadership for Higher Education from Capella University and earned his Plus 30 in Music Education from McNeese State University. It was then, in 2006, Haymer returned back to Southern as the Assistant Director of Bands. He was tasked as the chief arranger for the marching band, leader of band rehearsals; supervisor of the dance routine committee; director of the Jaguars basketball team's pep band; instructor of the sight-reading and development courses, and conductor of the well-regarded symphonic band.

Though many may believe all of those roles may be too many for one person, Haymer didn't shy from handling additional roles as the Human Jukebox's director, where his role surpasses music and delves into education and administrative capacities.

Haymer, who became the Director of Bands in Summer 2014, was responsible for every aspect of the Southern University Band program. He conducted and oversaw all department ensembles, including the world-renowned Human Jukebox. In addition, he was a recruiter, mentor, and ambassador of the university. As an endowed professor in the Department of Visual and Performing Arts, he was charged with researching and developing innovative strategies to secure grants and other funding for recruitment and retention. Haymer is an educator and was charged with the preparation of other music educators in elementary and secondary education.

Ever the proverbial multitasker, Haymer also serves as an adjudicator and clinician to middle and high school bands throughout the U.S., including the Virgin Islands; and was the coordinator of the annual Southern University Summer High School Band & Dance Team Camp.

Life after Southern University has been challenging, yet interesting for Haymer. Always seeking a new venture, Haymer has served as an elementary school music teacher from 2019-2021 in Houston, Texas. With more time on his hands than he was accustomed to throughout his unique career, Haymer also pursued his second passion in culinary arts and serves as a caterer proving yet again that success and grind is ingrained in his DNA. His latest bragging rights include being the first-place winner of a Greater Houston area chili cookoff competition.

Haymer's professional affiliations include Kappa Alpha Psi Fraternity, Inc., Kappa Kappa Psi National Honorary Band Fraternity, Mu Phi Epsilon, International Professional Music Fraternity, Music Educators National Conference, Louisiana Music Educators Association and HBCU National Band Directors Consortium.

Made in the USA
Middletown, DE
16 December 2023